The Obama
Administration
and the Americas

The Obama Administration and the Americas

Agenda for Change

Abraham F. Lowenthal
Theodore J. Piccone
Laurence Whitehead
editors

BROOKINGS INSTITUTION PRESS
Washington, D.C.

Copyright © 2009
THE BROOKINGS INSTITUTION
1775 Massachusetts Avenue, N.W., Washington, D.C. 20036
www.brookings.edu

Library of Congress Cataloging-in-Publication data
The Obama administration and the Americas : agenda for change / Abraham F. Lowenthal, Theodore J. Piccone, and Laurence Whitehead.
     p.   cm.
  Includes bibliographical references and index.
  Summary: "Argues that the Obama administration should focus early and strategically on Latin America because of its impact on issues from energy, narcotics, and immigration to trade and jobs. Contributors emphasize case-by-case, sophisticated, and multilateral approaches to dealing with such hard cases as Bolivia, Colombia, Cuba, Haiti, Mexico, and Venezuela"—Provided by publisher.
  ISBN 978-0-8157-0309-9 (pbk. : alk. paper)
  1. United States—Foreign relations—Latin America. 2. Latin America—Foreign relations—United States. 3. United States—Foreign relations—2009– 4. Obama, Barack. I. Lowenthal, Abraham F. II. Piccone, Theodore J. III. Whitehead, Laurence.
  JZ1480.A53.O23 2009
  327.7308—dc22   2009000893

9 8 7 6 5 4 3 2 1

The paper used in this publication meets minimum requirements of the American National Standard for Information Sciences—Permanence of Paper for Printed Library Materials: ANSI Z39.48-1992.

Typeset in Minion and Univers Condensed

Composition by Peter Lindeman
Arlington, Virginia

Printed by R. R. Donnelley
Harrisonburg, Virginia

Contents

Foreword   vii
Strobe Talbott

Preface   xi

Part I. Overview

1 Renewing Cooperation in the Americas   1
Abraham F. Lowenthal

2 Building a Constructive Inter-American Partnership   22
Daniel Zovatto

3 Supporting Democracy in the Americas:
The Case for Multilateral Action   47
Theodore J. Piccone

Part II. Getting Down to Hard Cases

4 Seven Steps to Improve U.S.-Colombia Relations   69
Michael Shifter

5 Human Rights and Free Trade in Colombia   83
Rodrigo Pardo

6 Haiti's Political Outlook: 96
What the United States Should Do
Daniel P. Erikson

7 Responding to the Challenges in Haiti   109
Juan Gabriel Valdés

8 Cuba in Transition: The Role of External Actors   119
Marifeli Pérez-Stable

9 Turning the Symbol Around: 136
Returning Guantánamo Bay to Cuba
Bert Hoffmann

10 Engaging Venezuela: 2009 and Beyond   145
Jennifer McCoy

11 The United States and Bolivia: Test Case for Change   167
George Gray Molina

12 The Rule of Law in Mexico: 183
Challenges for the Obama Administration
Carlos Elizondo and Ana Laura Magaloni

Part III. Looking Ahead

13 A Project for the Americas   203
Laurence Whitehead

Contributors   225

Index   227

Foreword

The Obama administration faces a difficult legacy when it comes to U.S. relations with its neighbors to the south. Often neglected, or other times viewed through the lens of global struggles against communism, terrorism, or narcotics, the Latin America and Caribbean region has not received the kind of attention it deserves. Looking ahead, if viewed only as a function of the urgent, the countries of the region are likely not to make the list of top priorities for the new president. Yet such a "top ten" approach would sell short our own stake in a prosperous, secure, and democratically stable hemisphere.

Fortunately, the Obama administration has a number of policy opportunities in the region that are ripe for prompt advance. Our neighbors in the Western Hemisphere share core values and interests with the United States. They also share an agenda of concerns that, in the era of globalization, can best be tackled together: the need to preserve and create jobs in the face of the global economic downturn; expand growth and trade; reduce poverty and inequality; combat organized crime and drug trafficking; protect the environment and reverse climate change; develop sustainable energy resources; manage migration flows; and strengthen international institutions of governance. On all these important issues, many Latin American countries have important roles to play, and they share many of the fundamental interests of the United States. At the same time, Latin American countries that are natural partners of the United States have been expanding their relations with other powerful countries. New leaders antagonistic to the United States are cultivating approaches that undermine U.S. interests and erode the prospects for inter-American cooperation.

It is in this context that the Brookings Institution decided last year to launch a Latin America Initiative, directed by Mauricio Cardenas, aimed at exploring the main challenges in the Americas and how U.S. policies might be improved to help confront these effectively. We felt that the time had come to focus more of the resources and talent at Brookings on identifying and understanding opportunities for cooperation and progress in the Americas.

Our first major step in 2008 was to convene the Partnership for the Americas Commission to examine the important changes under way in the relationship between the United States and the hemisphere and to propose practical, forward-looking recommendations to secure a brighter future for all citizens of the Americas. Led by Ernesto Zedillo, former president of Mexico, and Thomas Pickering, one of America's top diplomats, the distinguished members of the commission, drawn from throughout the region and representing decades of experience in politics, diplomacy, business, research, and the media, defined and debated the critical challenges facing the hemisphere and what steps Washington should take to set a better course. The final report, *Rethinking U.S.–Latin American Relations: A Hemispheric Partnership for a Turbulent World*, addresses five key themes that the group felt could serve as common ground for securing better inter-American relations: developing sustainable energy resources and combating climate change; managing migration effectively; making hemispheric economic integration work for all; protecting the hemisphere from drugs and organized crime; and reforming U.S.-Cuban relations. We are pleased by the response this timely report has received not only in Washington but throughout the Americas.

This book, *The Obama Administration and the Americas: Agenda for Change,* represents a further contribution by Brookings to the reconsideration of United States–Latin American relations on a set of issues that was not taken up directly by the commission: whether and how the United States can effectively support the strengthening of democratic governance and the more consistent application of the rule of law in the Americas today.

We encouraged the authors and editors to focus on the issue of democracy for two important reasons: first, because the countries of the Americas share a normative preference for democracy even though many of them face major shortfalls in delivering effective democratic governance and the rule of law. The rise of populist authoritarianism, the strength of organized crime, the corrosive effects of the drug trade, and the prevalence of gross inequalities and dire poverty all threaten the conditions for democracy. It is important to consider what can be done to reverse the deterioration of democratic institutions. The second reason is a sense that the democracy agenda has been tainted in recent years by aggressive U.S. attempts to export democracy, even by force. The authors in the collection, therefore, focused on hard cases for democratic governance in the Americas and set forth more nuanced policies that might be effective, if the Obama administration is ready to adopt a more patient approach to this long-term aim.

Indeed, the democracy and rule of law agenda remains an important item of unfinished business, particularly in countries facing internal tumult or repression. It also has a weighty presence in the substance and style of U.S. foreign policy itself, as noted in these chapters, and the way Washington conducts itself matters. Brookings, therefore, commissioned a series of papers by top experts from Latin America, Europe, and the United States to consider the democratic development questions that will demand the attention of the U.S. administration. These range from resolving the four-decades-long conflict in Colombia in a way that protects "democratic security," as President Uribe advocates, to the thorny question of whether to return the Guantánamo Naval Base to Cuba. In between, the impressive and diverse authors in this volume tackle big questions like improving the quality of Washington's limited attention to our relatively secure neighborhood, strengthening multilateral avenues for cooperation for democracy, bolstering fragile political change in Haiti, dealing with a controversial regime in Venezuela, navigating dramatic political change in Bolivia, and confronting the breakdown of the rule of law in Mexico. All attempt to treat their topics in real time, with practical and, in some cases, bold recommendations for President Obama and his team.

The three coeditors of this collection, each of whom made important contributions to the commission's deliberations, worked assiduously to ensure that the book's chapters reflected the most current issues of the day, while grounding their work in the great historical arc that has shaped U.S.–Latin American relations. The book's timing could not be better: as President Obama joins the thirty-three democratically elected leaders of the region in Port of Spain for the fifth Summit of the Americas in April 2009, they are challenged by a complex agenda and a turbulent economic environment. To navigate through the prevailing headwinds, the United States will need to take a fresh approach based on mutual respect and finding common ground with our increasingly independent and globalized partners. These chapters provide a host of good ideas for how the Obama administration can do just that, by keeping an eye focused on the enduring goal of strengthening democratic institutions and the rule of law for the benefit of all.

STROBE TALBOTT
President
Brookings Institution

Washington, D.C.
February 2009

Preface

The Obama administration has inherited a daunting set of domestic and international policy challenges. It is coping with a cascading and interconnected series of financial and economic problems on a greater scale than any faced since the Great Depression of the 1930s. At the same time, it must handle a large accumulated legacy of other tough problems: two wars, the continuing threat of international terrorism, the proliferation of weapons of mass destruction, global climate change, an impasse in international trade negotiations and rising protectionist pressures, energy and food insecurity, and the ever more complex management of relations with the Middle East, Europe, Russia, China, the South Asian subcontinent, and sub-Saharan Africa.

It is unlikely, therefore, that the new U.S. administration will find much time to think about the countries of Latin America and the Caribbean. These Western Hemisphere nations do not pose an imminent security threat to the United States, nor are they likely to be the cause or target of significant international terrorism. At first blush, the countries of the Americas do not appear to be critical to resolving the most immediately pressing problems of U.S. foreign policy.

Latin American nations, meanwhile, are undergoing their own important changes. They are increasingly diversifying their international economic relations by weaving closer cooperation among themselves as well as deepening trade ties with China, India, Russia, and Europe, making many of them less reliant on the United States. But this growing confidence and autonomy, in addition to regional progress in governance and economic development, suggest that some of Latin America's governments would likely be stable and effective partners if the United States could engage them in cooperative efforts to confront shared problems.

We believe that it would be very smart for the Obama administration to focus early and strategically on U.S. relations with Latin America and the Caribbean. The new administration should not promise to pay more attention to the region than it can deliver, nor should it offer soaring rhetoric about pan-American partnership that would inevitably fall short of expectations. Rather, the Obama administration should aim to improve the *quality* of the limited attention it can devote to the Americas. It should work with key Latin American nations to achieve progress on a few select and crucial issues that can be addressed soon, without investing enormous resources.

We make this central argument because we believe that Latin America's course will have a profound impact on the daily lives of U.S. citizens, on issues ranging from energy to narcotics, immigration to public health, global warming to trade and jobs. On all these issues, sustained and intimate cooperation from Latin American and Caribbean neighbors could make a critical difference to the United States, because of the high degree of interdependence that already exists in the Americas, especially between the United States and its closest neighbors to the south. We also believe that the countries of the Americas, to a high degree, share profound values, deep culture, and major core interests. Common commitments to democratic governance, market economies, social justice, and the rule of law establish the potential for genuine cooperation. We urge the Obama administration to recognize and seize upon this opportunity, understanding the diversity within the region but also its underlying shared aspirations and concerns.

This book began as a series of papers and memoranda commissioned for the Partnership for the Americas Commission, convened by the Brookings Institution and co-chaired by Ernesto Zedillo, former president of Mexico, and Ambassador Thomas Pickering, former U.S. under secretary of state. First drafts of the chapters by Abraham Lowenthal, Daniel Zovatto, and Laurence Whitehead (chapters 1, 2, and 13, respectively) were prepared for and discussed at the commission's first meeting, in May 2008. They were intended to provide broad perspectives by specialists from the United States, Latin America, and Europe on how the commission might approach its mandate to formulate recommendations for building a genuine partnership between the

United States and its southern neighbors. We are very pleased that the commission took our analyses and recommendations into account in developing the intellectual framework of its report, *Rethinking U.S.–Latin American Relations: A Hemispheric Partnership for a Turbulent World*. The commission chose to focus on five topics we emphasized as central: energy, migration, narcotics and crime, economic growth and trade, and the opportunity for a new approach to U.S. relations with Cuba. We highly recommend the commission's report for fuller discussion of these key issues.

In concentrating on these five important topics, the commission decided not to discuss two key questions we believe the Obama administration should consider: whether or not to continue the bipartisan emphasis of the past two U.S. administrations on efforts to support the consolidation of stable democratic governance and strengthen the consistent application of the rule of law in Latin America and the Caribbean; and, if so, how best to do so in Latin America's current circumstances. We think these questions deserve attention because of their substantive merits and historic importance, because of the special quality of the Americas as a region that shares a normative bias for democracy, and because the backlash from Iraq and other recent experiences, reinforced by the global economic crisis, may well swing the pendulum of U.S. policy and public opinion too far away from the long-standing commitment to use U.S. influence to nurture and support democratic governance.

With the support of Carlos Pascual, vice president and director of foreign policy studies at Brookings, and of Mauricio Cárdenas, senior fellow and director of its Latin America Initiative, we decided to put together a symposium volume that combines substantially revised and updated versions of the three original overview essays; a special essay by Theodore Piccone that advocates multilateral approaches to U.S. policies to strengthen democratic governance and a strong emphasis on international cooperation in this field; and contributions by highly qualified Latin American, North American, and European specialists on the half dozen most challenging cases for strengthening democracy and the rule of law in the Western Hemisphere today: Bolivia, Colombia, Cuba, Haiti, Mexico, and Venezuela.

Each of these six countries is unique and complex. All can be dealt with in practice only through policies tailored to their specific contexts. None provides easy opportunities for the United States to export its own institutions and practices. All will present the Obama administration with difficult policy challenges and choices. We believe these country case studies will help the administration, the U.S. Congress, nongovernmental organizations, and others better understand the real problems each country faces and the prospects for positive external involvement. The chapters also underscore that the United States can still have meaningful influence in supporting democratic development in Latin America if it adopts patient, well-crafted, and multilateral approaches.

We are grateful to the Brookings Institution and its Latin America Initiative for the opportunity to prepare this volume; to Brookings Institution Press, especially Janet Walker and Katherine Scott, for handling the publication quickly so that the book would be available before the Summit of the Americas Conference in Trinidad in April 2009; and to Emily Alinikoff of the Foreign Policy Studies program at Brookings for outstanding work in managing this far-flung enterprise. Abe Lowenthal and Laurence Whitehead offer their special thanks to Melissa Lockhart and Jane Jaquette and to Sarah McGuigan and Alexandra Barahona de Brito, respectively—this volume would not have been produced without their help. We express special appreciation to all our fellow authors for responding positively to our requests for more precision in fewer words. This has been a genuine, enjoyable, and fruitful intercontinental collaboration.

Abraham F. Lowenthal   Theodore J. Piccone   Laurence Whitehead
Santa Monica, California   *Washington, D.C.*   *Oxford, United Kingdom*

PART I

Overview

one

Renewing Cooperation in the Americas

Abraham F. Lowenthal

The Obama administration faces daunting challenges at home and abroad, the most demanding agenda that any U.S. government has inherited in many decades.

From the start it has had to cope with an economy in distress, reeling in the aftermath of the subprime mortgage meltdown, the broader financial turmoil, and the wider and deepening recession—while trying to prevent both the risk of rising inflation and the possibility of debilitating deflation. Beyond that immediate crisis, the new administration must deal with energy security, growing health care expenses, underfunded entitlements, the contentious impasse over immigration, and the massive fiscal and trade deficits. In the longer term, the new administration and Congress also must confront decaying infrastructure, inadequate K–12 educational performance, unprecedented rates of incarceration and the need for criminal justice reform, and increasingly frequent and severe natural disasters, themselves likely a result of broader climate change.

Internationally, the Obama administration has inherited the wars in Iraq and Afghanistan, the continuing threat of international terrorism, Pakistan's dangerous instability, tensions with Iran and North Korea, the festering Israel-Palestine quandary, and renewed conflict with Russia—not to mention the rapid economic growth of China and India and the implications of this growth for resource use, commodity prices, food insecurity, global warming, world trade, and international governance.

Under these circumstances no one should expect the new U.S. administration or the new Congress to make relations with Latin America and the Caribbean a high priority. None of the countries of the Americas presents an imminent threat to U.S. national security. None is likely to be the source or target of significant international terrorism. None will be critical to resolving the most immediately pressing problems of U.S. foreign policy.

Why Latin America Matters

But although the countries of Latin America and the Caribbean pose no urgent issues for the United States, they will be increasingly important to the U.S. future—not as areas of dramatic crisis but in a quotidian way. In fact, Latin America has great impact on the daily lives of U.S. citizens, for four main reasons that are not the hoary axioms about Western Hemisphere security, extra-hemispheric threats, and Pan-American solidarity often cited in the past as reasons for Washington to pay attention to the region.

Instead, Latin America matters to the United States today and will matter even more tomorrow, because of:

—Transnational issues that neither the United States nor any Latin American nation can successfully handle by itself, without close and sustained cooperation from regional partners, including energy security, global warming, pollution and other environmental issues, narcotics, crime, and public health.

—Demographic interdependence, arising from massive and sustained migration that has blurred the borders between the United States and its closest neighbors and given rise to complex issues with both international and domestic facets—so-called "intermestic" issues—ranging from education to health care, immigrants' remittances to driver's licenses, youth gangs to portable retirement pensions, narcotics trafficking to human and arms trafficking.

—Latin America's economic importance to the United States as a prime source of energy and other key resources vital for the U.S. economy and as a priority market for U.S. goods and services. The United States obtains over half of its energy imports from countries of the Western Hemisphere, more than half of that from Latin American and Caribbean suppliers, and the potential for expanded energy production in the Americas is high. Conversely, U.S. firms export goods and services to Latin America valued at $225 billion annually, four times the value of current U.S. exports to China. U.S. firms still have, but need to sustain, their competitive advantage in Latin

American markets, arising from proximity and familiarity plus cultural and demographic ties.

—Shared values as expressed in the Inter-American Democratic Charter, in particular, fundamental human rights, including free political expression, effective democratic governance, and consistent application of the rule of law. These core values are unlikely to prevail internationally if they cannot take root in the Western Hemisphere. At a time when the very difficult experiences in Iraq, Afghanistan, and elsewhere have discouraged many Americans about the prospects for expanding the international influence of U.S. ideals, the shared commitment throughout the Americas to the norms of democratic governance and the rule of law should be recognized as important and worth emphasizing in practice.

The State of U.S.–Latin American Relations

Despite Latin America's quotidian significance for the United States, U.S. policies toward the region in recent years have often been ineffective. Instead of focusing on truly shared concerns, since 9/11 Washington has tended to view Latin America mainly through the prism of international terrorism, just as, earlier, anti-Communism was the core of Washington's approach in the Americas. The administrations of both Bill Clinton and George W. Bush emphasized Western Hemisphere summits, but these meetings typically produced little beyond photo opportunities and mutual but mainly rhetorical commitments to cooperation. Both administrations continued to emphasize a proposed Free Trade Area of the Americas (FTAA) long after this goal had become unfeasible. Instead of building better bridges toward our closest neighbors, the United States started construction of a fence at the border with Mexico. Whereas early in the nineties Western Hemisphere cooperation had been strengthening, in the first decade of the new century resentment of this kind of treatment by Washington as well as of some of its global policies, and of its intermittent attentiveness to this hemisphere, have been building in much of Latin America. This resentment has in turn been stoked by the aggressive public and checkbook diplomacy of Venezuela's Hugo Chávez.

Meanwhile many Latin American and Caribbean countries have been deepening their processes of subregional integration, in part through formal institutions, but even more through trade, investment, Latin America–based multinational corporations, professional and business networks, and pragmatic cooperation. They have also been diversifying their international relationships, building cooperation with the countries of the European Union, members of the Asia Pacific Economic Cooperation (APEC) forum, China, India, Russia, and Iran. Many Latin American countries no longer look to Washington for leadership or even for close cooperation. The Organization of American States has been a disappointment, and other hemisphere-wide institutions, including the Inter-American Development Bank, have weakened. Western Hemisphere approaches to problem solving have waned. But the increasing international confidence of many Latin American nations and the emergence of shared concerns, reinforced by the severe international economic crisis, may make such approaches more attractive once again.

This chapter and others in this book argue that the Obama administration and the new Congress should seize an early opportunity to reengage the countries of Latin America and the Caribbean in building mutually productive cooperation on a number of shared concerns. As the new administration moves to redefine the U.S. role in the world, a realistic focus on how to relate more successfully to its Western Hemisphere neighbors in order to confront common challenges could yield important dividends for the United States and for all the Americas.

The Immediate Challenge: Restoring Confidence and Dynamism to the U.S. Economy

President Obama's first priority must be to gain the confidence of the American people and of the whole international community in the commitment and competence of his administration in working to brake the deterioration of the U.S. economy and to restore it to a course of dynamism and growth. How well the new administration succeeds in meeting this urgent need is highly relevant to the countries of Latin America, especially to those in the northern tier—Mexico, Central America, and the Caribbean—which are so dependent on U.S. trade, investment, tourism, and remittances. By the same token, these countries are relevant to the new administration's central economic challenge, for Latin America has been an expanding and important market for the export of U.S. goods and services, and its ability to respond to the current economic downturn will affect the chances for a prompt and solid U.S. recovery. The Obama administration should make it clear to Latin American leaders, at the Trinidad Summit of the Americas in April and in other settings, that the United States is prepared to work closely with its hemispheric neighbors in restoring economic dynamism, creating jobs, and avoiding depression.

Improving the Quality of Attention

Rather than promising to pay much more attention to Latin America and then falling short, the new administration and Congress should instead enhance the quality of the limited attention that can realistically be devoted to the region. Instead of offering soaring rhetoric about partnership from Alaska to Tierra del Fuego, the new administration should work with Latin American and Caribbean nations on a few select and crucial issues that can be addressed soon, if only partially, such as bolstering financial institutions, restoring credit flows, and tackling the problems of energy, the environment, crime, health, housing, and education—thus building credibility that has been damaged after years of unfulfilled pledges. Rather than scramble to counter Hugo Chávez and the "Bolivarian alternative" of anti-U.S. movements, Washington should concentrate on confronting the underlying issues that have created space for Chávez's inflammatory rhetoric and populist programs, and for other radical populist movements.

The new U.S. authorities should be thoughtful and consistent in disaggregating Latin America and the Caribbean. It is not new or profound to recognize that Latin American and Caribbean nations vary enormously. During the past twenty years, however, there has often been a tendency in Washington, within administrations of both political parties, to emphasize convergence within the region: toward democratic governance, market-oriented economics, and policies of macroeconomic balance and regional integration. Although these convergent trends have indeed been important, key differences persist among the many countries of Latin America and the Caribbean, and some of these differences are growing, not shrinking. This can be seen along five dimensions:

—*Demographic and economic interdependence with the United States:* highest and still growing in Mexico, Central America, and the Caribbean, and lowest and likely to remain low in South America, especially in the Southern Cone.

—*The extent to which the countries have opened their economies to international competition:* most fully by far in Chile; a great deal in Brazil, Colombia, Mexico, Peru, Panama, and some Central American nations; and less so in other countries.

—*The relative advance of democratic governance (checks and balances, accountability, and the rule of law):* historically strong in Chile, Uruguay, and Costa Rica; increasingly, if quite unevenly, robust in Brazil; gaining ground in Mexico over the past twenty years but with ups and downs, hard struggle, and major recent setbacks; arguably declining, or at least at risk, in Argentina; under great strain in Venezuela, most of the Andean nations, much of Central America and Paraguay; and exceptionally weak in Haiti.

—*The relative effectiveness of civic and political institutions beyond the state (the press, trade unions, religious organizations, and nongovernmental entities):* strongest in Chile, Uruguay, Costa Rica, the Dominican Republic, and perhaps Argentina; growing but still severely challenged in Brazil and Mexico; slowly regaining stature but still quite problematic in Colombia; weak in Peru, Bolivia, Ecuador, Paraguay, Venezuela, most of Central America, and Haiti;

—*The extent to which traditionally excluded populations are incorporated:* relating to more than 30 million marginalized, disadvantaged, and increasingly politically mobilized indigenous people—especially in Bolivia, Ecuador, Guatemala, the Peruvian highlands, and southern Mexico—and Afro-Latin Americans in countries where they are still the object of racial discrimination.

Only when all these important structural differences and their political consequences are consistently understood can the countries of Latin America and the Caribbean come into clear focus for U.S. policymakers. Hemisphere-wide summit conferences or very broad regional initiatives are less likely to be effective than subregional efforts that bring together smaller clusters of countries with comparable or complementary issues and concerns. Recognizing this reality should be one starting point for a reconsideration of U.S. policies in the Americas. A second, discussed more extensively later in this chapter, is to understand that questions of style, tone, and broad foreign policy outlook will matter a lot in the Americas.

Changing Mindsets

The Obama administration has a brief window to show that it is not imprisoned by damaging mindsets imposed by traditional ideology and rhetoric and that it can therefore respond more constructively than its predecessors did to the realities of Latin America and the Caribbean.

Instead of dividing Latin America and the Caribbean into two groups—friendly "democracies" and hostile "dictatorships"—Washington would be wiser to realize that many Latin American and Caribbean nations still have weak political institutions, low levels of accountability, and highly uneven application of the rule of law. Although the normative goal of democratic governance has been nearly universally embraced in the past generation— a welcome advance—effective democratic performance and the consistent application of the rule of law remain far from reality in many countries. Central questions posed in this book, in danger of getting short shrift in the backlash to the frustrating Iraq imbroglio, are whether and how the United States can help play an appropriate and effective role in bolstering the prospects for meaningful democracy, at least in some nations.

The familiar mantra of promoting free markets and pushing the "Washington Consensus" has lost traction, and citing Chile as the poster child for this formula no longer persuades. Washington should understand that most Latin Americans see things quite differently. They point out that Chile's success in fact demonstrates the value of pragmatically combining market-opening reforms with strengthened state capacity, sound public policies, including controls on foreign investment, and vigorous state action. Some of Latin America's governmental institutions need to become stronger, more competent, and more effective—not smaller or weaker—in order to deal with such issues as poverty, inequity, exclusion, crime, personal security, and competitiveness. After a period of excessive faith in markets, Washington needs to fully grasp this point as part of a more general rethinking of the role of government, both at home and abroad.

The key distinctions in Latin America today are less whether an economy is entirely market-driven or partly state-led and more how well the government and other institutions incorporate feedback and accountability into their decisionmaking and course correction processes, and whether competition among parties and sectors is constructive and energizing or polarizing and destructive. Moving toward more democratic politics and toward economies that are more market-driven than centrally planned certainly can help nations meet these imperatives. But many Latin Americans believe, understandably, that these nostrums are insufficient without effective institutions, including independent central banks and autonomous political parties, and without sufficient state capacity to regulate, allocate resources, and provide essential public services. In some cases the market-opening and state-shrinking policies recommended by Washington have come to be seen as damaging, or as facades meant to advantage narrow interests. The crisis of American financial institutions in 2008, requiring massive government intervention, further undermined the case for international market fundamentalism.

Starting at Home: The "Intermestic" Agenda

Four changes in U.S. policy that would have great positive impact in the Americas are strictly speaking not "Latin American policy" issues as such, but in many ways are primarily domestic questions: immigration reform, a revised trade policy, a new emphasis on energy conservation and development, and a fresh approach to the narcotics trade.[1]

Immigration

As soon as domestic economic stimulation and other truly urgent business permit, the Obama administration should work intensively with the new Congress to achieve comprehensive and proactive immigration reform, based on the premise that labor markets and family dynamics will likely produce substantial immigration flows for the foreseeable future. A new U.S. immigration policy should seek to manage and regulate these flows; enhance their benefits to the receiving communities; mitigate, compensate for, and more fairly distribute their various costs; and also affirm core U.S. values, including fundamental respect for law.

Any viable plan will require cooperation with Mexico, Central America, and the Caribbean on economic development, job creation, labor, health, education, youth employment, law enforcement, and infrastructure. To secure that cooperation, Washington must avoid name calling and finger pointing. The Obama administration should consult early with governments in Mexico, Central America, and the Caribbean regions with the goal of fashioning joint and practical approaches to those transnational issues.

A feasible and sustainable U.S. immigration policy must include improved border control and management, temporary worker programs, meaningful sanctions against employers who hire unauthorized residents, and concerted efforts at various levels to integrate unauthorized immigrants who have been contributing to the United States and who want to become part of the U.S. community—including practical paths to citizenship or long-term legal residence. It will take considerable political leadership and will to achieve immigration reform, but the need is evident. Immigration reform would be important, not only for the United States but for many other countries of the Americas, especially Mexico and the Caribbean and Central American nations.

Trade

It is not enough to stress the benefits of expanded trade for those who prosper from it while downplaying its costs and risks for others, especially in the context of mounting anxiety about a prolonged recession or worse. Much more needs to be done to compensate, protect, retrain, and provide technical assistance and access to credit to those who are displaced by expanded trade and by technology, both in the United States and in the economies of its trading partners, especially in the Americas. These provisions need to become part of new trade agreements, not just the subject of side accords or of vague promises to deal with the issue later. For their part, Latin American countries will need to improve protection of labor conditions and workers' rights if trade agreements are to have any prospect for U.S. approval. The 2007 negotiations—first between the Bush administration and congressional Democratic leadership and then with the government of Peru, on labor rights and environmental issues to make possible the free trade agreement with that country—show the way toward reconstructing expanded and sustainable inter-American commercial cooperation.

The new administration and Congress will need to win support from both business and labor to keep the United States globally competitive but also to open greater export opportunities for developing countries, including those of Latin America, rather than to intensify targeted protectionism. The United States cannot expect open access for its exports while retaining pockets of strong protectionism for itself precisely in sectors where developing countries, including Latin American economies, have competitive advantages.

Energy

With the price of oil fluctuating wildly, at times around unprecedentedly high levels; declining production of petroleum in Mexico, Venezuela, and Ecuador; rising demands for energy in China and India; geostrategic concerns about the Middle East and Africa; and growing consensus on the harmful impact of carbon emissions; the Obama administration and Congress will surely focus early on energy security. New policies will include conservation initiatives and the development of new supplies, particularly from renewable sources. The potential is great for significant collaboration among Western Hemisphere nations to ensure the provision of adequate energy, involving investment in producing oil and natural gas in Mexico, Brazil, Venezuela, Bolivia and Cuba; some expansion of nuclear power production in Argentina, Brazil, Chile, Venezuela, and Uruguay; carefully targeted support for some biofuel development, especially sugarcane-based and cellulosic ethanol, in Brazil, Colombia, Central America, Cuba, and elsewhere in the Caribbean; investments in wind, hydro, and geothermal energy; and collaborative research on both alternative fuels and options for conservation. Concerted efforts to build

Western Hemisphere cooperation on energy could substantially advance U.S. interests at home, in the Americas, and around the world.

Narcotics

The Obama administration, the new Congress, and Latin American governments all need to fundamentally rethink the "war on drugs." The "war" metaphor should be dropped, because it reinforces the tendencies to look for "victory" against a defined enemy and to favor mainly coercive methods. Even though there are undoubtedly some links between drug traffickers and guerrillas, Washington and Latin American governments should stop emphasizing "narco-terrorists," because the narcotics issue is not really primarily about terrorism or military security. It is, rather, a complex societal, cultural, medical, and institutional problem that has as much to do with deep-seated failures in advanced industrial countries as with weak governance, crime, corruption, and poverty in Latin American and other producing nations. The more honestly Washington deals with the societal roots and social consequences of this destructive business, the more likely is the development of the international cooperation needed to reduce this traffic and to diminish its scope and harm.

The new administration and Congress should give priority to prevention, treatment, rehabilitation, and youth employment programs at home. They should increase investment in well-structured alternative development and youth employment programs for regions in developing countries where growing drug crops currently seems like the only alternative to dire poverty, and where local conditions and stakeholders provide some chance for success. They should concentrate less on spraying herbicide on crops and interdicting shipments, and correspondingly more on disrupting both the money and the arms flowing from the United States that lubricate and facilitate the drug trade and undermine fragile states. And they should redouble efforts to constructively engage Latin American and Caribbean cooperation in countering all aspects of the corrosive narcotics enterprise, which increasingly damages the whole region, and in tackling the broader but connected issues of organized crime, including not only narcotics but also human trafficking, kidnapping, auto theft, and contraband smuggling. The drug trade is devastating the institutions and law enforcement capabilities of several countries in Central America, the Caribbean, and Mexico, as it had earlier ravaged Colombia. The Obama administration should be open to new analysis and approaches, and invite prompt multilateral and bilateral discussions of what to do.

Closest Neighbors

In rethinking its policies in the Western Hemisphere, the Obama administration will need to be selective but strategic, concentrating on major issues and regions where new initiatives could be most productive.

It should focus special attention on U.S. relationships with the countries of the Caribbean Basin region: Mexico, Central America, and the Caribbean islands. Together these countries, with about a third of the total population of Latin America and the Caribbean, account for nearly half of all U.S. investment in the entire region; more than 70 percent of legal U.S.–Latin American trade; a very high proportion of drug trafficking; and some 85 percent of all Latin American migration to the United States.

However much they differ among themselves, as they certainly do, Mexico and the Caribbean and Central American nations are, almost without exception, becoming ever more fully integrated with the United States. Many of these countries rely on large flows of remittances sent home by their diasporas in the United States and increasingly use the dollar as their informal and in some cases their formal currencies. They send most of their exports either to the United States or to each other, and rely mainly on U.S. tourists, investment, imports, and technology. They all send many migrants northward, and some accept increasing numbers of (often retired) North Americans as long-term residents, as well as large numbers of U.S. citizens seeking vacation homes, inexpensive medical care, and other services. All these trends will continue, and soon almost certainly Cuba, too, will reflect them, albeit with special characteristics. Transnational citizens and networks will grow in importance throughout the region based on such issues as portable international health insurance, extraterritorial applicability for Medicare benefits, and bilingual education.

The "intermestic" issues that flow directly from the unique and intense mutual interpenetration between the United States and its closest neighbors—immigration, narcotics and arms trafficking, youth gangs, citizen security, auto theft, money laundering, responding to and mitigating the effects of hurricanes and other natural disasters, protecting the environment and public health, law enforcement and border management—pose complex policy challenges. In both the United States and its neighbors, the democratic political process often results in policies that push in directions that are diametrically opposed to what would be needed to secure the international cooperation required to manage thorny problems that transcend borders. Immigration policy is a vivid example of this catch-22 dynamic: congressional approval of the border fence undoubtedly was a response to domestic opinion, but that made it harder for Mexico and the countries of Central America to work with the United States on immigration and other issues. This dynamic has also obtained in the case of anti-narcotics policy and of agricultural subsidies that are demanded by domestic lobbies and are difficult to undo, but impose disproportionate costs on neighbors.

The fact that the policy approaches most attractive at home often hinder needed international cooperation is certainly not limited to the United States. The impulses to place responsibility for tough problems on the other side of the border and to assert "sovereignty" even when strictly national control is no longer possible in practical terms are mutually reinforcing. Existing concepts and institutions are inadequate for managing these increasingly complex and intimate relations.

The Obama administration and Congress should undertake and promote official and nongovernmental consultations with counterparts in Canada, Mexico, Central America, and the Caribbean on the full range of challenges posed by the increased and irreversible interdependence of this whole close-knit region. The aim should be nothing less than to forge a shared vision of the entire Caribbean Basin's future—including Cuba and Puerto Rico—and of how to achieve it.

Brazil

A second strategic policy focus should be Brazil, where the long-trumpeted future has arrived, or at least is much closer. Since 1990 Brazil has opened important parts of its economy to international competition, modernized much of its agricultural sector, and developed a number of industries with a continental and even worldwide presence. Brazil has slowly but surely strengthened its state, private sector, and nongovernmental institutions. It has secured financial and political stability, has attracted very substantial foreign investment ($34 billion in 2007, more in 2008), participated aggressively in the world economy, and produced steady if still modest economic growth. Successful recent petroleum exploration reinforces the likelihood that Brazil's growth will further accelerate in the years to come. Together with Chile and Panama, Brazil has also begun to reduce absolute poverty and gross inequity, two of the most intractable problems faced by Latin America and Caribbean nations. And Brazil is making notable though still far from sufficient progress in combatting corruption, crime, violence, discrimination, impunity, and lack of accountability.

These transformations make it desirable and possible for the United States to work more closely with Brazil. The two countries have many shared interests: enhancing energy security, promoting regional stability, protecting the environment and public health, liberalizing and expanding international trade in agriculture and services, and strengthening global governance. Washington and Brazil can also improve the way they work together to manage conflicting international economic and commercial interests. This involves striving to overcome short-term domestic interest group pressures in both countries in order to facilitate long-term trade, investment, and prosperity. That will not be easy, but if the Obama administration communicates a strategic vision toward Brazil, it might well make headway, provided that the government of Brazil is ready to do its part.

The Andean Ridge

The nations of the Andean range are quite diverse, but all, to differing but invariably high degrees, are plagued by weak political institutions. Most face the unresolved integration into the market economy and the body politic of large indigenous and historically excluded populations. All must address the incorporation of many millions of persons, not only indigenous, who live in extreme poverty. Grinding poverty, gross inequities, social exclusion, rising ethnic and subnational consciousness, violence, the weak presence of the state in rural areas, and the further undermining of already feeble institutions are a volatile combination. The faith that free markets and democratic politics inevitably strengthen and support each other in a powerful virtuous circle simply does not capture the realities of this highly fragmented subregion.

The narcotics trade is at least as much symptom as cause of these conditions; dealing with the drug trade in isolation from other issues will therefore have little effect. By the same token, combating guerrilla and paramilitary movements primarily through military means is unlikely to have any enduring impact. Only if and when the underlying and interrelated problems of extreme poverty and political disenfranchisement are confronted in an integrated fashion can the Andean nations hope to achieve sustained political stability and economic development. Strengthening the state's capacity to provide order depends fundamentally on bolstering its capacity to deliver economic growth, basic services, improved equity, and the consistent application of the rule of law. Nothing the United States can do will substitute for local leadership that deals effectively with these fundamental problems.

Where such leadership emerges, the United States should support its efforts, without being so intrusive as to become part of the problem.

All of the Andean countries are distinct, their situations are fluid and uncertain, and in some cases they are in deep conflict with each other and with the United States.

Peru's democratic government has to overcome profound alienation in the country's highland (sierra) and jungle (selva) regions by delivering concrete results, not mere rhetoric or gestures. If the dramatic alienation of Peru's sierra and selva populations cannot be reduced, Peru will remain highly vulnerable to antisystem politicians and to destabilization by external actors ready to exploit this alienation.

In Bolivia and Ecuador, two very different and innovative efforts to "refound" national identity, build new and more inclusionary political institutions, and capture more of the benefits from natural resources face the constraints of the international economy and deep suspicion on the part of established national and provincial elites and also of many middle-class professionals. Each of these efforts is a work in progress: uncertain, unpredictable, and subject to conflicting internal currents and international influences.

Colombia has made progress in overcoming insurgent movements, restoring urban peace, and expanding the influence of nongovernmental institutions, but still faces embedded violence, pervasive corruption, and authoritarian tendencies.

Venezuela is deeply polarized. Chávez's march toward more consolidated authoritarian and personal rule on the basis of popular support from sectors previously without voice or influence has been slowed but by no means halted by an increasingly organized and vocal opposition, which has strengthened its position in Caracas and other populous regions. Further instability is likely, particularly as economic difficulties mount in the wake of falling petroleum prices and gross mismanagement, and as Chávez renews and intensifies his effort to extend his rule and expand his power.[2]

Advancing U.S. interests and the prospects for inter-American cooperation in these complex circumstances requires patient, nuanced, sensitive, and case-by-case treatment, not assertive and indiscriminate broad-brush policies. Career U.S. diplomats, led by Assistant Secretary of State Thomas Shannon, for the most part were skillful in the latter years of the Bush administration in managing Washington's relations with the diverse Andean countries by avoiding confrontation and trying to find ways to be constructive, but the mutual recriminations exchanged by the United States and both Bolivia and Venezuela late in 2008 further complicated these relationships.

The Obama administration would be well advised to revert to a nonconfrontational approach, to seek low-key cooperation from like-minded governments in the region, and where possible to find ways to work quietly with each country on concrete issues of shared concern. The country chapters in this volume provide specific guidance on how to do this.

Cuba

The question of Cuba cries out for fresh U.S. responses to changing circumstances.[3] The long-standing U.S. policy of denial, embargo, and exclusion, developed in the Cold War context, was not demonstrably successful even then. The Obama administration should promptly redefine the objectives of U.S. policy in the light of fundamentally altered international realities, the ongoing leadership transition in Cuba, the evolution and generational transformation of the Cuban American community, and of broader U.S. interests beyond the importance of Florida's votes in the electoral college. The 2008 election results give the Obama administration the political space to reframe U.S. policy in terms of national objectives, not pressure group influence, and to relate Cuba policy to the broader objective of refashioning the world role of the United States and how it is perceived internationally.[4]

The primary aim of U.S. policy at this stage should be to increase the likelihood that Cuba and the United States can cooperate pragmatically on migration, energy, narcotics, the environment, public health, and on response to hurricanes and other natural disasters. At the same time Washington should do all it can to repair badly frayed communications and trust by expanding family, academic, and other nongovernmental contacts with Cuba. As an indication of its intentions and a symbolic step potentially important in the broader international context, the new administration could offer Cuba a clear and respectful path toward resuming normal diplomatic relations with the United States. Pragmatic negotiations should be initiated to find a realistic solution to the claims arising from nationalizations and expropriations by the Castro government nearly fifty years ago, and to agree on a mutually acceptable future for the Guantánamo base. The United States can best encourage those in Cuba who want to nurture eventual democratic governance, and the Cuban American community can more likely come to play an appropriate role in the island's economic recovery and development, if steps are first taken to improve communication and expand practical cooperation in concert with other countries.

Reducing Extreme Poverty and Inequity

Perhaps most important, the Obama administration needs to both understand and explain to the American public that the United States would gain more stable neighbors, expanded markets, more attractive investment opportunities, and more congenial tourist destinations if the countries of Latin America and the Caribbean could be helped to reduce grinding poverty, gross inequities, and ethnic exclusion and to head off rising unemployment. These conditions fuel polarization, lend themselves to demagogic exploitation, and undermine both democratic governance and sustainable policies of economic growth and development.

Today, especially after the 2008 financial meltdown, U.S. public policy instruments and available resources are much too limited to make an immediate and dramatic impact on Latin America's poverty, inequity, and exclusion; this is certainly no time to consider another "Alliance for Progress." But the United States can certainly do much more to help confront the regional development agenda than the pale imitations of the Venezuelan and Cuban educational and health programs announced on President Bush's 2007 trip to Latin America. Washington can work to enhance the positive social impact of remittances, support microfinance programs, and build on the experience of the Millennium Challenge initiative to help establish a regionwide social development fund to target poverty-reduction efforts and to engage especially vulnerable populations, not only in the poorest countries but in the specific subregions of each country where dire poverty exists. The United States, the European Community, Canada, and the OPEC countries should consider providing multilateral credit to help energy-importing developing countries adjust during periods of very high costs. Washington could take the lead in financing a special fund for recovery and adaptation targeted at the countries most affected by consequences of climate change, including the highly vulnerable Caribbean and Central American nations. The international community could also do much more to support innovative educational reforms and to deal with youth gangs as a transnational problem that requires improving education and employing more young people. Dealing with arms trafficking, people trafficking, and money laundering all require coordinated international treatment.

Many of the necessary programs already are in place on a modest scale, but the Obama administration and the new Congress should give them additional and more secure support. Well-crafted and astutely implemented policies could make a big difference without being expensive. Washington should mobilize both public and private sector efforts to invest in infrastructure in Latin America and to expand energy production and distribution—major ways of accelerating the region's growth and providing much needed employment that are very much in the interest both of the United States and of its neighbors. On all these issues the Obama administration should favor multilateral approaches. In particular, it should support redoubled activity by an upgraded and reinvigorated Inter-American Development Bank.

Rebuilding *Confianza*

Finally, it is vitally important that the Obama administration and Congress work together to build mutual respect in the Americas as part of a broader reconsideration of the U.S. role in the world. President George W. Bush traveled to Latin America and the Caribbean more than any other U.S. president, and his administration produced some positive, though inadequate, U.S. policies specifically targeting the Western Hemisphere, especially during Bush's second term. But the stature and appeal of the United States in the region plummeted, primarily because of U.S. policies elsewhere in the world but also because the style of U.S. interaction with Latin Americans was so often dismissive or intrusive: from customs and immigration procedures at the individual level to irksome pressures on Latin American governments regarding various votes in international organizations.

After many years of responding to U.S. pressures regarding human rights abuses, including the use of torture in interrogation, Latin Americans have been understandably critical of U.S. conduct in the "war on terror," especially the use of Guantánamo to circumvent legal protections of the rights of prisoners detained there. The Guantánamo abuses, criticized by both candidates during the 2008 campaign and by U.S. federal courts, should be addressed immediately by closing down the detention camp and transferring the prisoners to facilities in the United States or other appropriate countries, where they should be charged expeditiously and brought to trial.

The Obama administration should make every effort to rebuild multilateral cooperation and international institutions in the Western Hemisphere as elsewhere. It should support the unprecedented efforts made by Brazil, Chile, and Argentina to help Haiti reverse its decline. It should enlist these and other countries to take the lead in building new relations with Cuba.[5] Washington should warmly welcome Canada's growing role in the Americas, and should encourage Canada to step forward on some issues and relationships where a high U.S. profile could be counterproductive.

The new administration should recommit the United States to active support of a more active and confident Organization of American States as well as the United Nations. Washington should endorse and adhere to the International Criminal Court, and should drop pressures on Latin American nations to grant U.S. personnel exemptions from the court's jurisdiction. It should engage actively and urgently in global cooperation in response to climate change, and should urge Latin American governments, too, to do their part. As Ted Piccone's chapter emphasizes, the Obama administration should assure that its efforts to promote and nurture democratic governance are approached on a multilateral and international basis. The United States should also recognize and help celebrate the bicentennial of South American independence from colonial Spain, perhaps by offering funding and technology for new Western Hemisphere educational initiatives.

Above all, the substance and tone of inter-American relations will be most quickly and substantially improved if and when the United States visibly returns to a world role that is respectful of international law and opinion, cooperative rather than domineering, clearly committed to multilateralism and international institutions, sensitive to Latin American aspirations for broader international recognition, and true to the fundamental values that are shared by citizens throughout the Americas. The Obama administration should make it clear, not only in Barack Obama's Inaugural Address but in concrete actions soon thereafter, that it plans to steer U.S. foreign policy consistently on this new course. Nothing would contribute more to rebuilding *confianza*, the essential trust on which Western Hemisphere cooperation ultimately will depend, both at the government level and among the broad public throughout the region.

Notes

1. For a fuller and illuminating discussion of these four topics, drawing on the deliberations of an outstanding inter-American commission of notables, see *Re-Thinking U.S.-Latin American Relations: A Hemispheric Partnership for a Turbulent World*, Report of the Partnership for the Americas Commission (Washington: Brookings Institution, November 2008). An early draft of this chapter and of those by Laurence Whitehead and Daniel Zovatto were prepared for and discussed at the commission's first meeting.

2. The specific circumstances of Bolivia, Colombia, and Venezuela are discussed in helpful detail in the chapters by George Gray Molina, Rodrigo Pardo, Michael Shifter, and Jennifer McCoy.

3. Complementary perspectives on how to proceed are offered in the chapters by Marifeli Pérez-Stable, Bert Hoffmann, and Laurence Whitehead.

4. This point is discussed in innovative detail in the Hoffmann chapter.

5. The difficult case of Haiti is discussed in the chapters by Daniel Erikson and Juan Gabriel Valdes.

two

Building a Constructive Inter-American Partnership

Daniel Zovatto

In their limited discussion of Latin America, both of the U.S. presidential candidates, Senators John McCain and Barack Obama, promised to pursue a closer, more collaborative relationship with the region. The question, now that President Obama has taken office, is whether the United States is ready, willing, and able to do so.

In this chapter I urge the new U.S. president to reassess this country's relations with Latin America. The United States has much to gain from a more constructive, collaborative, and respectful relationship with its hemispheric neighbors and partners, whose destinies are increasingly entwined and indivisible. This new relationship must recognize Latin America's increasing confidence and competence in addressing national and regional problems and strengthen U.S. partnerships with the region's trusted leaders.

The world is changing at an accelerating rate. The fall of the Berlin Wall in 1989 put an end to Marxist dogma, and the disintegration of the Soviet Union two years later put an end to the bipolar world. Today, almost two decades later, we are witnessing fundamental transformations of equal or greater magnitude. As a result of the financial and economic crisis that has quickly spread throughout the world, a new relationship between the state and the market is beginning to develop, as is strong demand for a reconfiguration of the archi-

The author would like to thank Alberto Adrianzen, David Kupferschmidt, Rafael Roncagliolo, and Kristen Sample for assistance in the preparation of this chapter.

tecture of global governance—it is being called a Bretton Woods for the twenty-first century. The financial markets were unable to regulate themselves and had to resort to the state to survive. Because the markets did not adequately allocate resources, the government will have to assume a greater role in the economy. A number of progressive governments in Latin America look favorably on this trend toward a more active role for the state in the economy.

But the profound changes we are witnessing are not limited to the financial and economic realm; they have also shifted international politics. As the journalist Fareed Zakaria notes in his book *The Post-American World*, we are transitioning from a unipolar world to a world that is post-American, global, multipolar, and decentralized because of the strategic regroupings of key global actors and the urgent need to find effective, common solutions to shared global dilemmas. The changes that are rapidly occurring worldwide, combined with those taking place on our continent, present a unique opportunity for the United States and Latin America to increase the scope and improve the quality of their relationship.[1]

Regional Solutions to Regional Problems

Some three decades after launching the third wave of democracy, Latin America now finds itself democratically more mature, more diversified in its relations with Europe, China, India, Russia, Iran, and other countries, more autonomous in its decisionmaking, and more inclined to seek solutions to its own problems.

For a peripheral region like Latin America, multilateralism, along with increasing power and autonomy, is a priority. As Roberto Rusell notes, "Washington is prepared to establish 'spheres of responsibility' with countries in the region to achieve common goals by means of a certain division of labor."[2] The coordinated effort of Brazil, Chile, Argentina, making Haiti their "sphere of responsibility," is one good example of this. Similar efforts should be made in the cases of Cuba, Colombia, and other countries. Unfortunately, internal problems and differences and conflicts between countries have often affected the region's willingness and ability to act collectively. The stagnation of Mercosur and the Andean Community,[3] the two principal entities advancing the process of Latin American integration, and the tensions, conflicts, and disagreements between various presidents in the region are evidence of unresolved difficulties. Nevertheless, two events in 2008 attested to the political will and capacity of the region's countries to resolve their conflicts without the participation of the United States.[4]

The first event was the Rio Group meeting in the Dominican Republic, following a Colombian military incursion into Ecuador to attack an FARC (Revolutionary Armed Forces of Colombia) camp. At the meeting, the host, Dominican president Leonel Fernández, facilitated dialogue among the presidents of Colombia, Ecuador, and Venezuela to reach a preliminary agreement that defused a potentially explosive situation.

The second event was the successful mediation by UNASUR (Union of South American Nations) in the Bolivian crisis that erupted when the state of Pando threatened to secede from the country. At its September 15 meeting in Santiago, Chile, UNASUR adopted the Moneda Declaration, which gave full support to the government of Bolivian president Evo Morales, demanded preservation of Bolivia's territorial integrity, condemned those who sought to destabilize democracy in that country, called for the parties to return to talks, and headed off an escalation of the bloodshed that had taken dozens of lives. For the first time, a South American organization acted as the guarantor of democracy, affirming in the Moneda Declaration that "governments will not recognize any situation that involves an attempt at a civil coup or the rupture of institutional order, or that compromises the territorial integrity of the Republic of Bolivia." Although the secretary general of the Organization of American States (OAS), Jose Miguel Insulza, was present at the meeting, negotiations were clearly carried out in the framework of UNASUR; the OAS was not a party to the declaration.

Crisis and Opportunity?

Although no one can predict the duration and extent of the global financial crisis, reforms already in place have left most Latin American economies better prepared to resist external disruptions than in the past. They have implemented improved macroeconomic practices and, as of 2007, reserves have increased from $174 billion in 1997 to $460 billion. Public debt has decreased, from 60.7 percent of GDP in 2002 to 31.8 percent in 2007, and external debt also decreased, from 46 percent of GDP in 1997 to 31 percent in 2008. At the beginning of 2008, concerns about inflation, previously the principal economic obstacle, were being dispelled by the threat of a recession. Economic growth remained strong, although 2008 estimates may not have fully taken into account the impact of the financial crisis. In October 2008 the Inter-American Development Bank estimated that the region's 2008 GDP growth would be 4 to 4.5 percent, and the projection for 2009 was 2.5

to 3.5 percent. However, these figures are likely to change, given the extreme volatility of the 2008 global financial crisis.

Latin America is also well positioned to weather the challenges of food and energy shortages, thanks to its rich resource base. Used strategically, these resources could give the region a competitive advantage on the international stage. Nevertheless, the causal links among deforestation, floods, and climate change demand a cooperative regional approach to conserving the region's natural resources and planning for a sustainable future.

Three additional challenges shared by the United States and Latin America are drug trafficking, public security, and immigration, issues that exemplify the need for closer U.S.–Latin American cooperation. Combating terrorism has been a central feature of U.S. policy since 9/11, but it appears that drug-financed organized crime is a bigger threat to hemispheric health and safety than terrorism. Meanwhile, even as migration has bound Latin America and the United States together ever more closely, a satisfactory long-term approach to managing these flows has yet to appear.

The Case for a New Partnership

Despite increasing inter-American trade and shared values and principles, especially those of democracy and human rights, Washington's relationship with the region has grown more distant, although it is more balanced than ever before.

The neglect to which the Bush administration condemned Latin America after September 11, 2001, together with the missteps of American foreign policy, especially after the World Trade Center attacks—the disaster of the Iraq War, the human rights abuses in Abu Ghraib and Guantánamo, and the violations and even repudiation of international law, to cite only the most notorious examples—have reinforced in the region a negative vision of the United States' international influence, while inflicting enormous damage on American soft power. The Bush administration's insistence on the free market and advocacy of policies designed to favor business have also helped intensify the United States' differences with a region whose governments and people advocate a stronger role for the state and more social programs.

Latin Americans expect relations with the United States to include consultation on political and economic issues and a shared vision of the region's future, and not be limited to financial and technical cooperation or trade. If the United States would like to have greater influence on democratic governance and the rule of law and pursue other shared interests with countries in the region, it must regain its prestige and moral authority. U.S. policy toward Latin America must take into account and build on the region's undeniable diversity. Change is occurring in the region in multiple directions and at different paces. An accurate and productive understanding of Latin America requires deep analysis of each national reality, yet it may also be possible to identify a few broad trends.

This complex set of new circumstances in the United States and Latin America requires a fresh approach based on a constructive inter-American partnership rooted in mutual respect, multilateralism, coordination, cooperation, and the quest for reciprocal benefits.

Cause for Optimism?

President Barack Obama faces the huge challenge of reestablishing U.S. credibility as an effective, trustworthy world leader. He also has to face the financial and economic crisis, budget deficits, wars in Iraq and Afghanistan, and a whole menu of international challenges: Iran's nuclear threat, instability in Pakistan, the Israeli-Palestinian conflict, Russia's new international assertiveness, and China's growing power. Meeting these challenges will leave few resources and little attention available for Latin America.

Nevertheless, the Obama administration is expected almost certainly to pay more, and hopefully better, attention to Latin America than the Bush administration did. During the U.S. presidential election, both candidates asserted that they were multilateralists, and this bodes well for a richer and more productive dialogue between the United States and Latin America.

In these economically and politically challenging times, to what extent is a new constructive partnership possible? Many Latin American observers are moderately optimistic. Diminished U.S. influence in the region could compel it to improve relations with Latin America, take a more nuanced approach using "soft" rather than "hard" power, and tailor its approach to both the unique opportunities and challenges of each country and the issues that bind the region together. And the first years of the Obama administration are seen as crucial.

Obama's inauguration in January 2009 marked the start of an extended campaign season in Latin America. Between 2009 and 2011, presidential elections have been scheduled for fourteen of the region's eighteen countries, offering yet another opportunity for improving U.S.–Latin American relations. The Fifth Summit of the Americas in Trinidad and Tobago in April

2009 presents an important opportunity for the Obama administration to set a tone for future relations with Latin America. Although it is not realistic to expect dramatic change, modest modifications in focus and style could create a climate more conducive to cooperation.

An Agenda for Cooperation

Overall there has been significant progress during the last two decades in the rule of law and democratic governance, although challenges to public security are becoming more intense in some countries, particularly those linked to drug cultivation and shipment. The United States is widely recognized in Latin America as having tried to play an active, positive role in judicial and police reform and support for civil society, human rights, and fair elections. Despite overall positive trends, however, there have been setbacks in some countries, such as Venezuela and Nicaragua. Furthermore, the existence of the prison at Guantánamo and strong U.S. support for the government and military in Colombia, which some accuse of complicity with paramilitary groups, have raised doubts concerning U.S. commitment to human rights and the rule of law.

Perhaps no country better exemplifies the need for sustained international cooperation than Haiti. The country is in a perpetual crisis driven by a lack of governmental competence and exacerbated by insufficient arable land, deforestation, and the related problem of floods triggered by hurricanes. As the poorest country in the region, Haiti is a test case for the effectiveness of multilateral cooperation. In such sensitive cases, better coordination with countries such as Brazil, Mexico, Chile, and Argentina and the strengthening of regional and subregional bodies should aid the pursuit of common goals.

The Rule of Law in Latin America

Progress on rule of law in the region has been uneven. Overall there is greater awareness of and respect for human rights. Judicial systems and police forces are engaged in reforms and innovation that are increasing access to justice and providing fairer enforcement of the law. Freer media and a dramatic growth in civil society stakeholders have led to greater oversight of the state and uncovered government malfeasance, a dramatic change from the decades during which authoritarian rule placed the state above the law. Nevertheless, countries that serve as sources of and transit points for drugs find their societies threatened by well-armed and organized criminal bands, sometimes with the complicity of the police, portions of the military, politicians, and judges.

Crime and corruption pose the greatest threats to rule of law, and violence remains rampant in many countries as a result of weak institutions and the presence of organized crime and youth gangs. Much of the violence and instability in the region can be traced to the drug trade. Supported largely by consumers in the United States and Europe, this problem requires a better coordinated and more realistic regional, if not global, response. With Mexico and other countries under siege from drug traffickers, the presidents of Mexico, Honduras, and Argentina recently called for decriminalization of possession of small amounts of some drugs. This proposal, unthinkable a few years ago, may become more prevalent in the region and may force the new U.S. administration to consider new approaches to limiting the damage caused by the drug trade.

Establishing the rule of law in Latin America seems to take two steps forward and one step back—or sometimes two steps back, when weak governments and judicial systems find themselves overwhelmed. Nonetheless, progress has been made since the end of the dictatorships in Uruguay, Chile, Argentina, and Brazil (among others) and the cessation of Central American conflicts, as seen from the following developments:

Human rights. Respect for human rights has increased, and the legal framework for human rights protection is relatively strong. Argentina, Chile, and Peru have combated impunity in human rights cases while ensuring respect for legal procedures and due process.

Civil society. At the regional level, long-established bodies such as the Inter-American Commission on Human Rights and the Inter-American Court of Human Rights have become in many cases real mechanisms for handling citizens' complaints. Active civil society networks also monitor human rights, and many governments are willing to cooperate with international and regional human rights bodies.

Rule of law. One highly visible manifestation of the rule of law has been the relative success with which free and fair elections have been established. In many countries ensuring the right to vote through independent and professional election commissions and the existence of independent election-monitoring groups have helped strengthen the rule of law, even though illicit sources of campaign funds still make headlines regularly. Strong foreign involvement in the professionalization of election administration and support for civil society election-monitoring groups have had a positive influence. Even in Venezuela, which has been criticized for concentrating power in the executive branch, President Hugo Chávez lost a referendum in 2007 that would have expanded his powers.

Fighting corruption. Anticorruption efforts have been aided by greater judicial autonomy and freer and more independent media that are increasingly willing to expose government officials to public scrutiny.

Security. Although public security is perceived as deteriorating in most countries of Latin America, there have been some successes. Bogotá once had the highest homicide rate among the region's capitals, but a multidimensional program, the Development Security and Peace Program (DESPAZ), dramatically lowered the rate from about eighty murders per 100,000 people in 1993 to twenty-one in 2004. São Paulo, using a variation on the measures implemented in Colombia, has seen a steady decline in homicide rates since 1999, in contrast to Brazil's overall upward trend in the homicide rate. Crime fighting through the development of new institutions and policies, such as those used to reduce homicides in Bogotá, Cali, and São Paulo, appears to be most successful when driven and designed locally.

Much of the progress in addressing a legacy of human rights abuses and impunity can be attributed to institutional developments spurred by greater awareness of and demand for basic rights. In Peru, Colombia, Chile, Argentina and Brazil, the supreme courts, constitutional courts, and ombudsman's offices have played an important role in bolstering democracy and respect for human rights.

In Guatemala, Argentina, Chile, and Peru, truth commissions have proposed ways of addressing the aftermath of violence, aiding victims and deepening democracy. These bodies have helped affirm countries' commitments to human rights, even if perpetrators of abuses have been brought to justice only infrequently. The prosecution of several high-profile corruption and human rights cases has shown that governing elites are no longer assured of peaceful retirement if they commit crimes while in office, as illustrated by the trials of Chile's dictator, General Augusto Pinochet, and Peru's former president Alberto Fujimori.

Democratization in the region is accompanied by a flourishing civil society that assumes oversight functions when the state is unwilling or poorly equipped to audit itself. Independent media and freedom of information acts also provide greater access to government information.

Despite these successes and advances, establishing the rule of law in Latin America is still an uphill battle. Although measurement is still inadequate and imprecise, the World Bank estimates that the rule of law in Latin America declined by about 18 percent between 1996 and 2006, and the region faces serious challenges:

Homicide rates. Latin America has a homicide rate of 22.9 per 100,000 inhabitants, second only to that of Africa and twice the worldwide average. Despite the local security successes previously described, in most of the region's eighteen countries, crime is the number one public concern. In Rio de Janeiro, an estimated 700 people are shot to death by police each year. It is a bitter irony that murder and crime rates have soared in El Salvador, Guatemala, and Honduras since armed conflicts ended in the 1980s.

Drug trafficking. Drug trafficking fuels both high-level organized crime and street-level youth gangs, which are an increasing source of terror for urban residents of Guatemala, El Salvador, and Honduras. In some countries, drug barons finance the election of some candidates and assassinate others who do not pledge fealty. Dozens of candidates were murdered during Guatemala's recent congressional election campaign. The United Nations reports that despite the "war on drugs" and increased drug seizures, the street price of cocaine has been dropping steadily and significantly in the United States, indicating greater supply and failure of interdiction even as interceptions increase.

Corruption. Although there are great variations within the region, Latin America is ranked overall by Transparency International as the world's second most corrupt region, after Africa. Thirty-two percent of people who have had contact with the police report having paid bribes. In general, poorer countries suffer disproportionately from corruption. Central American and Caribbean nations, which serve as transit points for drug trafficking, find their government institutions infiltrated and sometimes hijacked by organized crime. Despite international conventions and anticorruption collaboration between civil society and international organizations, some governments still lack the political will and resources to take decisive action. Corruption poses a substantial obstacle to development. There must be a renewed effort to find new, more creative methods to combat corruption and incentives for promoting good governance and rule of law, such as those recommended by the World Bank Institute.

Judiciary. Judicial systems are generally mistrusted and underfunded, and the poor often lack access to justice. Judges are underpaid and prisons overcrowded. There has been progress in modernizing judicial systems, but larger budgets are needed, especially in the Andean countries.

Democratic Governance

Latin America and the Caribbean are caught in a political paradox. While democracy is becoming more firmly entrenched, it is also being questioned.

According to Latinobarómetro, support for democracy dropped from 58 percent to 54 percent between 1995 and 2007.[5] Costa Rica and Uruguay show the highest levels of support for democracy, with 83 and 75 percent, respectively and Bolivia and Venezuela take third and fourth place, with 67 percent of citizens in both countries agreeing that democracy is preferable to any other system of government. Countries with the lowest scores are those facing public security crises—Honduras, El Salvador, and Guatemala.

Citizens who are disenchanted with democracy do not seek a return to authoritarian regimes; rather, they are "dissatisfied democrats." The dissatisfaction is not with democracy as a system of government, but with its failure to deliver on its promise. This citizen dissatisfaction suggests the urgency of reforms that would transform these systems from electoral democracies into true citizen democracies.[6]

One of the most important positive developments in Latin American democracies in recent years has been increasingly inclusive politics. The 2000 presidential elections in Mexico and the Paraguayan elections in 2008 have brought new political movements to power, breaking the long-standing political monopolies of the PRI (Partido Revolucionario Institucional) in Mexico and the Partido Colorado in Paraguay.

Traditionally excluded groups have also gained ground. The percentage of women elected to Latin American parliaments nearly doubled between 1997 and 2007, from 10 percent to 18 percent, and the number of women cabinet ministers increased from 9 to 24 percent during the same period of time. Although Latin America has had only four elected female presidents in its history, two have taken office since 2006. In Bolivia, indigenous people's increased political participation experienced a turning point in municipal elections in the mid-1990s and has been transformed since the December 2005 election of President Evo Morales. Though the situation in Ecuador is less dramatic, that country has also seen indigenous movements succeed in municipal and legislative elections and, as part of a coalition, in the executive branch. Although women and indigenous people still have a long way to go to achieve representation proportionate to their numbers, their increasing inclusion has begun to make a difference in terms of equity.

Other significant strides have been made in democratic governance in recent years:

Resolution of political crises. Political crises in Ecuador, Bolivia, Venezuela, Peru, and Argentina were managed through legal constitutional means, accompanied by political pacts and reforms to improve the quality of elections, political representation, and sometimes democracy itself.

Transparent elections. Increasingly fair, transparent elections have helped increase the legitimacy of governments and electoral authorities and ensure peaceful transfer of power and alternating parties in power. In most countries, elections have reflected the will of the people and helped consolidate democratic governance. In many elections, the international community, particularly OAS observer missions, has played a key role in ensuring transparency. Election monitoring by civil society groups has been important in Mexico, Guatemala, Nicaragua, Panama, Colombia, Ecuador, Venezuela, Bolivia, Paraguay, and Peru.

Improved dialogue. The international community and national and international NGOs have promoted dialogue, consensus, support for a stronger party system, and public participation in and oversight of democratic culture. Events such as the development of Peru's National Accord and or the naming of Ecuador's Supreme Court in 2005, after the resignation of President Lucio Gutiérrez, are examples of positive relations among the international community, civil society, and political parties.

Inter-American Democratic Charter. The Inter-American Democratic Charter was adopted by the OAS on September 11, 2001. While governments' lack of commitment has prevented it from functioning as it should, it is important to strengthen it to serve as a mechanism for defending democracy and fair elections.

What, then, are the challenges to democratic governance? A few countries have experienced an actual deterioration of civil and political rights, but a return to authoritarianism is not the gravest governance issue facing Latin America: the greatest challenge today stems from the complexity presented by expanding and strengthening democracies that cannot respond adequately when large numbers of citizens, long sidelined from political life, demand inclusion. Much has been learned in recent years about building on a foundation of constitutional legality, free elections, electoral oversight, defense of human rights, and the consolidation of democratic institution, but some serious and complex problems persist in the region as a whole:

Weak states. In most countries, the state is weak. A responsible fiscal policy that would promote equality, legality, equal opportunity, and substantial improvement in public services (justice, health, education, public security, water, and so forth) is lacking. Despite economic growth throughout Latin America, poverty has increased or held steady in subregions—the Andean countries and Central America, particularly. This is a call for the United States and European countries to cooperate in solving the food and energy crises and reducing poverty and inequality, as well as to discuss ways to decrease the negative impact of developed countries' farm subsidies.

Dissatisfaction with government. Dissatisfaction with government and politics is a response to inequality, poverty, and social exclusion, as well as the poor functioning of institutions. The 2007 Latinobarómetro survey concluded that respondents were calling for more state involvement: "The region's inhabitants perceive that the fruits of economic progress do not reach everyone. It is the hand of the state that somehow reaches them with development." In other words, "lower poverty and unemployment rates are not enough to make people believe that the market economy is the only system that will bring development."[7]

Pessimistic outlook. There is disenchantment with politics and pessimism about democratic institutions (legislative and judicial branches and oversight bodies) and political parties. "Hyper-presidentialism"—a concentration of power in the executive—is the norm in a number of countries, with parliaments and opposition parties too weak to provide effective checks and balances.

Media monopoly. The media have increasing influence in politics and democracy. The danger is that they may obey powerful economic interests and are increasingly concentrated in fewer hands, undermining the public debate that is a cornerstone of democracy.

Certain countries also face specific hurdles.

Venezuela and Nicaragua. Both face a risk of what some call authoritarian involution and others call radical populism. Radical populism is characterized by highly concentrated power that threatens the alternation of parties in power and the guarantees necessary for effective political opposition; greater influence exercised by the executive branch and control over democratic institutions; violation of civil and political rights, such as freedom of expression, of association, and the press. In Venezuela, however, President Hugo Chávez's defeat in the December 2007 referendum suggests that the government respects election results.

Bolivia. The October 2008 agreement between the government and the opposition paved the way for a January 25, 2009, constitutional referendum. Judging by the support (68 percent) President Morales received in defeating a recent presidential recall (August 2008), the constitution is expected to win approval. The opposition has not offered a viable alternative to the vision of Morales's Movimiento al Socialismo, but it has blocked some of the president's initiatives, leading to political conflict and even violent confrontation.

Ecuador. With the support of an overwhelming national majority (64 percent), Ecuador's new constitution took effect October 20, 2008. The current "transition regime" will oversee the elimination of the country's existing legal institutions and the creation of new ones. A presidential election as well the election of a new legislature has been slated for February 2009.

Colombia. The persistence of guerrilla forces, paramilitaries, and drug trafficking threatens democratic governance. The country is implementing reforms in an effort to decrease the influence of drug trafficking on the government, but the dispute sparked earlier this year by Colombia's bombing of a FARC camp in Ecuador highlights the danger that the internal conflict could spill over the country's borders.

Eight Steps toward a More Constructive Partnership

There are many positive trends in the region, but there are also a number of persistent or emerging challenges to the rule of law and governance. The response of the new U.S. administration should be based on the principles of dialogue, collaboration and multilateralism. Here are eight of the most important steps the Obama administration can and should take to encourage improved democratic governance and rule of law in the Americas.

Encourage Dialogue with Politically Sensitive Countries

Dialogue, consultation, and informal multilateralism are essential tools for furthering the rule of law and democratic governance. It is crucial to respect and encourage regional and subregional political and economic integration and security efforts in Latin America and the Caribbean to lay the groundwork for dialogue and joint actions involving as many countries as possible. Particular attention should be paid to Cuba, Mexico, and Colombia.

Cuba. A genuine U.S. opening toward Cuba is a policy shift that would be welcomed throughout Latin America. U.S. policy has failed to foster democratic governance and rule of law in Cuba. The embargo only provides the Castro brothers with justification for prolonging their repressive hold on power. Greater engagement with Cuba could only improve this situation, and there is no issue that carries more symbolic weight for the rest of Latin America. The U.S. government should recognize that it remains alone in its embargo of Cuba, the justifications for which appear increasingly ridiculous in light of close U.S. relations with Communist China and Vietnam.

Cuba recently accepted the European Union's invitation to engage in a formal political dialogue—the first step toward normalizing relations between Cuba and the twenty-seven EU member states. The United Nations, with the support of all Latin American countries, has voted repeatedly on measures to end the embargo. Engagement with Cuba should be undertaken in cooperation with the European Union, Canada, and Latin America. The United States should join forces with the EU, the OAS, and especially with the Rio Group (that recently welcomed Cuba as a full member) to develop a common policy to foster democratic development in Cuba. Brazil and Mexico could be helpful in this regard. Human rights in Cuba should, of course, remain a paramount concern. A new U.S. Cuba policy should include:

—An immediate end to heavy-handed pressure on other countries to isolate Cuba

—Initiation of official dialogue and lifting of the embargo

—An offer of incentives, in cooperation with the other Latin American countries (especially Brazil and Mexico), Canada, and the EU so that Cuba can achieve basic milestones in democracy and rule of law, while insisting on pluralization of the political landscape and free and fair elections with multilateral assistance

—Economic assistance to dissidents, starting with a review of their needs and development of an effective, realistic people-to-people strategy

—Implementation of a policy of engagement, which would be beneficial for Cuba's economic and political development and increase pressure for increased economic and political liberties.

U.S. leaders' demonization of Cuba's leadership is short-sighted, juvenile, and counterproductive. Engagement and dialogue with Cuba, and easing of restrictions on Americans visiting Cuba, will immediately boost U.S. prestige in the region and help restore the moral authority that must undergird calls for democratic governance and respect for rule of law and human rights in Cuba. As with Venezuela and other politically sensitive countries, heavy-handedness by the United States will further retard development of democracy and rule of law in this island nation.

Mexico. The government of President Felipe Calderon is fighting a war with drug cartels that extends to the U.S. border. Many police and government officials have been assassinated, and national and local government agencies have been sidelined or corrupted. Because of extensive police corruption, President Calderon has begun relying on the army to confront the traffickers, with mixed results. The issue of drugs links the two countries very closely, as Mexico is a producer and transporter, and the United States is the consumer. In addition, many of the arms used by the traffickers appear to come from the United States. So far, both countries are losing the "war on drugs." As part of the Mérida Initiative, the United States has offered Mexico $1.4 billion in training and equipment between 2008 and 2010, but this pervasive problem will not be solved only through training and equipment. A long-term solution will require deeper cooperation and more coordinated, systematic, and imaginative policies. Because of their proximity and increasingly shared problems, the emphasis must be on bilateral relations between the United States and Mexico. The Mérida Initiative can be a source of some help to Mexico, but most of the resources and political resolve must come from that country.

Recommendations as to how the United States can foster greater rule of law in Mexico focus primarily on the interconnected issues of public security, drugs, and immigration.

—*Immigration.* Migration of Mexicans has created a massive rule-of-law issue in the United States, as much of the migration is illegal and benefits cartels who traffic the illegals. A simple solution to discourage illegal migration might be to allow Mexicans and perhaps other Latin Americans to purchase guest-worker visas. This would benefit all parties except the traffickers, who charge thousands of dollars to smuggle people across the border and yet sometimes abandon them to dire fates. Most migrants would rather pay a U.S. consulate for a visa if they could do so.

—*Public security.* The United States and Mexico need to tighten and coordinate mechanisms for restraining weapons and increase penalties for illegal gun possession. Mexico must also reduce the number of illegal guns through programs such as amnesties and the purchase of weapons from individuals.

—*Drug policy.* The United States and other regional actors need to reassess drug policy. The current policy of prohibition has led to the growth of huge multinational drug mafias that are undermining the rule of law in Mexico and many other countries. Regulation and harm reduction should figure prominently in the discussion of new policies, which will involve choices between lesser and greater evils.

Colombia. The U.S.-led Plan Colombia, with an average annual investment of $600 million, changed the balance of power in Colombia. President Álvaro Uribe and his administration won wide support for public security improvements while weakening the insurgency group FARC. Uribe is now Latin America's most popular president, and many believe Colombia's constitution should be modified to allow him to run for a third term in 2010. First, if the United States wishes to avoid supporting a new era of regional strongmen, or *caudillos,* it should signal its disapproval of such a constitutional change enabling a third term, particularly in light of similar aspirations on the part of Chávez in Venezuela, President Rafael Correa in Ecuador, and Bolivia's Morales to extend their terms of office beyond what their constitutions allow.

Second, as Plan Colombia resources shrink in the wake of the economic crisis and with fewer troops available to maintain public order and security, it is important that the United States join with the Colombian government and the democratic opposition to plan for this eventuality and head off a crisis in Colombian security policy. This strategy should focus on consolidating democracy, above and beyond security considerations, to guarantee the sustainability of the gains achieved so far. Third, approval by the United States of the U.S.-Colombia Free Trade Agreement would signal U.S. support for the measure and could help Colombia weather the global financial crisis. Finally, U.S. commitment to broad, multiparty dialogue is the best strategy for avoiding the election of a government that could ally itself with Venezuela's President Chávez.

Venezuela. The situation in Venezuela must be monitored carefully to ensure that political and civil rights do not deteriorate further. It is important to avoid unilateral policies that lead to greater polarization and complicate possibilities for dialogue between the government and the opposition. The irony here is that the United States has been President Chávez's biggest trading partner: more than 60 percent of Venezuela's oil exports go to the United States, and trade between the two countries has grown steadily, not only in the oil sector. Meanwhile, Venezuela's GDP grew by about 76 percent between 2003 and 2007, and the country pursued a commendable policy of investing heavily in literacy, education, and health. That investment is the source of Chávez's popularity among many Latin Americans. A dramatic decline in the price of oil from above U.S.$150 in the summer of 2008 to below U.S.$45 in December 2008 could result in a disproportionately large loss of influence for Chávez, domestically as well as internationally. In addition, Venezuela's oil production has dropped by about 25 percent since 1997, reflecting politicized and incompetent handling of the national oil company, PDVSA, the goose that lays Venezuela's golden eggs. So President Chávez may be headed for difficult times. Instead of engaging in saber rattling with the Venezuelan leader, the United States should attempt to counter more effectively his regional influence. If the Venezuelan president's power wanes, the United States should avoid any move that might undermine the country's active, homegrown opposition.

Bolivia. President Evo Morales, whose convincing mandate in the 2005 elections was overwhelmingly reaffirmed in a 2008 referendum, is using his popularity to try to adopt a new constitution in a process that echoes the constitutional revisions that took place in Venezuela in 1999 and Ecuador in 2008. There is substantial political tension between the natural gas–rich lowlands, where there is a separatist movement, and the highlands, where most of the indigenous majority lives. As the Morales government attempts to incorporate this indigenous majority into the political mainstream, active cooperation from Washington and other states is needed to support dialogue between the government and the opposition and to avoid greater polarization and political instability. Unfortunately, relations between Washington and La Paz have reached a low point with the expulsion of the U.S. ambassador, Washington's "decertification" of Bolivia as a trusted partner in antidrug efforts, and President George W. Bush's proposal to suspend trade preferences for Bolivia.

Although direct U.S. engagement in Bolivia's domestic mediation efforts is not an option, the United States and its European partners should support regional efforts to defuse potential violence and discretely encourage efforts by other Latin American countries such as Brazil, Argentina, Chile, and Colombia to facilitate reconciliation. The United States should correct imbalances in its bilateral relationship by decreasing funding to opposition regional governments and focus instead on activities coordinated with the central government and a broad range of municipal actors. Because Bolivia is a major producer of coca leaves, it should also be part of a regional initiative to mitigate the damage that results from the drug trade.

Ecuador. The country is undergoing a challenging political transition as it seeks to implement a new constitution, ratified with strong popular support in September 2008, which will expand and concentrate previously weak executive power and increase state intervention in the economy. Facing a weak and fragmented opposition, President Rafael Correa is seeking to leverage his popularity to create a new political framework—and win reelection in 2009, as he is likely to do. The country is suffering from high inflation, however, and the economy will be hit hard by the decline in oil prices; the reduction in revenues is likely to force the government to cut back on social programs. It is critical that the United States avoid the temptation to treat Ecuador as part of a Venezuela-led bloc; the contexts are distinct and there are tensions between the countries, as evidenced by their different positions regarding the future development of the Andean Community.

Haiti. The problems besetting the hemisphere's poorest country are many, including a degraded environment, urban crime, and challenges to state authority stemming from circumstances arising from the drug trade, low literacy rates, and poverty. More than half the population lives on less than one dollar a day. Haiti is a failed state. Laurence Whitehead, an Oxford University political scientist, writes elsewhere in this volume, "As various state-building exercises have shown, one cannot implant democracy in the absence of solid state structures." If intervention is to be successful, the United States should work closely with Latin American countries, Canada, and the European Union, within the OAS and United Nations, toward longer-term goals and develop a realistic plan to help Haiti address its fundamental problems.

Generate a New Post-Washington Consensus

Although the Washington Consensus is widely considered defunct, a clear successor has not emerged.[8] The European Union's support for discussion of "social cohesion" as a response to inequality and exclusion fills part of the gap. The Venezuela-led Bolivarian Alternative, which emphasizes the role of the state in economic affairs, has also gained ground in many circles. But it is time for the United States and Latin America to produce new ideas and proposals for joint action, especially now that the world is rethinking the relationship between the state and the market and seeking new foundations for the global financial system.

Create an Inter-American Democracy Fund

As part of a broader review of U.S. foreign assistance, cooperation with Latin America on governance and the rule of law requires closer, more empirical examination. Democracy is the dominant form of government in Latin America, and there is substantial agreement that the focus in the region must be on improving the efficiency, competence, and integrity of democratic institutions.

Latin America, having experienced several decades of democratic governance and having a range of available bilateral and multilateral assistance providers, no longer feels dependent on the United States for the transfer of technical skills. Instead, there is interest in access to a broader range of ideas, innovations, and experiences from within Latin America and from other regions.

A framework for cooperation is needed, along with a greater push to strengthen democracy, focusing on empirical assessment of needs, demands, and policies for governance and the rule of law. Such a framework could be provided by the creation of an inter-American democracy fund, to be financed by contributions from the United States, Canada, the European Union, and Latin American countries, and managed through either an existing multilateral organization or an ad hoc structure. The fund's mission would include the following:

Support civil society. Latin America has developed a vibrant civil society, sometimes with the support of foreign donors. Well-targeted financial support for civil society organizations can enrich democracy and the rule of law by enhancing democratic and legal institutions' educational, advocacy, and oversight functions and helping them become a training ground for future government officials. Efforts to build civil society's advocacy capacity can be strengthened by disseminating a clearer understanding of state–society interactions and supporting organizations with solid membership and political clout. Proper targeting of financial support does not mean that organizations become wholly dependent on foreign funds or serve as mouthpieces for U.S. or other partisan interests; rather, they develop genuine foundations of popular support and are managed efficiently and transparently.

Expand political representation. Despite the flaws in parliaments and political parties, there is no substitute for them. The proposed inter-American democracy fund would strengthen parties' outreach, transparency, internal democratic processes, and programmatic capacity. The inclusive, nonpartisan approach increasingly adopted by U.S. party foundations (for instance, the National Democratic Institute and the International Republic Institute) should continue. Funding to strengthen parliaments could help to facilitate demand-driven political reforms that enhance party cohesion, research, policy planning, and ability to review and analyze national budgets.

Encourage diversification of the media. In Mexico, Brazil, and Colombia, as well as in several other Latin American countries, the media are owned by monopolies or duopolies. Declining trust and participation in political parties have allowed the media to increase their influence on agenda setting and election outcomes. The United States can help increase freedom of the press by promoting links between U.S. and Canadian media and those in Latin America, transparency in media ownership, equitable media access during elections, monitoring of press coverage and freedom by the OAS and civil society groups, and the development of alternative media.

Cooperate in pan-American education. The ability of Latin Americans to solve their own problems depends to a great extent on the quality of education and the sharing of ideas and experiences in the region. The United States, while providing strong military support and coordination to Latin American countries, has underinvested in education. Ironically, while helping train Latin America's political and economic elites, U.S. universities also have promoted a brain drain from the region. Meanwhile, many Latin American students lack access to U.S. universities or find it increasingly difficult to obtain visas. The United States should support greater academic cooperation in the social sciences, including scholarships or funding to expand Latin American institutions such as FLACSO (the Latin American School of Social Sciences) and programs that would help professionalize public administration. Scholarships and support should be expanded, and government officials should be allowed sabbaticals to reinforce and share their intellectual capital, increase the professionalism of public administrators, and provide incentives for good governance. Generous investment in education would be repaid many times over in greater regional cooperation and integration and improved bilateral and multilateral relations.

Promote justice. U.S. and European cooperation agencies should evaluate previous efforts at justice and police reform and identify opportunities to more effectively support genuine improvements in juridical and law enforcements institutions' competence and impartiality. The international community should also support the development of better internal controls, anticorruption measures, and civil society participation in reform and oversight, and assist with the design of indicators for the judiciary and public-defender and stronger justice-of-the-peace systems. Facilitating the sharing of local experience is crucial to finding creative solutions to common problems.

Recognize That the Rule of Law Begins at Home

U.S. influence on Latin American rule-of-law policies has been severely undermined by its perceived lack of moral authority. To change this, the new U.S. president should promptly address three issues: the prison at Guantánamo, American human rights practices, and the Cuba embargo.

The Guantánamo prison has had a negative effect on U.S.–Latin American relations. For many Latin Americans, it reflects disregard for human rights and the rule of law and is an affront to the region, which has not forgotten its own dark history of decades of state-sponsored abuse of human rights and civil liberties. Closing the prison immediately would go a long way toward restoring Latin Americans' trust and confidence in the United States.

Similarly, U.S. advocacy for human rights rings hollow as long as the United States defers joining the inter-American human rights system. Becoming a member of the Inter-American Court of Human Rights and recognizing the jurisdiction of the International Criminal Court would help improve the United States' image in the region as a defender, and not just a preacher, of human rights.

The United Nations and all Latin American countries have voted repeatedly for resolutions to end the U.S. embargo against Cuba. Closing Guantánamo and opening up relations with Cuba would send the strongest possible message to Latin America that the United States is ready to be a partner with the region.

Build a Domestic Constituency for Hemispheric Cooperation

U.S. citizens are woefully ignorant of Latin American processes and politics. A 2007 Zogby poll found that only 10 percent of those polled were familiar with Brazilian president Luiz Inácio "Lula" da Silva, and only 20 percent had heard of Mexican president Felipe Calderon.[9] Americans also lack knowledge about development aid: most vastly overestimate the percentage of the federal budget allocated to foreign assistance. Sustainable political support for improved U.S.–Latin American relations depends on the development of a domestic constituency with greater awareness of and commitment to hemispheric issues:

—Latino and Hispanic communities should play a special role in educating U.S. citizens about Latin America.

—Education on hemispheric issues and cooperation should be part of a broader overhaul of the U.S. educational system, with the goal of forming citizens who are better prepared to live in a globalized world and in particular have a better understanding of the interpenetration of U.S. and Latin American societies and interests.

Strengthen the Inter-American Democratic Charter and OAS Electoral Missions

So far the Inter-American Democratic Charter has served primarily as a statement of principles; in addition it should incorporate economic and social rights as substantive elements of democracy. There are various ways to strengthen the charter. The secretary general of the OAS should be empowered to promote greater application of the charter in the region. Article 17 of the charter, in section IV, "Strengthening and Preservation of Democratic Institutions," states: "When the government of a member state considers that its democratic political institutional process or its legitimate exercise of power is at risk, it may request assistance from the Secretary General or the Permanent Council for the strengthening and preservation of its democratic system."[10] The invocation of this article by a member country would also provide an opportunity to apply and legitimize the charter. The charter should be reinforced through the creation of a civil society monitoring network and an international coalition of "friends of the charter" countries to promote its implementation.

Strengthening OAS electoral missions also offers an opportunity to promote regional cooperation for reform and greater transparency in electoral systems. In addition, these missions have the support of most of the region's countries.

Support Global Anticorruption Instruments and Practices

The U.S. Foreign Corrupt Practices Act, passed in 1977, provides a legal basis for prosecuting bribery of foreign officials, politicians, and political parties. It is a credible deterrent, and the United States should urge the European Union to implement a similar measure. The United States should actively support other complementary measures aimed at achieving mutual accountability and transparency between businesses and governments. One example of such a measure is the Extractive Industries Transparency Initiative (EITI), a public-private effort aimed at increasing the transparency of payments by mining and related companies to governments. Announced by British prime minister Tony Blair at the World Summit on Sustainable Development in Johannesburg in September 2002, EITI sets a global standard for companies to publish what they pay and for governments to disclose what they receive.[11]

Establish High-Level Dialogue on Sensitive Issues

U.S.–Latin American relations are profoundly affected—and often driven—by two issues: drugs and immigration. Even though the particular circumstances of drug trafficking and immigration are largely determined by domestic considerations in separate countries, success in meeting the challenges they pose depends on a new multilateral approach based on regional dialogue and cooperation. It is crucial for the United States, Canada, and Latin American countries to start talks on a new regional security strategy that should especially highlight problems related to drug trafficking, public security, and immigration.

Drug trafficking as a security threat. Regional security is more affected by the drug trade than by terrorism. The "war on drugs" has had numerous unintended effects, including the funding of organized crime (by some estimates, 70 percent of organized crime proceeds come from drug trafficking) and the creation of a narco-industrial complex that creates jobs for financial institutions, prisons, security forces, government bureaucracies, weapons manufacturers, and criminal groups. Recognition that the negative effects of prohibition may outweigh the benefits has led some serious analysts in the region to call for some degree of drug legalization. As we have said earlier in this paper, three Latin American presidents recently proposed decriminalizing possession of small amounts of some drugs. A respected independent inter-American panel should investigate and explain to the public the effects and costs of drug control and the ways in which government agencies and illegal organizations have become mutually dependent. The outcome could signal the need for a paradigm shift from "war" to a more realistic focus on the reduction of harm from taking drugs, while recognizing the complex legal, moral, and public health issues involved in decriminalizing drugs. There does seem to be growing consensus that combating drug-related criminal networks requires enhanced regional cooperation to train and assist police, prosecutors, and judicial institutions.

Violence and inadequate public security. The lack of public security constitutes the principal threat to stability, stronger democracy, and economic development in Latin America. Along the U.S.-Mexican border, the violence that is common on the Mexican side is increasingly likely to spill over into the United States. Violent behavior is closely connected with thwarted economic development. According to the Inter-American Development Bank, the cost of crime in Latin America, including the value of stolen property, is about $16.8 billion, equivalent to 15 percent of the region's GDP. Besides human and economic losses, violence also threatens the integrity of the state and democratic institutions and ultimately spurs migration, as drug lords supplant the state in towns and regions. This pressing concern with establishing public security is reflected in an agreement, the Commitment to the Public Security of the Americas, which was adopted October 2008 during the first meeting of ministers on public security in the Americas in Mexico City.[12] Ensuring public security must be balanced by full respect for human rights and requires reinforced cooperation between ministries of public security throughout the hemisphere. Policies should include modernization of police management, including the OAS's inter-American police training program, and a stronger role for the Inter-American Coalition for the Prevention of Violence, "an alliance of inter-American and international agencies formed to develop strategies and solutions to address high levels of violence and crime in the Americas."[13]

Role of armed forces. One troubling trend is the degree to which the armed forces in some countries are called on to maintain internal order, especially to combat crime and drug trafficking. This leads to the militarization of civilian life and undermines the professionalism of the armed forces by involving them in matters that are outside their purview and for which they have neither the training nor the resources. Although migration, drugs, and crime are important regional concerns, they must be addressed by civilian institutions, particularly police forces, which need strong support and training to prevent them from being undermined by competition from the military.

Impact of U.S. immigration policies. U.S immigration policies have a direct impact on the rule of law and therefore merit regional consideration. About

85 percent of immigrants to the United States are from Mexico and Central America, and millions are in the country illegally. Far from deterring illegal immigration, U.S. policies have spurred the growth of a vast human-trafficking industry that fuels organized crime and undermines the rule of law in both Latin America and the United States. Deportation of gang members to countries to which they have only tenuous ties exacerbates crime and aggravates relations as in Guatemala, Honduras, and El Salvador. A recent Zogby poll suggests that many Americans would like to address illegal immigration by supporting job creation in Latin America.

The November 2008 U.S. presidential election gave Americans the chance to rethink the country's course, to improve relations with their Latin American neighbors, and to encourage a more effective and clearly defined role in shaping and supporting the region's democracies. President Barack Obama should not be afraid to review past policies, break with them where necessary, and present a new vision and approach that emphasizes constructive partnership instead of paternalism. For both the United States and Latin America, the benefits of such a change of course would be enormous.

Notes

1. The National Intelligence Council, *Global Scenarios to 2025, February 2008*. For the full report, please see www.dni.gov/nic/PDF_2025/2025_Global_Scenarios_to_2025.pdf.

2. Roberto Rusell, "America Latina para Estados Unidos: ¿especial, desdeñable, codiciada o perdida?" *Nueva Sociedad*, no. 206 (November-December 2006), available at www.nuso.org.

3. On Mercosur (Mercado Común del Sur, Common Market of the South), see http://news.bbc.co.uk/1/hi/world/americas/5195834.stm. The Andean Community (Comunidad Andina) is a subregional organization pursuing economic and social development through cooperation and integration. See www.comunidadandina.org/endex.htm.

4. Another good example is the December 2008 summit of Latin American and Caribbean leaders in Costa do Sauipe, Brazil, under the leadership of President Luiz Inácio "Lula" da Silva. Previous summits of Latin American and Caribbean leaders have always included former colonial powers Spain and Portugal or the United States.

5. Informe Latinobarómetro 2007 (www.latinobarometro.org).

6. The United Nations Development Program's 2004 report, *Democracy in Latin America: Towards a Citizens' Democracy*, refers to electoral democracies and citizens' democracies. While an electoral democracy is merely a "set of conditions for electing

and being elected," a citizens' democracy "requires a state capable of guaranteeing the universality of rights." The report goes on to explain that "for weak and ineffective States, hopes are limited to the preservation of electoral democracy." For further reading, see www.democracia.undp.org/Informe/Default.asp?Menu=15&Idioma=2.

7. Informe Latinobarómetro 2007 (www.latinobarometro.org).

8. The so-called Washington Consensus reflected broad agreement among international financial institutions and donor governments that free markets, deregulation, and privatization were the most likely factors to lead to economic growth.

9. Zogby, "Majority of Americans Understand Little about Latin American Neighbors," August 10, 2007.

10. See www.oas.org/OASpage/eng/Documents/Democractic_Charter.htm.

11. For further information, see www2.dfid.gov.uk/news/files/extractiveindustries.asp.

12. "Compromiso por la Seguridad Pública en las Américas [Commitment to Public Security in the Americas]," OEA/Ser.K/XLIX.1. MISPA/doc.7/08.rev.3, October 7, 2008 (adopted by the Organization of American States, October 8, 2008, Mexico City). The full text can be found through www.convivenciayseguridadciudadana.com/contenido/images/.

13. See www.who.int/violenceprevention/about/participants/iacpv/en/index.html.

three

Supporting Democracy in the Americas: The Case for Multilateral Action

Theodore J. Piccone

The mere fact of Barack Hussein Obama's decisive election as the first African American president can be a pivotal turning point in a much-needed repositioning of the United States' role as an ally of democratic reform around the world.

Of course, much more than an election and soaring rhetoric are needed to complete the revamping necessary to make U.S. policies to support democracy and promote human rights more credible and effective. This is particularly true in the Western Hemisphere, where democratization trends are fragile and U.S. influence is waning. The Obama administration needs to overhaul U.S. strategy for assisting democratic governance by investing serious time and resources in strengthening and, where necessary, creating new multilateral tools for supporting democratization in Latin America and around the world. This will require a significant shift in thinking, away from traditional bilateral channels of diplomatic pressure and assistance and toward multilateral cooperation with like-minded partners.

Why Washington Needs to Expand Multilateral Mechanisms

According to a number of polls, democracy is seen as a strongly held aspiration around the world. Most Latin Americans, like the vast majority of people from other regions, believe that democracy is better than any other form of government. But Latin Americans are largely dissatisfied with the way democracy works in their countries, particularly when it comes to distributing income and providing social protections. Corruption is seen as a huge impediment to improved governance. Trust in politicians and political parties ranks particularly low. In the 2008 Latinobarómetro poll, 54 percent believed that there is more corruption in politics than in any other sector of society.[1]

In essence, the positive democratic trends that have unfolded in the region over the last twenty years contain serious vulnerabilities. To prevent backsliding toward authoritarian rule, democracy assistance needs to translate into tangible improvements in the judicial system, accountability of public institutions and politicians, greater transparency, and improvement in public services.

Even though the United States has a vital interest in seeing a hemisphere of prosperous democratic states governed by the rule of law, its historical legacy in the region and more recent errors beyond—including conflating short-term security objectives with longer-term democratization goals in Iraq—handicap its credibility in working toward that goal. Public opinion polls around the world show U.S. favorability ratings at historic lows, including disapproval of U.S. unilateral action and democracy promotion.[2]

Latin America, a region with a complicated history of hot and cold relations with Washington, is generally in sync with this global trend. Only 34 percent of respondents in a 2007 Barómetro Iberoamericano survey had a positive opinion of the United States.[3] According to the 2008 Latinobarómetro poll, President Bush was tied with Fidel Castro with a 4.3 approval rating (out of 10), followed in last place by Daniel Ortega of Nicaragua, with a 4.0 rating.[4]

These low ratings could impair the Obama presidency. According to a special Latinobarómetro survey about the 2008 U.S. presidential election, 30 percent of those who were asked which candidate would be better for their country said that it made no difference who won the November election, and another 31 percent had no opinion.[5] This widespread indifference, according to Marta Lagos, director of the poll, shows the extent to which the United States has lost influence in the region in recent years.

Meanwhile, Latin American publics' perception of other international actors is more positive. The United Nations, for example, is trusted by 57 percent of respondents to the Barómetro Iberoamericano poll, and the Organization of American States (OAS) received 40 percent approval. The European Union met with approval by an average of 48 percent, and in nine Latin American countries the score was above 50 percent (see figure 3-1).[6]

Figure 3-1. How Positively the Latin American Public Perceives International Organizations

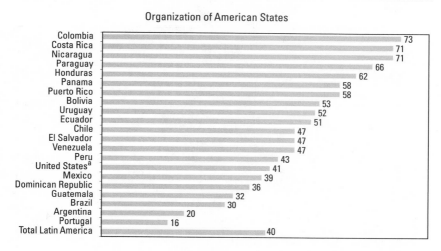

Organization of American States

Colombia	73
Costa Rica	71
Nicaragua	71
Paraguay	66
Honduras	62
Panama	58
Puerto Rico	58
Bolivia	53
Uruguay	52
Ecuador	51
Chile	47
El Salvador	47
Venezuela	47
Peru	43
United States[a]	41
Mexico	39
Dominican Republic	36
Guatemala	32
Brazil	30
Argentina	20
Portugal	16
Total Latin America	40

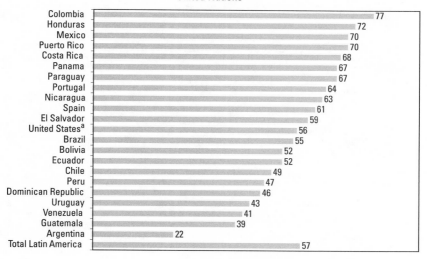

United Nations

Colombia	77
Honduras	72
Mexico	70
Puerto Rico	70
Costa Rica	68
Panama	67
Paraguay	67
Portugal	64
Nicaragua	63
Spain	61
El Salvador	59
United States[a]	56
Brazil	55
Bolivia	52
Ecuador	52
Chile	49
Peru	47
Dominican Republic	46
Uruguay	43
Venezuela	41
Guatemala	39
Argentina	22
Total Latin America	57

Source: CIMA, *Barómetro Iberoamericano de Gobernabilidad 2008* (Bogotá), pp. 26–28. For more information, see www.cimaiberoamerica.com.

a. Hispanic respondents.

Figure 3-1. How Positively the Latin American Public Perceives International Organizations (continued)

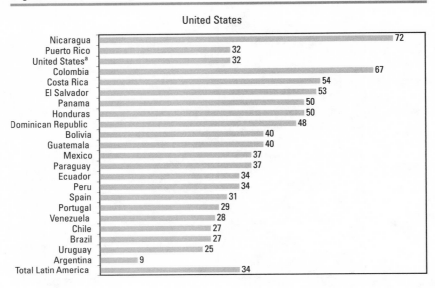

United States

Nicaragua	72
Puerto Rico	32
United States[a]	32
Colombia	67
Costa Rica	54
El Salvador	53
Panama	50
Honduras	50
Dominican Republic	48
Bolivia	40
Guatemala	40
Mexico	37
Paraguay	37
Ecuador	34
Peru	34
Spain	31
Portugal	29
Venezuela	28
Chile	27
Brazil	27
Uruguay	25
Argentina	9
Total Latin America	34

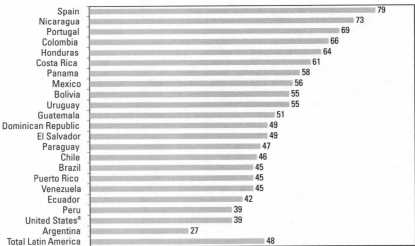

European Union

Spain	79
Nicaragua	73
Portugal	69
Colombia	66
Honduras	64
Costa Rica	61
Panama	58
Mexico	56
Bolivia	55
Uruguay	55
Guatemala	51
Dominican Republic	49
El Salvador	49
Paraguay	47
Chile	46
Brazil	45
Puerto Rico	45
Venezuela	45
Ecuador	42
Peru	39
United States[a]	39
Argentina	27
Total Latin America	48

Source: CIMA, *Barómetro Iberoamericano de Gobernabilidad 2008* (Bogotá), pp. 26–28. For more information, see www.cimaiberoamerica.com.

a. Hispanic respondents.

Given these realities, and the inherent sensitivity of providing external support to indigenous actors involving their own political affairs, it is critical that Washington move in partnership with others. It needs to reboot its image in the region as an ally of democracy by working closely with countries and international organizations that are accepted as credible actors, share basic assumptions about the positive link between democracy, development, and peace, and are willing to join in a deliberate though more muted effort to strengthen respect for democracy and the rule of law in the region. Washington needs to walk softly, talk quietly, and join hands with others.

Partners are needed as well to help share the financial and diplomatic burdens of this task. U.S. foreign aid will likely face significant cuts as a result of the global financial crisis, but a serious reduction in democracy assistance, which demands a long-term and consistent commitment of resources and expertise, would be a mistake: it would undermine our own interests in making sure that our scarce taxpayer dollars go to transparent and accountable governments.

The United States also needs to work with others in order to offer a more varied menu of democracy assistance to the increasingly diverse set of democracies and political cultures in the hemisphere. The democratic challenges faced by Bolivia, Paraguay, and Guatemala, for example, are different from each other and even more different from those faced in the United States. President Evo Morales of Bolivia, with its large indigenous population, is more interested in learning from South Africa's experience after apartheid than from North America's treatment of its native population. Fortunately, as democracies in the developing world mature and grow, there are abundant examples of democratic reform to study. A mechanism is needed, therefore, to bring these diverse actors and experts to the democracy assistance table. Latin American governments should step up to the plate by devoting their own resources and expertise to this joint venture. They should create a unit within their foreign ministries dedicated to democracy and human rights concerns and provide training and education for their diplomats—for example, on how they can help civil society play a positive role in democratic development.[7]

The Obama administration is inheriting over two decades of democracy aid experience with both diplomatic and development assistance strategies. Were it seriously to embark on a more multilateral course, it could build on this experience and consider new avenues for collaboration. Diplomatic and development assistance aspects of a comprehensive democracy assistance strategy, both separately and together, would serve the United States well in the Latin American region.

Diplomatic Tools for Democracy Assistance

Building on the lessons learned over the last several years, a number of diplomatic approaches could be employed to improve the outcomes of U.S. democracy initiatives in Latin America. They require a willingness on the part of the United States, however, to yield some control and share the burden with others.

Depersonalize Our Relations with the Region's Leaders

Early in its first term, the Bush administration committed a cardinal sin of democracy assistance: it signaled support for an unconstitutional coup against the democratically elected president of Venezuela, Hugo Chávez. It did not matter that Chávez himself had been jailed for plotting a coup during his days in the army, or that he was dedicated to an anti-U.S. agenda. What mattered was that an administration ostensibly committed to democratic freedoms abroad chose instead to engage in an old-style game of picking winners and losers, and did so in contravention of both the letter and spirit of important and positive regional norms built up since the 1980s. As a result, the Bush administration lost face in the region, just eight months after it had signed the Inter-American Democratic Charter committing all governments in the region to respecting constitutional government, and gave Chávez further ammunition for his anti-U.S. program. The U.S. image in the region was further damaged when it intervened in national elections in Bolivia, El Salvador, and Nicaragua by endorsing pro-U.S. candidates and threatening to withdraw bilateral benefits if voters supported the leftist candidate.

Advisers to Barack Obama explicitly rejected this kind of approach during the campaign and will likely handle similar situations with greater respect for the wishes of Latin American voters. President Obama has an opportunity to assert his administration's bona fides in this area by making clear at the April 2009 Summit of the Americas that the United States will refrain from interfering in internal elections and work constructively with whoever wins free and fair elections and respects the fundamental tenets of the Inter-American Democratic Charter. In addition, when President Obama and members of his cabinet visit countries in the region, they should meet with relevant political leaders of different parties and sectors as a way to convey the intention of the United States to work with the legitimate democratic leadership of the country broadly speaking, and not personalize relations with just the head of state. As democracies in the region mature and diversify, it is particularly important for the United States to strengthen ties with leaders of parliaments, cities, nongovernmental organizations, and other sectors of society that have or should have influence in the body politic.

Restore Civilian-Military Balance and Improve Interagency Coordination of U.S. Policy

One worrisome trend in U.S. policy toward the region and globally has been the expanding role of the Defense Department and its regional commands as the face of U.S. foreign policy. This is particularly true in the case of the U.S. Southern Command (SOUTHCOM), headquartered in Florida, which has Latin America and the Caribbean as its area of responsibility (excluding Mexico).

During the 1990s, as military officers in the region gradually retreated from the presidential palace to the barracks, civilian leaders struggled to assert democratic control of the armed forces. Given the legacy of U.S. support for military regimes in the region, the role of the U.S. military at that time was especially delicate. The Clinton administration sought to ameliorate that situation by investing resources in civilian capacity building to train a new generation of civilian leaders in defense management and national security policymaking.[8] In addition, U.S. policymakers in both the Clinton and Bush administrations sought to strengthen anti-coup provisions of the inter-American system as a way to ward off a return to military or authoritarian seizures of power, although the Venezuela debacle noted earlier revived fears of a return to the old ways of U.S. unilateralism.

Despite these efforts, however, over the last decade a demonstrable shift of power and resources from U.S. civilian to military agencies has occurred, starting with the disproportionate emphasis on military aid of Plan Colombia (see also chapter 4). Between 1997 and 2008, U.S. military and police assistance to the region grew from approximately $325 million to $973 million a year, mostly for counternarcotics assistance to Colombia and its Andean neighbors.[9] The new Mérida Initiative, approved by Congress in the fall of 2008, adds $450 million for Mexico and $100 million for Central America in military and police aid for 2008, and another $550 million for 2009.[10] Over this same period, an increasing proportion of U.S. assistance funds was handled directly by the Pentagon—which is subject to less congressional scrutiny and fewer restrictions on how aid is spent—instead of the State Department. Meanwhile, economic and social aid to the region grew from $594.4 million to $1.1 billion a year, a smaller rate of growth and a sharp reduction in the previous gap between traditional economic and security assistance (see figure 3-2). An additional $328 million was channeled through President Bush's Millennium Challenge Account (MCA) and the HIV/AIDS initiative, though only six of the poorest countries (El Salvador, Honduras, Nicaragua, and Paraguay for MCA; Guyana and Haiti for HIV/AIDS) qualified for these funds.

In addition to the shift toward security assistance, SOUTHCOM has emerged as a big player in the projection of U.S. soft power in the region. Over time, it has re-engineered its understanding of security threats in the hemisphere with a greater emphasis on poverty, crime, and inequality as the primary drivers of instability. Even though these underlying threats cannot be ameliorated through military means, SOUTHCOM has restructured its operations as if they could be. For example, a new SOUTHCOM Partnering Directorate "engages the public and private sector to coordinate and integrate with interagency, non-governmental organizations, and partner nations to facilitate good governance, the strengthening of economies, and a favorable investment climate in order to support economic independence, sustainable development, and prosperity throughout the region."[11] Operationally, this shift in focus also means more attention by the Pentagon to humanitarian assistance and disaster response, areas traditionally handled by civilian agencies. The elevation of SOUTHCOM's naval unit to the status of Fourth Fleet in 2008, which has caused a diplomatic stir in the region, gives SOUTHCOM additional resources to do even more humanitarian work through naval visits to various ports of call. During its 2007 deployment, the USNS *Comfort* treated almost 400,000 patients, conducted more than 1,100 shipboard surgeries, and provided veterinary services to almost 18,000 animals in twelve Latin American nations.[12]

This imbalance in civil-military relations and resources, while not a direct challenge to democracy assistance strategies, does present an image of U.S. military power at the expense of civilian capacities. Even Bush's secretary of defense, Robert Gates, has called for ramping up resources for the State Department and other civilian agencies of the U.S. government to redress this imbalance. Secretary Gates, as President Obama's choice to remain at the Pentagon, should support a White House move quickly to expand diplomatic and development resources, even if it means reducing the Defense Department's budget. A much stronger National Security Council is also needed to exert some discipline and pressure on the relevant national security agencies to rebalance the tools of U.S. power in the region so that the main challenges of the hemisphere—poverty, inequality, and crime—are addressed through direct economic, trade, and social aid delivered through civilian, not mili-

Figure 3-2. U.S. Aid to Latin America and the Caribbean, 1997–2008

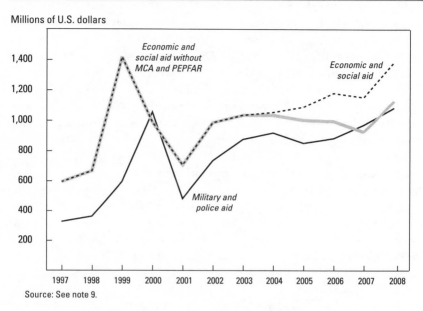

Millions of U.S. dollars

Source: See note 9.

tary, agencies. Implementing President Obama's plan to double the size of the Peace Corps by 2011 also would be a step in the right direction.

Strengthen the Organization of American States and Its Inter-American Democratic Charter.

At least on paper, the Organization of American States (OAS) and the associated Inter-American Court and Commission on Human Rights largely have what is needed to play a vital role in strengthening democracy and the rule of law in the region. Indeed, member states of the OAS have made some progress over the years toward constructing a set of principles and practices that have made concrete contributions toward stabilizing democratic crises, monitoring elections, and addressing systemic violations of human rights. What is missing from this picture is the political will and financial resources from the member states to make the OAS the go-to player in protecting democratic norms in the region. Instead, the organization has become bogged down in a series of rhetorical food fights between Venezuela, Bolivia, and Nicaragua, on the one hand, and the United States on the other.

Brazil has stepped in to fill the vacuum left by this stalemate by pursuing its own multilateral agenda through its initiative to create the Union of

South American States (UNASUR), a new forum that excludes the United States. UNASUR, which played an important role in defusing an impending civil conflict between opposing sides in Bolivia in October 2008, now has a charter that commits its members to promote democracy and human rights.[13] Yet the future direction of UNASUR appears opaque. It could evolve to become a competitor to the OAS with an ascendant Brazil determined to sideline Washington in the affairs of its immediate neighbors—or UNASUR could become a subregional actor capable of working constructively alongside the OAS as it seeks to resolve tensions and mediate conflict. Which course is taken will largely be decided by where Brazil wants to take UNASUR, and by Brazil's success in bringing other key players along. One could imagine a useful division-of-labor approach in which some localized subregional problems such as migration or other cross-border disputes are handled by the immediate players involved, while issues that affect the entire hemisphere, such as drug control, are the lead province of the OAS. Regardless of UNASUR's future trajectory, the ability of the OAS to play a leadership role in the political affairs of the hemisphere depends to a large extent on the relationship the Obama administration has with Brazil as well as with Venezuela and its allies.

The OAS and its Inter-American Democratic Charter need an infusion of new commitment and consensus building to function well as diplomatic tools for democracy (see also chapters 2 and 13). Notably, the charter's provisions concerning responses to democratic crises require a member state to initiate a request for assistance, making it less likely to be invoked. In fact, these provisions have never been used, despite abundant opportunity to do so since the charter was adopted in 2001. The charter also limits the secretary general's power to take the initiative to investigate deterioration in democratic standards only to situations involving "an unconstitutional alteration of the constitutional regime." Yet many instances of democratic backsliding do not rise to this level, leaving the OAS impotent to act. One way to generate momentum for greater activism on the part of OAS states is to support the efforts of the Friends of the Inter-American Democratic Charter, a panel of prominent figures from throughout the hemisphere organized by the Carter Center to serve an unofficial monitoring and advisory role for the secretary general and aimed at preventing tense situations from erupting into conflict.[14] The United States government should play a low-profile role in such an effort, quietly looking for opportunities to support this group's activities and, at a minimum, building consensus for the kind of neutral fact-finding function it could play.

Support South-South Cooperation through the Community of Democracies

As noted earlier, the sheer diversity of democratic systems emerging through-out the region and the world demands a different, more varied approach to supporting democratization. Already, a number of new or restored democracies have begun incorporating a concern for democracy and human rights into their foreign policies.[15] The Community of Democracies, a multilateral forum created in 2000 by the United States, Poland, Chile, and several other countries, is the only global forum devoted to mutual cooperation to support the consolidation of democratic governance. Under its auspices, the OAS and the African Union have begun working together on joint election observation activities and exchanging capacity-building experiences between the African and inter-American human rights systems. This is the kind of work that should continue and be expanded to other thematic and geographic areas. It creates habits of cooperation on democracy issues at the regional and cross-regional levels, and with time will help build an international architecture for like-minded states to reinforce and sustain the democratic wave into the twenty-first century.

A related area that deserves support from the Obama administration is cooperation on human rights issues at the United Nations and its new Human Rights Council. Since the creation of the council, in 2005, the United States has grown increasingly hostile and disengaged from the UN's principal forum for human rights, as evidenced by its failure to run for a seat on the council. At the same time, Latin American governments, with the main exception of Cuba and Venezuela, have constituted an important bloc of votes in favor of a stronger council. The State Department should reach out to Chile, Argentina, Brazil, and other council members to find common ground for partnering with them on a positive human rights agenda for the council. More important, the United States should seek to regain a seat on the council so that it can influence the council's work from the inside.

Development Tools for Democracy Assistance

The positive relationship between democratic governance and development is well documented and increasingly incorporated into mainstream development assistance programming at some donor institutions.[16] For example, the UN Development Program now gives 40 percent of its development assistance, $1.5 billion annually, to strengthening democratic governance and institution building as a way to improve state capacity to deliver public services and manage revenue effectively.[17] Canada also has made democracy assistance a priority, contributing 17.1 percent of its total aid budget—$473.8 million Canadian dollars, or $383.4 million U.S. dollars—to democratic governance programs, one of the focal themes of its 2006–07 agenda.[18] The United States, on the other hand, allotted only 9 percent ($2.14 billion) of its $24.6 billion FY 2007 foreign assistance budget to the State Department's strategic objective 2, Governing Justly and Democratically, which includes rule of law and human rights, good governance, political competition and consensus building, and support to civil society.[19]

The Obama administration, unfortunately, has inherited a fiscal disaster of unprecedented magnitude and likely may have to cut foreign aid programs dramatically. While the Latin America and Caribbean regions received increased assistance during the Bush administration, its signature initiatives to tackle HIV/AIDS, malaria, and other public health emergencies mainly went to Africa. The Bush administration also created the Millennium Challenge Account (MCA), a special incentives fund to reward low-income states that govern well with major infusions of grants to support infrastructure and other projects identified by the receiving government. Most of the countries of the Latin America and Caribbean regions, however, are not eligible for the fund because they have graduated out of the low-income category. Those that are eligible—Honduras, Nicaragua, El Salvador, and Bolivia—are at various stages of the complex process of qualifying for the money.[20] Paraguay, Peru, and Guyana must still meet threshold requirements regarding anti-corruption and rule of law and receive some targeted funding to help them become fully eligible.[21] The MCA program, while theoretically sound, is often criticized for its slow implementation. Nonetheless, as a democracy assistance tool, it deserves continued support because it requires states to adhere to basic principles of civil and political rights, anti-corruption, sound fiscal policy, and basic social welfare in order to receive funding. Questions remain about the MCA's enforcement of this conditionality. One test of this challenge was presented by Nicaragua, where flawed municipal elections in November 2008 led MCC to suspend future disbursements of its $175 million aid package.

Whether or not the democratic governance account receives sufficient funding, the United States seriously needs to ramp up its investment in multilateral mechanisms of democracy assistance. Unfortunately, the United States has inadequate and insufficient tools in the toolkit, preferring instead to conduct most of its democracy assistance through belated channels. It does this mainly through USAID (U.S. Agency for International Development), the Human Rights Democracy Fund of the State Department, and the National Endowment for Democracy and its four institutes, which operate on a budget of approximately $110 million, $80 million of which comes directly from the U.S. Congress.[22]

Over the last decade, funding for the Human Rights Democracy Fund, administered by the State Department's Bureau for Democracy, Human Rights, and Labor, has grown significantly, from a mere $7.82 million in 1998 to $317 million in 2007 (much of this increase went to Iraq state-building and democracy programs).[23] The program's supporters in the State Department say that the increased funding has strengthened the bureau's position so that its voice is more likely to be heard in internal battles in various policy debates in Foggy Bottom. Giving the State Department money to run democracy programs runs the risk, however, of politicizing what should be, to the extent possible, a nonpolitical foreign assistance endeavor. It gives political appointees and diplomats greater power to deploy democracy dollars in a way that supports short-term policy goals. For example, Democracy, Human Rights, and Labor funds have been directed quickly to priority cases, such as Venezuela or Bolivia, but this approach has sparked controversy in the region, with critics charging that the United States is funding groups that seek the overthrow of a democratically elected government. This method of delivering democracy assistance further feeds the perception that the United States continues to promote democracy on its own terms and bankrolls efforts to unseat those it does not like.

At the same time, it is critical that the United States continue to support sectors of civil society and the independent media that are, by their nature, at odds with the government in power. These groups are the lifeblood of a well-functioning democracy because they provide the kind of horizontal accountability essential to checking abuses of power between elections and providing voters with independent analysis during an electoral period. Receiving official assistance from the U.S. government, however, particularly under rules that require them to display the USAID logo on all their materials or to identify partners for the terrorist vetting list, makes them vulnerable to charges of being agents of a foreign government. This approach has been particularly troublesome in closed societies such as Cuba and Iran, in which dissident groups advocating for a new regime have received support via special congressional appropriations. Predictably, several advocates genuinely committed to democracy and human rights in those countries have refused Washington's money out of fear that they will face prison time from a hostile government. This is no way to frame a democracy assistance strategy.

The answer to this dilemma has two parts. First, the Obama administration should ask Congress to make the National Endowment for Democracy (NED) the primary channel of democracy assistance grants to civil society. An independent nonprofit organization that has enjoyed bipartisan support from its birth in the Reagan era, the NED is a relatively small and nimble grant-making entity whose mission is sustaining large and small civil society groups of democracy and human rights advocates around the world. Its work in building the World Movement for Democracy as a global network of civil society activists to share lessons learned and build solidarity as a transnational voice for democracy and human rights is important and should continue. The monies currently sitting in the State Department's Democracy, Human Rights, and Labor fund and devoted to civil society groups should be moved to NED as a way to depoliticize U.S. government support for democracy. Democracy funds directed to government and quasi-government entities, on the other hand, can continue to be funded through official State Department and USAID channels. The Democracy, Human Rights, and Labor fund can then refocus its energies on the challenging diplomatic and analytical work needed to strengthen multilateral mechanisms and coalitions for democracy and human rights.

The second answer is to multilateralize U.S. government funding for democracy assistance wherever possible. President Bush succeeded in doing this when he proposed, in 2004, the creation of a United Nations Democracy Fund (UNDEF). With the early support of India, Australia, and the Community of Democracies, this voluntary fund supports democracy-building initiatives mainly implemented by civil society groups around the world. Since its establishment in 2005, UNDEF has received donations and pledges totaling over $98 million from a wide range of countries, including India ($20 million), the United States ($25 million), and Japan ($20 million), with modest donations from smaller countries like Senegal, Slovenia, Chile, and Peru. These funds are nearly all dedicated to supporting local and regional nongovernmental organizations, as opposed to government bureaucracies or consulting firms. As noted earlier, the image of the UN in Latin America certainly surpasses that of the United States; furthermore, the UN has the legitimacy to be a credible defender of the universal nature of democratic and human rights principles and now has a proven track record that it can spend the money appropriately. Whereas the United States is only one of several voices on the UNDEF governing board (albeit one of great weight), the benefit of working with such a diverse array of partners outweighs the cost of losing some influence in deciding who should receive grant awards. Congress should continue regular and substantial funding for this account.

The United Nations Democracy Fund experience can serve as a model for U.S. democracy assistance funding in the Latin American and Caribbean region. An inter-American democracy fund, housed at the OAS and funded by the United States, Canada, the European Union, its member states, and, most important, some countries from Latin America, would be a regional vehicle to address regional problems (see also chapter 2). It could focus not only on supporting civil society monitoring and participation but also on development of independent media, legal reform, political party representation, and civic education. It would be a concrete, practical manifestation of the region's commitment to the principles of the Inter-American Democratic Charter and avoid the "regime change" taint associated with past U.S. government funding. It could also provide a source of funds for the Friends of the Inter-American Democratic Charter group, which could be an independent voice in the monitoring of hemispheric standards.

Another way in which the U.S. could multilateralize its democracy assistance is by teaming up more deliberately with other major donors working in the region. For starters, U.S. diplomatic and foreign aid officials should meet regularly with counterparts in Canada, Europe, and Japan to work out a common needs assessment followed by some joint funding projects or vehicles, particularly in countries in greatest need of support. A pooling of funds in one account would save enormous time, especially on the part of the recipient countries, which spend hours and hours of time fulfilling the myriad and distinct requirements of each donor.

Such a joint approach is not easy: A recent study of the political aid priorities of major European donors reveals a lack of coordination among six donors—Denmark, France, Spain, Sweden, United Kingdom, and European Commission—in identifying thematic priorities. Of this group, only three (Denmark, Sweden, and the European Commission) shared one thematic priority: human rights. The other leading thematic areas were democratic process, financial governance, civil society, governance policy, conflict prevention, justice, gender equality, public administration, and public sector reform (see table 3-1).[24] The Germans have traditionally emphasized political party development.

Of course, each bureaucracy follows its own internal logic for crafting its assistance strategies, usually in accordance with the political priorities of the government in power or its legislative overseers. There may be merit to some specialization of democracy assistance according to a particular donor's experience with, say, federalism.[25] Despite various attempts at the international level to change the traditional top-down, conditional approach to bilateral

Table 3-1. European Donors' Top Two Thematic Priorities within Political Aid Funding[a]

Donor	First thematic priority	Second thematic priority	Year
European Commission (EIDHR)	Democratic process	Human rights culture	2006
Denmark	Human rights	Conflict prevention	2005
France	Financial governance	Justice	2006
Spain	Civil society	Gender equality	2006
Sweden	Human rights	Public administration	2003
United Kingdom	Governance policy	Public-sector reform	2006

Source: Richard Youngs, "What Has Europe Been Doing?" *Journal of Democracy* 19, no.2 (April 2008): 166.
a. This information has not been compiled for Germany or the Netherlands.

development aid, the situation is unlikely to change anytime soon. What is needed is a complementary multilateral mechanism that will demonstrate to both donor and recipient states the efficiencies and impact of a coordinated approach.

One of the more challenging roadblocks any reform-minded president must overcome is the inertia of bureaucratic politics. A serious shift of political culture is needed in which the United States and other donor countries conclude that it is in their interest to pool resources with like-minded partners. This would entail a loosening of the traditional preference for bilateral aid, and the control of negotiations that goes with it. That said, a total abandonment of bilateral assistance would be a mistake. The U.S. ambassador to a country should still have access to funds to help achieve certain security and economic objectives in that country. But a new multilateral window of financing, professionally administered through an intergovernmental or quasi-independent agency, should also be available to handle the more delicate task of political and good governance reforms.

One multilateral tool the United States should consider is the International Institute for Democracy and Electoral Assistance (International IDEA), an intergovernmental organization created in 1995 on the initiative of the Swedish government. International IDEA, which has offices in Costa Rica, Bolivia, Peru, Colombia, and Ecuador, counts among its twenty-five members a diverse range of older and newer democracies worldwide; in this region Barbados, Canada, Chile, Costa Rica, Mexico, Peru, and Uruguay are full members (Japan serves as the sole observer). It provides knowledge resources, offers platforms for debate on democratic development policy issues, and assists in democratic reform processes, leveraging the comparative experience of its members. It already works closely with UN agencies, the OAS, and a number of donor governments on regional and national levels and is known for taking a consultative approach emphasizing dialogue. In Bolivia it provided assistance concerning the electoral system as well as land rights, indigenous rights, and the use of energy resources to promote democratic development. Unfortunately, the United States is neither a member nor an observer state and has rarely provided direct grants to the organization. The Obama administration should consider how it might partner with IDEA and other such organizations as vehicles for internationalizing its democracy assistance.

Conclusion

President Obama and his advisers have a special moment of opportunity to advance democracy and human rights in the Latin American and Caribbean region through old and new multilateral mechanisms. Seizing this opportunity will require not only making fullest use of these mechanisms but also bringing a new, more positive attitude toward collaborative partnerships, and away from top-down, unilateral prescriptions. It will also demand a greater willingness on the part of our Congress and Latin American partners to devote greater political will and financial resources to the task. As Latin American countries look forward to their bicentennials of independence, the United States should celebrate the shared heritage of democratic societies by funding new multilateral projects for building accountable, transparent, and participatory governance.

Notes

1. Corporacion Latinobarómetro, Informe Latinobarómetro 2008, Santiago de Chile, p. 26. For the full report, see www.latinobarometro.org/docs/INFORME_LATI-NOBAROMETRO_2008.pdf, or Latinobarómetro website at www.latino-barometro.org/.

2. Pew Global Attitudes Project, "Global Unease with Major Powers: Rising Environmental Concern in 47-Nation Survey," report, June 27, 2007. The summary of findings is at http://pewglobal.org/reports/display.php?ReportID=256.

3. CIMA (Consorcio Iberoamericano de Investigaciones de Mercados y Asesoramiento [Iberian American Consortium for Investigating Markets and Consultation]), *Barómetro Iberoamericano de Gobernabilidad 2008* (Bogotá: Centro Nacional de Consultoría), p. 29. For more information, see www.cimaiberoamerica.com/.

4. Informe Latinobarómetro 2008, poll (Santiago: Latinobarómetro Corporation, 2008), p. 110 (see also www.latinobarometro.org).

5. Latinobarómetro Corporation, "Las Elecciones Presidenciales en EEUU: Opinion de 18 paises de America Latina [The U.S. Elections: The Opinion of 18 Latin American Countries]," Informe Latinobarómentro 2008, p. 5 (Santiago, 2008) (not available on the Internet). This report was produced exclusively for *The Economist*. The statistics used can be found in "The Americas: The More Things Change; Latin America and the United States," *The Economist*, October 25, 2008.

6. CIMA, *Barómetro Iberoamericano de Gobernabilidad 2008*, pp. 26–30 (www.cimaiberoamerica.com/). The European Union scored just above the United States—59 percent—in Latinobarómetro's most recent poll (see Informe Latinobarómetro 2008, p. 17). For the complete document, see www.latinobarometro.org/docs/INFORME_LATINOBAROMETRO_2008.pdf.

7. A useful tool for training diplomats is "A Diplomat's Handbook for Democracy Development Support," a new publication launched under the auspices of the Community of Democracies and available at www.diplomatshandbook.org.

8. The Defense Ministerial of the Americas, which put civilian defense ministers as the primary policymaking actor in the defense arena, and the Center for Hemispheric Defense Studies, which provides defense management education to both civilian and military students, were two examples of this approach.

9. Latin American Working Group Educational Fund, the Center for International Policy, and the Washington Office on Latin America, "Below the Radar: U.S. Military Programs with Latin America, 1997–2007"(March 2007) (http://justf.org/files/pubs/below_the_radar_eng.pdf). In the 1990s U.S. military and police aid was less than half of economic and development assistance to Latin America. For full data of U.S. spending and further information, see http://justf.org/Aid.

10. For more information, see U.S. Department of State, "The Merida Initiative" (www.state.gov/r/pa/scp/2008/103374.htm). For a breakdown of the figures and further explanation, see Congressional Research Service, "Merida Initiative: Proposed U.S. Anticrime and Counterdrug Assistance for Mexico and Central America," Report RS22837, March 18, 2008 (http://fpc.state.gov/documents/organization/103694.pdf).

11. For more information on the SOUTHCOM Partnering Directorate, see www.southcom.mil/AppsSC/pages/staff.php?id=32&flag=1.

12. Lieutenant Commander Pat Paterson, "SOUTHCOM Turns to Soft Power," *U.S. Naval Institute Proceedings* (Annapolis, Md., July 2008).

13. The Constitutive Treaty of UNASUR, signed May 23, 2008, states in its preamble that South American integration and union "are based on the guiding principles of unlimited respect for sovereignty . . . democracy, citizen participation, universal, interdependent, and indivisible human rights," among others (see www.mre.gov.br/portugues/imprensa/nota_detalhe3.asp?ID_RELEASE=5466).

14. For further information, see the Carter Center website, "Americas Program" (www.cartercenter.org/peace/americas/friends.html).

15. Robert Herman and Theodore Piccone, *Defending Democracy: A Global Survey of Foreign Policy Trends, 1992–2002* (Washington: Democracy Coalition Project, October 2002).

16. See, for example, Morton H. Halperin, Joseph T. Siegle, and Michael M. Weinstein, *The Democracy Advantage: How Democracies Promote Prosperity and Peace* (New York: Routledge and Council on Foreign Relations, 2005).

17. UN Development Program, *Annual Report 2008*, "Democratic Governance" (New York: 2008), p. 19 (www.undp.org/publications/annualreport2008/pdf/ENG_IARforweb_Ch3b_Democratic_Gov0608.pdf).

18. Canadian International Development Agency, *Departmental Performance Report* (for period ending March 31, 2007), pp. 21–22. For more information, see www.acdi-cida.gc.ca/INET/IMAGES.NSF/vLUImages/Publications3/$file/DPR_2006%202007%20EN.pdf.

19. USAID, *Fiscal Year 2007 Foreign Assistance Performance Report* and *Fiscal Year 2009 Performance Plan* (www.usaid.gov/policy/budget/cbj2009/101446.pdf); on Strategic Goals, see www.state.gov/s/d/rm/rls/dosstrat/2007/html/82952.htm.

20. Although Bolivia became eligible for an MCA grant in 2004, its approval process has been stalled because of "adverse conditions" in the country. Currently, Bolivia's status is listed as "Compact Proposal Received"; El Salvador, Honduras, and Nicaragua have either signed or already implemented their contracts. See Millennium Challenge Corporation website, "Compact Development Status Report, Bolivia: Update on Progress" (www.mcc.gov/documents/qsr-dev-bolivia.pdf).

21. MCA applies a set of seventeen indicators to determine which countries are eligible for assistance. For countries that do not score high enough on these indicators, threshold programs are available to help them improve their performance so that they can become eligible for an MCC grant later on. Paraguay and Guyana were selected as threshold countries in 2005 and Peru in 2007.

22. The International Republican Institute, the National Democratic Institute for International Affairs, the AFL-CIO Solidarity Center, and the Center for International Private Enterprise are affiliated with the U.S. Chamber of Commerce.

23. For more information, see U.S. Department of State, "DRL Programs, Including Human Rights Democracy Fund (HRDF)" (www.state.gov/g/drl/p/index.htm).

24. Richard Youngs, "Trends in Democracy Assistance: What Has Europe Been Doing?" *Journal of Democracy* 19, no. 2 (April 2008): 166.

25. Canada took the lead in creating the Forum of Federations, which specializes in studying and promoting different models of federalism. For more information, see www.forumfed.org/en/index.php.

PART **II**

Getting Down to Hard Cases

four
Seven Steps to Improve
U.S.-Colombia Relations

Michael Shifter

The state of democratic governance and the rule of law in Colombia is decidedly uneven and remains marked by paradoxes and contradictions. Very positive trends coexist with notably negative ones, so sweeping characterizations of Colombian democracy should be greeted with skepticism. Unfortunately, however, Colombia's highly charged political debate in recent years has discouraged a balanced understanding of the country's many complexities. In this chapter, I first outline the contradictory currents within Colombian democracy, and then describe how external actors, particularly the U.S. government, can constructively support improved governance in the country.

A Barack Obama administration and Democrat-controlled Congress offer an opportunity to reassess the overall U.S. approach toward Colombia as well as to figure out which policies should be emphasized and which should be scaled back or even discontinued. The Obama administration should go beyond an aid- and trade-centered focus on Colombia to vigorously pursue greater multilateral diplomacy and political engagement. It is also important for U.S. relations with Colombia and Latin America, as well as for its own global interests, that Congress pass the pending U.S.-Colombia free trade agreement—negotiated in 2006—likely contingent on Colombia's further progress on human rights and the creation of an adequate social safety net for U.S. workers.

The State of Democratic Governance in Colombia

Colombia has a rich democratic tradition. It is South America's oldest democracy and, in contrast to its neighbors, the country experienced military rule only once in the last century, from 1953 to 1958. Although its party system has become attenuated in recent years—reflecting a broader regional, even global, trend—it is still among the most institutionalized in Latin America, and especially among the Andean nations. The Liberal Party remains the strongest party, while the other traditional powerhouse, the Conservative Party, has been substantially weakened. Significantly, in recent years the Democratic Pole party has emerged as a political force on the left—several members of Congress and the last two mayors of Bogotá have come from its ranks—but the party has remained relatively marginal on the national political scene.

President Álvaro Uribe, a dissident member of the Liberal Party, has dominated the political scene since his election in 2002 and is currently backed by an array of political parties including Radical Change (Cambio Radical) and the Social Party of National Unity (Partido de la U). After having the 1991 constitution amended in 2005 to permit his reelection the following year, Uribe enjoys an approval rating of over 70 percent. He has generated widespread support among the Colombian people by delivering results on the security front, under the rubric of his "democratic security" framework. Homicide rates are lower than they have been in over two decades, kidnappings have dropped sharply, and trust in government institutions is up, as reflected in public confidence that it spends tax dollars wisely (see figure 4-1). There has been widespread speculation that Uribe, in response to public pressure, will once again attempt to have the constitution changed to allow him to serve a third term. He has not ruled out the possibility, and his supporters have presented a petition to the Colombian Senate with over 5 million signatures encouraging a referendum on the constitutional amendment. As of this writing, Uribe has given ambiguous signals about his intentions, alternately identifying possible successors and warning that he needs to be assured that the security policies he has put in place would continue once he leaves office. Along with the institutional hurdles Uribe must clear if he is to serve again, economic difficulties, controversy from the collapse of pyramid schemes, and the November 2008 vote in the lower house of Congress against holding another reelection referendum indicate another reelection may be more problematic than previously thought.

There is a clear tradeoff between Uribe's effectiveness as president, at least as perceived by most Colombians, and the robustness of the checks and bal-

Figure 4-1. Trust That Tax Revenue Will Be Well Spent by the Government, 2003 and 2005

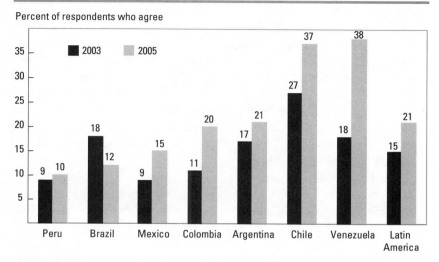

Percent of respondents who agree

Source: Organization for Economic Cooperation and Development, *Latin American Economic Outlook 2008*, based on Latinobarómetro, Informe 2003 and Informe 2005.

ances in the political system. Changing the rules of the game midcourse is always questionable and suggests a departure from democratic norms, but in Uribe's first term it was at least arguable that exceptional circumstances—Colombia was truly moving back from a violent abyss—justified such a move (see figure 4-1). Although Colombia has made impressive progress on the security front—the police presence throughout the country is much greater and the military is generally more professional—there is legitimate concern that another term for Uribe could pose serious risks for the country's institutional accountability and equilibrium.

The state of Colombia's judiciary is similarly uneven and complex, though there have been impressive advances in recent years. The Constitutional Court of Colombia, one of the innovations of the 1991 constitution, is the envy of the rest of Latin America for its quality and independence. In addition, the country's judicial system has recently shifted from a written, inquisitive system to an oral, accusatory system. This noteworthy reform has, by all accounts, improved the level of transparency in the judiciary, by opening proceedings to the public and speeding up trials. At the same time, however, levels of impunity from criminal prosecution remain extremely high. To be sure, impunity is a common and pervasive problem in many Latin American countries, including some that have made important strides in other critical areas. But in this respect, adherence to the rule of law in Colombia remains incomplete at best.

Nothing better illustrates the simultaneous progress toward and retrogression from democratic governance in Colombia than the ongoing so-called "para-political" scandal, the subject of regular media reports. Uncovering links between the illegal, brutal paramilitary forces and sectors of the country's political establishment revealed the rot and corruption that had become rampant in Colombia. It is particularly troubling that many of the accused are close associates of President Uribe, as illustrated by the April 2008 arrest of Mario Uribe, a former senator as well as the president's cousin and confidant.

At the same time, the attorney general's office is able to investigate these para-politics cases only because roughly 30,000 paramilitary forces have been demobilized following the passage of the Justice and Peace Law in July 2005. Though legitimate concerns have been raised by the human rights community and others that the demobilization process should have been tougher and mandated more severe punishments for crimes, it has at least resulted in new confessions and revelations, less violence, and some sanctions on the paramilitary groups. It demonstrates, as the government argues, that the judiciary is functioning and that, for the first time, an attempt is under way to cleanse the system of the corruption that has accumulated over decades. As of this writing, over sixty members of Congress have been investigated and more than thirty have been arrested for ties to paramilitary groups. The truth is that Colombia is going through a collective catharsis in an attempt to deal with many years of violence, corruption, and trauma. The improvements in security are significant, but the damage to Colombian political institutions and the rule of law caused by decades of criminality has not yet been repaired.

Colombia's progress in moving toward the end of its long-standing internal armed conflict has been similarly mixed. For years that conflict and the accompanying violence have posed the major threat to the country's democratic governance. The government is combating two groups, the Revolutionary Armed Forces of Colombia, or FARC (Fuerzas Armadas Revolucionarias de Colombia), and the National Liberation Army, or ELN (Ejército de Liberación Nacional), though the latter is much smaller and has been in decline for years. The conflict continues, but the government has considerably strengthened its military capacity in recent years and is now on the offensive.

The FARC today numbers an estimated 8,000 to 10,000 combatants and retains some military strength, largely due to revenue from the drug trade and other criminal activity. But it has suffered severe setbacks, both on the battlefield and in its internal organization. Communications have broken down and there have been growing defections, including the high-profile case of Karina, a guerrilla commander who surrendered in May 2008 because she was starving and had not had communication with FARC leadership in two years. Colombia's March 2008 air strike and raid into Ecuadoran territory and the July mission that freed the most high-profile hostages held by FARC were both made possible through the Colombian government's increasingly effective intelligence-gathering and communication-interception abilities. Three members of the FARC's seven-man ruling secretariat died in March, including Manuel "Tirofijo" Marulanda, the leader of FARC since its inception in 1964. Together, these guerrilla setbacks point to the Colombian government's growing capability and competence.

Nonetheless, it is unrealistic to expect that Colombia's serious problem with violence will disappear, even in the unlikely case that a formal peace was reached with the weakened FARC. In spite of hope that FARC will engage in an open and genuine dialogue with the government following its recent military setbacks, real negotiations are unlikely in the short term. After decades in the jungle, FARC has a different sense of time and is unlikely to surrender anytime soon. Even if the FARC leadership entered in negotiations, it would not necessarily lead to immediate peace. Just as the Medellín and Cali cartels fragmented into smaller, more dispersed drug-trafficking groups in the 1990s and early 2000s, so it is most likely that FARC will similarly morph and fracture into new violent entities. While demobilized paramilitary leaders were confessing their crimes in prison, their lieutenants were forming new mafias, sometimes in cooperation with their former enemies, the guerrillas, as both groups become less motivated by ideology. Now fourteen of the top paramilitary leaders are in U.S. prisons, serving sentences or awaiting trial on cocaine trafficking charges after Uribe extradited them to the United States in May 2008. The end of FARC as a national armed group would mark an important advance, but as is so often the case in Colombia, other problems are bound to emerge.

One unexpected adverse consequence of the security gains in Colombia is the spread of the conflict into neighboring countries, including the notable FARC presence in the border areas of Venezuela and Ecuador and the displacement of significant drug production in Bolivia and Peru. Colombia's ideological differences with the neighboring governments of Ecuador and particularly Venezuela had already set the stage for potentially tense relationships. President Hugo Chávez was originally involved in a hostage negotiation process with FARC, but the Colombian government's termination of his involvement and its subsequent air strike on a FARC camp in Ecuadoran territory sparked a regional crisis that simmered for months. Long-term solutions to guerrilla and drug-trafficking challenges require extensive, genuine cooperation among the Andean countries. Though it certainly will not be easy and will call for a shift in emphasis and approach in its foreign policy, Colombia needs to work through low-level diplomacy and multilateral channels to gradually rebuild trust at the highest levels and restore cordial relations with its neighbors.

Another fundamental problem is that the drug trade remains essentially intact, despite significant investments from Colombia and the United States in efforts to diminish the flow of cocaine and heroin. These measures are carried out under the framework of Plan Colombia, a comprehensive program designed to reduce drug trafficking and restore security to the country by providing military equipment and training to the Colombian government. Although antidrug policies enacted under the Plan Colombia umbrella have registered some gains in terms of interdiction or lower levels of production in particular regions, they have been more than offset by the agility and sophistication of the actors involved in the illicit trade. Much has been achieved in restoring security to Colombia, but wherever the drug trade is flourishing there will inevitably be high levels of criminality and corruption. An October 2008 report (GAO-09-71) from the Government Accountability Office found that Plan Colombia had helped improve the security situation in Colombia but had failed in its goal of reducing the cultivation, processing, and distribution of illegal narcotics by 50 percent in six years. Instead, coca production levels actually increased 15 percent between 2000 and 2007.

The persistence of the drug problem has important implications for democratic governance in Colombia. For example, journalists and others engaged in informing the public have been the target of violence and, increasingly, threats from both paramilitaries and guerrillas, who are sustained by the drug trade. Although the number of killings of journalists has declined from previous years, there has been a rise in the number of threats and a corresponding increase in self-censorship. This is particularly the case outside of Bogotá and other major cities, which tend to be significantly more secure than the provincial areas. It is crucial to bear in mind when discussing the state of democratic governance that there are actually *many* Colombias, some enjoying the benefits of economic prosperity and security improvements and others for whom the conflict is a part of their daily life. These sharp differences are seen clearly through the contrasting conditions facing media in large cities and those in conflict zones.

Other vulnerable sectors include union officials and human rights workers, many of whom also receive threats from armed groups and require protection from the Ministry of the Interior. Although the murder of union officials has become less frequent over the past six years, as of October 2008 there had been a disturbing increase in assassinations in 2008 compared with 2007. In addition, some senior Colombian officials have leveled baseless accusations that respected human rights representatives are associated with guerrilla groups, which has contributed to a tense climate and complicated the important work of these representatives.

Human rights organizations have reported a recent jump in the number of extrajudicial executions committed by the Colombian armed forces. Particularly disconcerting is the increase in the so-called "false positives," civilians killed and dressed up as FARC guerrillas to meet unofficial army benchmarks for military success. The 1997 Leahy Amendment is designed to ensure that any Colombian armed forces unit receiving aid under the Plan Colombia framework have been certified as trained to respect human rights. That several of the units implicated in the "false positive" scandal and other atrocities had been certified under this process reflects poorly on Plan Colombia overall. The United States should reassess the verification process and assist in the full investigation of these killings.

Since the peak of violence in 2001, the military had increasingly performed more professionally and in closer adherence to human rights norms, but the recent increase in extrajudicial killings represents the disturbing reversal of a long-term positive trend. This spate of killings is indefensible, particularly as security gains are being consolidated. Fortunately, the unprecedented dismissal of several top Colombian military officers in October 2008 signals that the Uribe administration has recognized the seriousness of these crimes and is responding to pressure to deal with them decisively.

Colombia also faces the imperative to respond in defense of those who have the fewest resources and are least able to defend themselves, many of whom are Afro-Colombian, indigenous, women, or all three. Sadly, these vulnerable groups are disproportionately represented among the estimated 3 million to 4 million people internally displaced by decades of violence in Colombia (the second highest number in the world after Sudan). The internal refugee population, which continues to grow as a result of guerrilla raids and military incursions, undeniably constitutes a serious problem of democratic governance.

The crisis further underlines Colombia's problems of persistent poverty and inequality, which are particularly severe in the rural sector of the country. The massive and occasionally violent protests among indigenous communities in 2008 reflected the frustration felt in forgotten or neglected areas of the country. Any serious, long-term effort aimed at improving democratic governance in Colombia must focus attention on redressing the country's underlying social ills and endemic injustices. Although the economic growth experienced in recent years has been important in mitigating poverty and inequality levels, the global financial crisis is already beginning to take its toll in Colombia. The country's social agenda remains urgent and must be tackled through more comprehensive and sustained education and health reforms.

In conclusion, Colombia's current state of democratic governance is highly complex and involves many overlapping dimensions. In recent years there have been some notable advances, acknowledged by even the government's harshest critics. In many parts of the country the security situation has improved dramatically. At the same time, however, Colombia has experienced reversals on some critical measures: the state has become overly centralized and paramilitary and organized crime groups have once again started to accumulate economic and political power. There are indeed many Colombian realities, and it is crucial to take all of them into account when assessing the state of democratic governance. On balance, the gains have outweighed the setbacks and have prepared the ground for an ongoing process of institutional and security improvements.

What Can and Should Be Done by External Actors?

It is important to have realistic expectations about what can and cannot be done by external actors to assist Colombia in improving the prospects for making progress on democratic governance. Colombia is sophisticated and highly developed in many respects, and as the second most populous country in South America after Brazil, has an enormous sense of pride and independence. Any policies and programs involving Colombia should be carried out with great respect and sensitivity, in close consultation and in concert with key national actors.

Three principal lessons can be derived from Colombia's experience since 1990. The first is that there are severe limitations on how much can be done

Figure 4-2. Retail Price of Cocaine in the United States, 1990–2005

U.S. $ per gram

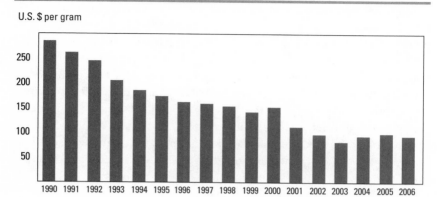

Source: United Nations Office on Drugs and Crime, *World Drug Report* (Vienna: 2007), p. 80.

in pressuring Colombia to improve its democratic practices in accordance with some external standards. Pressuring or lecturing Colombian officials about human rights norms through channels that are not predictable or institutionalized can prove counterproductive, cutting off important lines of communication and limiting the effectiveness of persuasion. Human rights should be a key part of the bilateral conversation, but one conducted in an environment of cooperation and mutual respect.

Second, the United States in particular has committed a serious mistake by overemphasizing the drug question in its relationship with Colombia. The dominance of this issue has often resulted in the relative neglect of other priorities, such as building the democratic institutions needed for good, effective governance. The U.S. emphasis on the drug trade over security has been a response more to U.S. domestic politics than to Colombia's needs. And it has failed to measurably diminish the drug trade, as the 2008 GAO report noted previously makes clear. Contrary to the principal goal of U.S. aid targeting the drug trade, the purity levels of cocaine on American streets have generally increased while prices have consistently fallen, suggesting an increase in supply (see figure 4-2).

Third, the case of Colombia illustrates that the United States got it backward by focusing narrowly on the drug question at the cost of other key issues, but some antidrug aid can nevertheless have beneficial effects in other areas. Colombians deserve the utmost credit for reasserting state authority over the past several years, but the U.S. contribution—even if it could have been more wisely and efficiently channeled—has helped in key ways, most notably in the security and justice sectors. Compared to other U.S. policies in Latin America in recent years—and even to its other international policies more generally—the U.S. effort in Colombia has been relatively successful.

The international community, including the United States, should have a sense of modesty and realism in working with Colombia in the coming years. The effectiveness of any outside support will depend significantly on the will and commitment of democratic actors in Colombia. It is hard to know how the country's domestic politics will evolve, but fortunately such actors are present and active in Colombia and there is generally a genuine determination to improve the situation and build on an existing institutional foundation. In contrast to its position in many other countries throughout the world, the task confronting the United States in Colombia is not one of "nation building." Rather, it is trying to assist a country that has been battered on many fronts and is seeking to recover from a period of deterioration.

There is ample opportunity for constructive action by the Obama administration, a Democrat-controlled Congress, and the wider international community. The following seven steps should be considered:

Rebalance U.S. aid toward social development. Too much of the public debate, particularly since Plan Colombia was adopted in 2000, has concentrated on security assistance, a single, relatively narrow piece of what should be a broad strategy to help bring peace and the rule of law to Colombia. How much U.S. support should be directed to military programs and how much to social development and institution building? Congress has moved toward greater balance between security and development aid, and it would be wise to maintain that equilibrium in future budgets.

Unfortunately, aid decisions are rarely geared toward larger policy purposes. In the Colombian case, one primary goal should be to further enhance the capacity of the state to carry out elementary functions more effectively, in accordance with democratic norms and the rule of law. It would be a mistake to try to project exactly how much assistance should be directed toward social development activities or security hardware over the next four years. The changing security and budgetary circumstances should determine how resources are best allocated, and it is crucial to retain some flexibility in policy response. The ratio of development aid to security aid in the funds set aside for Colombia has indeed shifted in the 2009 U.S. budget, from under 20 percent of total aid to Colombia to over 40 percent. This change reflects the reality on the ground, as Colombia works to translate security gains into more effective and responsive government institutions. In addition, government resources will become scarcer as a result of the current financial crisis, and the security situation will probably improve in the coming years, which means overall aid to Colombia is likely to wind down in the medium term.

In light of the crucial importance of consolidating Colombia's gains, the United States should continue its support at roughly the same absolute levels over perhaps the next four or five years, then gradually decrease aid. Cutting U.S. military aid to Colombia, though it would lead to cuts in the overall budget, would free up some funds for development aid. Politically, it will not be easy to sustain funding as the budget tightens in Washington, particularly with the purse strings in the hands of the Democratic Party, whose members have recently been more skeptical of support for security aid to Colombia than their Republican counterparts.

Support diplomatic strategies for initiating a peace process in Colombia. Another option that appears to have been underutilized in recent years is high-level policy consultation and advice on the Colombian government's strategy for peace. Senior U.S. government officials might usefully devote less time to ensuring that Colombians are meeting targets or satisfying bureaucratic requirements set in Washington and more in engaging with Colombians to reach compromises on fundamental strategic decisions. Such a focus would be in keeping with President Obama's stated desire and promise to be more engaged diplomatically. The United States can and should continue to pursue this course both bilaterally and through multilateral organizations, particularly the political secretariat of the Organization of American States (OAS).

Step up support for the reintegration of combatants into society. The United States should work closely with the OAS's mission in Colombia to assist in the reintegration of former combatants into society. As the OAS has noted, some progress has been made on this front, but there have also been some troubling setbacks, including difficulty finding legitimate employment for ex-combatants, the rise of organized crime and drug gangs to replace paramilitary units, and reluctance of guerrilla groups to join the process. To ensure democratic governance in Colombia, it is essential to prevent any further retrogression in the demobilization process. If former combatants cannot be productively reintegrated, it will be nearly impossible for Colombia to achieve greater peace and security.

Strengthen international organizations. The United States should help fortify the OAS—possibly by taking a more active role in devising a set of issues that the organization could realistically tackle, such as arms control and transparency, disaster relief, and energy cooperation—and should assist other governments in carrying out humanitarian missions in Colombia. The United

Nations has also been an active and valuable actor in Colombia, particularly in its work with the massive internally displaced population, and the United States should strongly support its efforts.

Work with Europe to craft a coordinated Colombia policy. Although resources will be limited in Europe, as they are in the United States, there is some concern and interest in European countries about the evolving situation in Colombia and there are opportunities for more productive collaboration with the United States than in the past. The traditional formula for the division of labor—the United States providing "hard" security aid and the Europeans "soft" development assistance—has failed, leading to incoherent and ineffective policymaking. There may now be possibilities for greater, more clear-sighted cooperation, provided the next U.S. administration has a more flexible attitude toward the drug question and is willing to seriously consider alternative approaches.

Emphasize human rights. Ensuring that human rights are respected should be the first step in the overall policy program of the Obama administration as it confronts the Colombia challenge. The work performed by international human rights organizations and the pressure they have put on the U.S government in support of human rights in Colombia has generally been helpful. Most democratic actors in Colombia view such efforts as constructive and encourage them. For example, the Leahy Amendment mentioned earlier has faced some implementation difficulties but has been useful in keeping human rights abuses on the agenda.

The U.S. government is in a better position to be effective in cooperating with Colombia on working toward stronger democratic governance and rule of law if it devises an overall strategy that guides work on diplomatic, security, and development levels. Only this way can it possibly succeed in helping to nudge the country along the constructive path it wants to pursue. As noted earlier, the surprise extradition of fourteen paramilitary leaders in May 2008 to face trial in the United States after they had violated the terms of Colombia's Justice and Peace Law is a perfect opportunity for strengthening bilateral collaboration. Two of the leaders have been sentenced to prison terms of more than twenty years, and they may be returned to Colombia to face justice once they are released. In the meantime, both Colombian and U.S. law enforcement agencies have promised that they will continue to solicit testimonies from the extradited paramilitaries and that any seized assets will be set aside for victim reparations. Making good on that pledge will build trust between the governments and within the broader Colombian population.

Table 4-1. U.S. Perceptions of International Trade

Percent of respondents (sample size: 1,026 adult Americans)

Cohort	Trade as a threat	Trade as an opportunity
Age		
18–49 years	47	47
More than 50 years	56	33
Income		
Less than $50,000	60	33
More than $50,000	51	42

Source: CNN/Opinion Research Corporation, poll conducted June 26–29, 2008.

Support the U.S.-Colombia Free Trade Agreement. This pact will deepen engagement between the two countries and enable the United States to more constructively work with Colombia on democracy and rule-of-law questions. Especially in light of the financial crisis, it is critical for the United States to focus on initiatives, such as the free trade agreement, that will contribute to job creation in the United States by removing the high tariffs placed on U.S. exports. At the same time, passing the agreement makes it clear to the world that the United States will not revert to isolationism or protectionism (see table 4-1). The agreement will also enhance confidence and stability in the bilateral relationship, as well as the United States' overall relationship with the region.

The U.S.-Colombia trade pact gained prominence in the U.S. presidential campaign as John McCain and Barack Obama sparred over its merits in the third presidential debate. Obama argued that there needs to be more progress on ending the murders of union leaders and prosecuting those responsible before he can back the agreement. Despite President Obama's concerns and the delays from the Democratic Congress, there is room to pursue the agreement. Politically, this will require two conditions. First, the Colombians need to demonstrate that they have taken successful steps and allocated significant resources to reduce levels of violence against union officials and to prosecute those responsible for those abuses. Second, President Obama and the U.S. Congress should follow up on their pledges to adopt a package of social benefits for Americans displaced by changing patterns of trade, including health care, job training and placement, and education loans. This action would help allay fears in the United States and also send an important signal to Colombia and the region that the United States follows through on commitments and intends to remain engaged. Once in office and free of campaign

Figure 4-3. How Latin American Publics View the United States

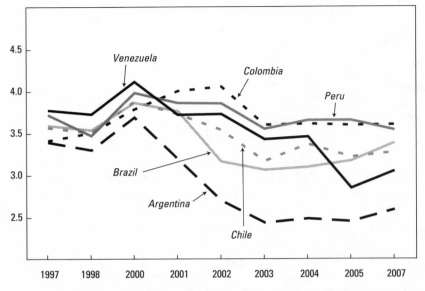

Mean score (0–5) scale

Source: Carol Graham and Soumya Chattopadhyay, "Poverty, Inequality, and Public Opinion Trends in Latin America (and the U.S.): How Strong Is Support for Markets, Democracy, and Regional Integration?" mimeo, based on *Latinobarómetro Reports 1997 to 2007* (Brookings, 2008).

pressures, Obama may find a way to get the agreement passed by the Democrat-controlled Congress.

The possibility that the agreement will not be approved is creating resentment in Colombians of varying political orientations, and failure to approve it would ultimately be harmful to U.S. national interests (see figure 4-3). Anything short of passage of the agreement would not satisfy allies in Colombia and the region, but both parties may still be open to amending the agreement or including a side letter on human rights and labor concerns, if that is what it takes to secure approval. Failure to approve the free trade agreement would further weaken the already diminished capacity of the United States to encourage respect for democracy and the rule of law in a critically important South American nation.

five
Human Rights and Free Trade in Colombia

Rodrigo Pardo

The Andean region is going through a very difficult, challenging period. The legitimacy of the democratic system is in grave danger. Neopopulism has sprung up in different forms in every country in the region (Colombia, Venezuela, Ecuador, Peru, Bolivia). Diplomatic tensions have called into question the countries' ability to coexist peacefully. Institutions of integration, particularly the Andean Community (Comunidad Andina de Naciones, CAN), are on the verge of collapse.

Even in this troubled region, Colombia has achieved important gains in the past six years; much improved security and economic growth have bolstered democracy and the rule of law. There has been a dramatic decline in violence, and President Álvaro Uribe's policy of "*seguridad democrática*" (democratic security)—a security strategy aimed at improving the armed forces' efficiency in combating crime—has sharply reduced the political and military capabilities of criminal groups, especially those of the Revolutionary Armed Forces of Colombia (Fuerzas Armadas Revolucionarias de Colombia, or FARC).

During the first half of 2008, FARC suffered the worst losses in its history: one of the seven members of its secretariat, the governing body, was killed in combat; another member was assassinated by his own men; and the top leader, Manuel Marulanda, died of natural causes. Various second- and third-level "commanders" have been captured, killed in combat, or turned themselves in. In addition, acreage under coca leaf cultivation has shrunk, while the numbers of drug confiscations, extradition of criminals to the United States on drug-trafficking charges, and capture of leaders of minicartels (which have replaced the large cartels of the nineties) have gone up.

But a modern and functioning democracy has not yet been created in Colombia. Internal conflict, authoritarian strains, tensions between modernity and underdevelopment, and the corrupting effect of drug trafficking all remain as troubling domestic issues, and regional disputes and tensions are creating further difficulties for Colombia.

Tensions within Colombia

There are two common images of Colombia. The first is that of a country with the strongest civil and government institutions in the region, a democratic system, and a long electoral tradition. In this image Colombia is a modern country characterized by pluralist debate, separation of powers, and a respectable record of defending the rule of law from the powerful domestic threats of drug trafficking, guerrilla warfare, and paramilitarism.

The first image of Colombia has become more common since the election, in 2002, of President Álvaro Uribe. The country's record of violence and drug trafficking has improved, and guerrilla groups have been weakened. The process of demobilizing the paramilitary United Self-Defense Forces of Colombia (Autodefensas Unidas de Colombia, or AUC) has been highly successful; security forces extradited fourteen top paramilitary leaders to the United States in 2008, destabilizing these powerful groups of assassins. Through interrogation conducted under the framework of the Justice and Peace Law first passed in July 2005, which is designed to deal with paramilitaries who are not extradited to the United States, Colombia has expanded its knowledge of the groups' structure and nature—an important tool for their ultimate eradication.

Yet there is a second common image of Colombia, which paints a different picture. This is of a country that has failed in its long history to overcome recurrent violence and consequently has been able to construct only a limited model of democracy. What democracy does exist is largely formal and elitist, and high percentages of the population remain marginalized. Those who challenge and question the established order—opposition groups, unions, independent journalists, and human rights advocates—are muzzled. This is a nation plagued by internal conflicts fueled by the corrupting influences of a huge illicit drug trade.

From this perspective one must assess Uribe's six years in power more cautiously. Ties that were revealed between the political class and paramilitary groups illustrate a high level of illegitimacy in state institutions, particularly in Congress. The slow progression of the Justice and Peace Law and the short five- to eight-year sentences it has established for ex-paramilitaries who have committed crimes—in exchange for the demobilization of their bands—are evidence of the judicial system's weakness. Indications that new paramilitary groups associated with drug trafficking are springing up in some of the regions where the demobilized groups operated previously show that demobilization efforts have been only partially effective.

The two images of modern-day Colombia may not be mutually exclusive—in fact, they may exist simultaneously. Indeed, there *are* two Colombias. One is a modern state, essentially urban, in which the rule of law functions successfully. The other is underdeveloped, rural, and influenced by powerful criminal factions—guerrilla groups and paramilitaries that are funded by drug trafficking and pose a great challenge to the authority of the law. The search for solutions in Colombia must begin by recognizing these two realities.

After the drug-trafficking trade's enormous structures of power (the infamous Medellín and Cali cartels) failed in the 1990s, the composition of this illicit industry changed in favor of powerful local mafias. Dozens of small organizations, many allied with paramilitaries and some with guerrilla groups, sprang up. In a number of regions the alliance of drug-trafficking and paramilitary interests resulted in a consolidation of local power, the displacement of traditional liberal and conservative political parties, and the infiltration of public institutions.

These regionally based mafia organizations have political influence on the national level as well, especially in the Congress of the Republic. Because congressional leaders are essentially regional representatives, during the electoral process many develop alliances with drug-trafficking establishments in order to campaign in certain areas or even gain direct support. In the "parapolitical" (paramilitary + political) scandal, sixty-three members of Congress are under investigation for having colluded with the AUC, and half of them are in jail.

The Corrupting Power of Drug Trafficking

Ten years after the special session of the United Nations General Assembly on the world drug problem in 1998, this issue remains deeply discouraging. John Walters, the antidrug "czar" of the United States, released a report in 2008 showing that cocaine trafficking had actually increased 40 percent between 2006 and 2007. Other studies show even bigger jumps. Two papers on the Latin American drug trade published by the International Crisis Group in 2008 ("Latin American Drugs I: Losing the Fight" and "Latin American Drugs II: Improving Policy and Reducing Harm," March 14, 2008) stated that strategies in Latin America, the United States, and Europe have not succeeded in controlling either coca cultivation or the production and consumption of cocaine, and have not been effective against drug-trafficking organizations.

The reports show that the number of acres of cultivated coca in Andean countries has not decreased. Colombia continues to be the largest cocaine producer worldwide, providing 62 percent of total supply, despite increases in fumigations of fields, confiscations of product, and extraditions of traffickers. The United States remains the largest consumer, with annual demand at about 250 to 300 tons.

The global drug industry has changed in the last decade in important ways. As noted above, large Colombian cartels have given way to nearly 140 smaller organizations. Global narcotics production has increased, trafficking by air appears to have decreased, and 78 percent of production is now transported by sea. Venezuela, although not a country of production, has become an oft-used transit route: according to Walters, it exported 89 percent more narcotics by tonnage in 2007 than in 2005. The Mexican cartels, meanwhile, have taken control of a growing portion of the supply in transit to the United States. Brazil, the main South American market for cocaine and marijuana, has now also become a transit country, and its security forces have deteriorated and become corrupted. Europe, the second largest market in the world, after the United States, has seen the greatest increase in consumption.

The domestic manifestations of the global narcotics trade are dangerous on many levels. First, the illegal armed groups that plague Colombia generate the funds they need to survive by extorting money from drug traffickers or by participating directly in production and distribution of narcotics. Successive Colombian governments have failed in their initiatives to combat guerrilla and paramilitary groups or to seek a negotiated end to their activities despite the groups' illegitimacy, growing unpopularity, and lack of any political dimension, because the enormous funds generated by drug trafficking allow them to maintain their structure. As long as the illicit drug industry maintains its current proportions, these groups will continue to be a challenge to democracy and the rule of law in Colombia.

Second, although the policies of many successive Colombian regimes (in cooperation with the United States) have been successful in reducing cultivated areas and combating large drug cartels, productivity has increased and the trade remains enormous. Moreover, drug traffickers have adjusted to interdiction pressures and policies by finding new routes as well as new transit and destination countries. This is the infamous "balloon effect": as long as global dimensions of production, trafficking, consumption, and profits remain unchanged, associated criminal activities will be able to stay a few steps ahead of law enforcement by moving easily from one country to another.

The Role of the International Community and of the United States

During the 1980s and the early 1990s there was great hope in Latin America that the end of the cold war would bring a new era of hemispheric cooperation. In the Andean region this was particularly relevant, as multilateral efforts to address the narcotics trade arose from the Cartagena and San Antonio summits in 1990 and 1991, respectively. President George H. W. Bush and his counterparts from Colombia, Bolivia, and Peru outlined compensation programs for those countries victimized by the drug trade, including a number of alternative development projects. They also agreed on the terms of the Andean Trade Preference Act (ATPA), which established preferential access to U.S. markets for export products from Colombia, Peru, Ecuador, and Bolivia.

But during the years since the first Summit of the Americas in Miami in 1994, where the participants committed to making cooperation on economic and social issues a greater focus than security concerns in the wake of the end of the cold war, the countries of Latin America have dropped the illusion of a hemispheric partnership and have become frustrated at the lack of attention from Washington. U.S. policies toward Latin America, including democracy promotion, have been inconsistent at best. Only ten years after the summit, the relationship between the United States and Latin America has become "securitized." The majority of U.S. attention is now targeted to military and security matters and a greater number of issues have come to be understood under the rubric of "security." Furthermore, by the end of George W. Bush's second term, the general feeling in Latin America was that U.S. foreign policy was focused on other continents.

Colombia has been the exception to this. Plan Colombia, financed with support from the United States, has been the lifeblood of Colombia's democratic security policy. It has strengthened the armed forces, improved the functioning of the nation's justice system, and cut ties between security entities and paramilitary groups. But as George W. Bush's administration came to a close, there were signs that U.S. support for the established policy toward

Colombia might be waning. The U.S. Congress did not pass the U.S.-Colombia Free Trade Agreement (FTA), chiefly because of Democratic Party opposition (including that of then Senator Barack Obama) based on concerns about the violation of Colombian union members' human rights. But linking these two important issues reduces the possibilities of improving either of them, and now voices in the Colombian government clamor for a "restructuring" of the bilateral relationship in the direction of diversifying Colombia's foreign policy and reducing its commitments with the United States.

Colombia Policy Pressure Points

From the viewpoint of strengthening democracy, the rule of law, and respect for human rights, the Obama administration could play a very positive role in Colombia by continuing some policies and by changing others.

Plan Colombia

Plan Colombia has been effective and should be continued in a form that incorporates strengthened support for the justice system and nongovernmental organizations (NGOs) that champion human rights. Plan Colombia's positive results in the security realm are widely recognized. The armed forces are now more effective and have in the last few years put guerrilla groups on the defensive, lessening their operating capacity and finally establishing a general sense of confidence that organizations like FARC can be defeated.

Other results are less well known but have been equally important in strengthening the rule of law. Since the passage in 2001 of the "Leahy Law," which prohibits U.S. military assistance to foreign military units that violate human rights with impunity, the United States has made military support to foreign units contingent on human rights observance, thus encouraging Colombia's military and government to cut ties with paramilitaries and adhere to human rights protocols. The discourse and practices of the army have changed accordingly. Until 2002 the military's official line was that the problem of paramilitarism was minimal and unimportant, and thus they often ignored the issue or treated it in terms of isolated cases. Official Colombian policy today is openly critical of paramilitarism, tolerance of such groups has diminished, and the government has taken serious measures to address the issue, including dismissing high officials and investigating those accused of having connections with paramilitary groups.

In recent years, especially since the Democratic Party won control of the U.S. Congress in 2006, the composition of U.S. aid to Colombia has changed in favor of nonmilitary components. The greater part of the relationship is still based on strengthening the armed forces, creating a more democratic and civilian-ruled state, and encouraging practices that are respectful of human rights; this shift has been largely positive. In particular, support for the judicial system (the Fiscalía General de la Nación, independent of the executive branch) has been valuable, as has that to NGOs that advance human rights objectives.

U.S.-Colombia Free Trade Agreement

The U.S.-Colombia Free Trade Agreement should be approved, with reasonable requirements for the protection of union workers' human and political rights. Blocking the passage of the FTA is harmful to U.S.-Colombian relations. Politically, Colombian public opinion reflects frustration as to why other countries of the region, with smaller economies and less politically aligned with the United States, have free trade agreements with the United States while Colombia does not. The long-term bilateral relationship is being negatively affected by the failure to pass the legislation, as is U.S. influence on key issues in Colombia, such as cooperation on union workers' rights.

There are strong commercial arguments for supporting the FTA. Beyond the obvious (the benefits of free trade, improved access to markets, the size of both countries and hence the opportunities they offer as markets for each other), the effect of an invigorated modern economy could be important in Colombia. A greater number of companies oriented toward the U.S. market would be one way to close the gap between the "two Colombias"—by opening up opportunities for growth to productive projects in rural and developing parts of Colombia.

With respect to the Democratic Party's demands for protection of union workers, the relationship that exists between this serious issue and the free trade agreement should be more closely examined. Certainly the security of union members and workers' movement leaders should be improved in Colombia. But the connection between this matter and that of the free trade agreement is potentially dangerous. It projects the image in Colombia that the United States cares more about internal politics than the commercial regime and human rights, posing additional problems for its passage. Voices against making human rights a priority in Colombia could also try to use anti–free traders as allies. Excessive politicization may also impede an accurate assessment of the situation, implying greater violence against union members than may really exist. The issue of human rights and protection of union workers should be addressed in separate forums from those used for the free trade agreement.

Improvements in both FTA and human rights are important, and each issue should be treated within a framework that assures urgency, comprehension, and effectiveness. Linking them would result in a delayed FTA and a shortsighted human rights policy, while separating them could accelerate FTA's approval in Congress and allow more coherent and integral cooperation in human rights. The murder of union leaders—the issue currently linked to the discussion of the FTA—is just a small part of human rights abuses in Colombia. The recent scandal regarding "*falsos positivos*"—dozens of civilians killed with participation of army officers and then presented as guerrillas killed in combat—is a far more serious problem. A complete human rights strategy should also address topics such as missing persons and "displaced families"—those who must leave their homes in order to protect themselves from local violence, kidnappings, and restrictions on the activities of human rights advocates. A special bilateral commission on human rights, parallel to but separate from the FTA congressional process, should draft a more sophisticated cooperation program, including and taking into account conditions already existing in Plan Colombia under the Leahy Amendment. The membership of this bilateral group should not be limited to government officials but also include representatives of human rights organizations and victims' associations.

U.S.-Colombia Policy as Model for Region

Policy toward Colombia should be part of a wider policy of the United States toward Latin America. Instead of treating Colombia in isolation, Washington should craft an approach to Colombia as part of a framework for a new strategy toward Latin America generally. The entire continent feels ignored by both countries, and recent chaotic events have shaken the region. Although the relationship between the United States and Colombia has been productive, negative effects have arisen because of the relationship's singularity. For instance:

—The two countries have been diplomatically cut off from the majority of the rest of Latin America.

—The United States–Colombia relationship has caused difficulties in the bilateral relationship between Colombia and Venezuela, one that is vital to both countries because of the very long shared border, the 7 million residents of both countries who live in the border region, and $5 billion volume in annual bilateral trade.

—It has generated friction and tension in the Andean region as a whole. The crisis in March 2008, caused by an attack by the Colombian Armed

Forces on a FARC camp in Ecuador, almost exploded into more violence before it was defused at the last minute.

—The relationship has contributed to the formation of ideological blocs that make cooperation difficult.

—The current agenda for cooperation is limited. Important issues such as drug trafficking and border security are being put on the back burner and there is no plan in place for dealing with them. This is not beneficial to either Colombia or the United States.

The special relationship between Washington and Bogotá must, therefore, change in substance and rationale. In recent years a split has opened up between the group of countries that have closely aligned themselves with the political vision of the Bush administration (Mexico, most of Central America, Colombia, and Peru) and the group that has continued to seek something closer to social democracy (Brazil, Argentina, Chile, Paraguay, Uruguay). Colombia and the United States should opt for a dialogue that is broader and more general than the "war on terror" (which in any case is hardly applicable in Latin America), one that includes the defense of democracy and wide areas of cooperation, and allows for a closing of the gap between the Washington-Bogotá pole and the majority of the countries of Latin America. In other words, Washington and Bogotá must seek conceptual lines of minimum consensus in order to encourage cooperation and counteract the tendency for the countries of Latin America to separate into two camps.

Barack Obama's arrival in the White House will facilitate movement toward a different discourse, based on democracy, human rights, and free trade. This will permit reestablishment of multilateral focuses and give greater credibility to instruments like the Summit of the Americas, which in turn will contribute to mending damaged bilateral relationships, such as those between the United States and Venezuela or between Colombia and Ecuador, and establishing a framework more conducive to cooperation.

The Illegal Drug Trade

Dealing with the illegal drug trade should be a renewed priority. The enormous problem of narcotics is not receiving the attention it merits. Progress made in the last decade has been negligible, yet the drug trade is not a central issue in summit meetings or in other types of official discourse. This has prevented confronting new realities (for example, the role of Venezuela and of transit through Brazil) and creating appropriate innovations in policy, strategy, and practice on the ground. Conversely, certain effective elements of the policy of the late 1980s and early 1990s have been forgotten and should be reinstated. Adjustments must be made by parties involved to maintain successful approaches and reform unsuccessful ones:

—Encourage more discussion of the issue, as well as improve visibility in political discourse.

—Create closer links between entities that have the best grasp of new realities in order to coordinate strategically between and among antidrug agencies, police, academic centers, NGOs, think tanks, and other actors.

—Pursue multilateral approaches to the issue, because by nature the problem is global, multinational, and damaging to countries on many continents. Reinstate special summits on the issue, such as those of Cartagena in 1989 and San Antonio in 1990, and connect these efforts with the United Nations. Seek participation by new countries without regard to their ideological inclinations.

—Extend antidrug strategy beyond this hemisphere, because other regions (such as Europe) have risen in importance as consumers. Initiate needed dialogue and cooperation on narcotics between the Americas and Europe.

During the first half of 2009, three Latin American former presidents— César Gaviria of Colombia, Ernesto Zedillo of Mexico, and Fernando Henrique Cardoso of Brazil—will present some general proposals for innovative thinking and a redefinition of antinarcotics policies. They have already begun an ambitious process of reflection. The proposals will not be radical—they will not propose legalizing drug production and trafficking—but will have authentically multilateral focuses with the goal of finding practical solutions to the problem of reducing demand and consumption. These recommendations should be welcomed.

Encourage Democracy

Cooperation to establish real and deeply rooted democracy should again be taken up. The perfection of democracy is not accorded the level of importance today that it was in the 1990s. The Democratic Charter of the Organization of American States, approved in September 2001 as a collective instrument of intervention to protect democracy, is now a dead letter. Current political difficulties—in particular, divisions between and among ideological blocs—have rendered the charter inoperative. But it is still necessary: great challenges to democracy remain. The global crusade against terrorism, the "securitization" of the hemispheric agenda, and the growth of anti-U.S. populism in Venezuela and elsewhere have all added to the value of geopolitics and weakened the pro-democracy position.

In the case of Colombia, antidemocratic practices have grown in scope but have not been opposed by the international community because these practices have not shared the authoritarian dimensions of those promulgated in Bolivia by Hugo Chávez. The U.S. and the international community should work to create a true democratic culture in Colombia by undertaking the following:

—Revive the efforts for strengthening collective mechanisms to improve democracy that were initiated at the beginning of the 1990s with the Miami Summit and in the Organization of American States charter.

—Collaborate with NGOs and academic centers studying democratic perceptions and practices. Undertake a new study to determine whether the 2004 conclusions of the United Nations Development Program—which concluded that people were open to limitations of democracy in exchange for government efficiency in solving economic problems—still hold today.

—Support practices and institutions that facilitate the healthy functioning of Congress, the institutional opposition, and independent media. These counterweights to presidential power must be fortified through upper-level dialogue, programs of financial support, and exchanges of ideas and "best practices."

—Prioritize requirements with regard to democracy over ideological considerations, short-term alliances, or geopolitical analyses.

—Immediately strengthen the credibility and legitimacy of the region's legislatures and political parties by convening congressional representatives and political party representatives from different countries to exchange "best practices" knowledge regarding methods, resource administration, and efficient operations.

Ending Paramilitarism

The defeat of paramilitarism in Colombia must be a real priority. The demobilization of paramilitary forces is a desirable goal, and the effort has produced positive results. Nonetheless, there are serious problems that have prevented progress: the impunity of various paramilitary members for crimes they have committed, the rise of new groups to replace those that are demobilized, and lack of a clear structure of the procedures to be followed when ex-combatants confess their crimes. The United States should support NGOs and academic centers within Colombia that put pressure on government institutions and systems of justice for strict management of the process. Otherwise, the positive results of the Justice and Peace Law passed in July 2005 and strengthened by the Constitutional Court in spring 2006—specifically, obligation of the "commanders" to reveal their crimes—in bolstering democracy and the rule of law might be lost. Among the steps to be taken:

—Institute a more disciplined administration of justice. The United States should support the Justice and Peace body of the public prosecutor's office, as well as Colombia's Supreme Court. In Plan Colombia there are already some provisions for the institutional strengthening of these entities. Maintaining this support should be a priority.

—Ensure interrogation of extradicted paramilitary leaders. The fourteen paramilitary leaders extradited to the United States to stand trial for drug-trafficking charges may later be subject to pending trials in Colombia for crimes against humanity. The extradition of these AUC "commanders" to the United States to face charges is key to the revelation of their human rights abuses in Colombia. Because of conditions included in the two countries' extradition regulations, they are being tried in American courts exclusively for crimes related to drug trafficking; they also should be interrogated by the Colombian judges and law enforcement entities that are investigating paramilitary crimes.

—Link victims of crimes committed by paramilitary groups (and the families of victims) in the study and decision of what actions to take to assure compliance with the Justice and Peace Law, in order to favor the obligations included in the Justice and Peace Law that entail compensation for the victims.

—Educate the public about how to avoid becoming entangled with paramilitaries and guerrilla groups.

—Create, through NGOs, mechanisms for cooperation by representatives of victims and human rights in the United States and Colombia.

Conclusion

There are several reasons for maintaining and strengthening the special relationship that the United States and Colombia have built in the last several years. Improvements in Colombia's democratic processes and the rule of law need to be consolidated. Bogotá's strategic importance for Washington remains high in the light of ongoing turmoil in the divided, chaotic, and dangerous Andean region. The menace of drug trafficking needs to be addressed aggressively and through international mechanisms. The two nations have also learned lessons and built cooperative tools that should not be abandoned. The investment already made in funds, political will, and commitment will continue to bear fruit.

At the same time, the advent of a new administration in the United States offers a good opportunity to rethink U.S.-Colombian relations and to ensure the relationship's continued success. In fact, now is the best time to launch a more active and politically relevant policy toward the whole Latin American region, a new agenda of which Colombia is a crucial piece. A multilateral approach would improve the effectiveness of cooperation in key areas.

Finally, the bilateral agenda should continue plans and programs that are already in place: passage of the Free Trade Agreement in the U.S. Congress; extending Plan Colombia; and the inclusion of a more serious, comprehensive, and committed strategy to improve human rights, democracy, and the rule of law. The last-mentioned point will require an adjustment of President Uribe's approach toward a more open, sincere, and productive dialogue and cooperation with human rights NGOs. Only with such additions and adjustments to the current framework of U.S.-Colombia bilateral relations can the two countries maintain, under evolving political conditions, the high level of cooperation that has benefited them in the past.

six

Haiti's Political Outlook:
What the United States Should Do

Daniel P. Erikson

Haiti's slow but steady climb out of its political and economic abyss was severely jeopardized in 2008 by a series of internal and external shocks. In the spring, escalating food prices prompted widespread riots as the population pushed back against a 40 percent rise in the costs of basic food commodities, which cut deeply into the standard of living in a nation where most people subsist on less than two dollars per day. The Haitian food crisis contributed to the ousting of Prime Minister Jacques-Edouard Alexis and the months of political instability that followed. After rejecting a string of prime ministerial nominees set forth by President René Préval, parliament eventually reached consensus on the nomination of Michèle Pierre-Louis, a respected figure in the development field. In the fall, Haiti was hit by a series of powerful storms in rapid succession that killed seven hundred people, virtually destroyed the major coastal city of Gonaïves, and caused hundreds of millions of dollars in damage. As Préval's presidential term reached its midpoint, Haiti's population was forced to contend with increasingly dire circumstances. The country's stability seems increasingly fragile.

This most recent crisis in Haiti cuts deeply into the U.S. government's efforts to portray Haiti as a modest "success story," following a decade of tumult and setbacks. In the 1990s, Haiti was on the front lines of U.S. efforts to help bind Latin America and the Caribbean into a "community of democracies." This was most dramatically demonstrated by the 1994 intervention by the Clinton administration to authorize the U.S. military to help restore the democratically elected president Jean-Bertrand Aristide to power. Aristide had been voted into office in free and fair elections in 1990, but he was ousted by a repressive military regime in 1991, and the subsequent migration crisis caused by tens of thousands of boat people fleeing political repression galvanized the Clinton administration into action. Following Aristide's return to Haiti, the United States and other international partners poured more than $1 billion into the country to build its police and judicial institutions, strengthen democratic practice, alleviate widespread poverty, and forge a more sustainable economy. Haiti twice more held presidential elections, once in 1995, when René Préval, an Aristide ally, won the presidency in a free and fair vote, and again in 2000, when Aristide was brought back into office in an election that was boycotted by the opposition, spurned by international monitors, and characterized by low turnout. The international community, led by Washington, responded by cutting off aid to the Haitian government, which began to unravel and eventually collapsed when an armed rebellion in the countryside forced Aristide from the presidency on February 29, 2004. Departing under intense pressure from a Haitian rebel uprising, domestic opposition groups, and the governments of the United States, France, and Canada, Aristide penned a resignation letter, boarded a U.S.-chartered plane, and was deposited in Africa, where he remains in exile.

During the next two years, from 2004 to 2006, the interim government of Gérard Latortue presided over a normalization of Haiti's relations with the international donor community and was kept in power principally by the Brazil-led United Nations stabilization force that entered Haiti with several thousand troops in the summer of 2004 and now numbers about 9,000 personnel. In February 2006, former President René Préval was elected with a slight majority of the total vote in the first round of voting, while the other thirty-three presidential candidates split the remaining half of the vote between them. During the next two years Haiti notched up several important successes: the restoration of an elected parliament, a return to economic growth (estimated at slightly less than 4 percent in 2007), and the establishment of basic security as a result of improvements in the UN mission. Despite this progress, and the confirmation of Michèle Pierre-Louis as the new prime minister, the events of 2008 demonstrate that Haiti remains a source of regional instability and a continuing political problem that will require the attention of the next U.S. administration.

Defining U.S. Interests in Haiti

The United States has long been in a quandary about where exactly to place Haiti in the context of its overall foreign policy in the Americas. The U.S. has only limited interests in Haiti. Haiti is not a major supplier of commodities or manufactured goods to the U.S. market and there is little in the way of trade and investment. Haiti is not a major recipient of American tourists and the U.S. expatriate population in Haiti is small, consisting mainly of aid workers and Haitians who also claim U.S. citizenship. Haiti is considered neither an important ally nor a strategic rival to the United States, nor is it effectively integrated into Latin American regional blocs. Haiti is a largely peripheral actor in hemispheric affairs, and its diplomacy abroad is mainly focused on winning more foreign aid. During the cold war, Haiti's right-wing Duvalier dictatorship was considered to be an important, if unsavory, ally, but the geopolitical importance of Haiti declined precipitously in the 1990s, with the exception of U.S. concerns about averting a major migration crisis. The estimated 1 million Haitians who live in the United States represent an important constituency for Haiti that sends back an estimated $1.6 billion in remittances annually, but it is not effectively organized as a political bloc in U.S. domestic politics.

Today, Haiti presents itself as an enduring concern for U.S. policymakers for four principal reasons, which can be identified separately but are not mutually exclusive. The first stems from Haiti's deep levels of poverty and ongoing humanitarian crisis, which manifests itself in high mortality rates, susceptibility to HIV, and widespread hunger. The very nature of Haiti's fragility means that it lacks the political and economic shock absorbers to deal effectively with economic or environmental turbulence, such as the current spike in global food prices, or the impact of tropical storm Jeanne in 2004, which killed more than 4,000 people, and the storms of 2008, which claimed at least 800 more lives.

The second reason is that Haiti remains a continuing source of out-migration and was, in the 1990s, at the center of a major refugee crisis when tens of thousands of Haitians took to the seas to escape the military dictatorship that ousted Aristide and ruled in his place from 1991 to 1994. Although it has been more than a decade since Haiti has produced a major wave of boat people heading to the U.S., there is a steady stream to Florida, and hundreds of thousands of Haitians have fled elsewhere, principally to the Dominican Republic, but also to the Bahamas, Turks and Caicos, and Cuba.

Third, Haiti is an important transshipment point for Colombian cocaine and also is a hub of arms trafficking and human trafficking that has significant effects on the United States.

Fourth, the establishment of democracy in Haiti, which has nominally been touted as a principal goal of U.S. policy, has been a long and winding road whose outcome is still unclear. Insofar as the United States has a stake in the consolidation of democracy in the Americas, Haiti remains a missing link in this agenda. True, the country has held semiregular elections over the past twenty years, but these have mainly been organized by, and held at the behest of, the United States and the international community. Few can doubt that Haiti's electoral practices would decline precipitously and perhaps collapse altogether without continued foreign involvement. Moreover, Haiti still lacks a functioning democratic structure at most levels, and the parliament, civil service, judiciary, and national police all remain quite weak.

It also must be noted that the fact that Haiti is a Creole-speaking black country (and one that has historically suffered a long line of injustices at the hands of Western powers) matters in terms of U.S. policymaking. Haiti's blackness has resulted in heightened interest in terms of American domestic politics, which is principally channeled through the Congressional Black Caucus; and it has prompted concerns, fair or unfair, that mistreatment or neglect of Haiti stems from a racial bias in areas such as migration policy; for example, Cubans who make it to U.S. shores automatically get refugee status, even when they are economic migrants; most Haitians are detained and deported without even an interview, even if they have credible claims as refugees. Moreover, the combination of Haiti's black population, Creole culture and French roots, and its low levels of development means that many policymakers do not view Haiti as a natural part of Latin America—and indeed it is often Washington's Africa hands that have the experience in post-conflict nations and French language skills that equip them to work effectively in Haiti.

Since Haiti's first democratic election in 1990, the U.S. approach to Haiti has vacillated wildly, even though the premise of promoting democracy and economic sustainability has ostensibly been at the core of the policy. U.S. policy toward Haiti has included support for the democratic transition (1990–1991); tough sanctions on the military government (1991–1994); an armed intervention followed by an effort at nation building (1994–2000); political disengagement and a cut-off in aid to the elected government (2000–2004); another, briefer, armed intervention followed by support for a multilaterally managed transition back to a new government (2004–2006);

and the present period, where the U.S. currently supports both the elected government of René Préval and the Brazil-led UN mission but eschews taking on a more robust leadership role in Haiti. True, most of these changes in policy have been precipitated by the changing political dynamic in Haiti and shifting U.S. priorities globally, but the reactive nature of U.S. policy has undermined efforts toward achieving the core goals of strengthening democratic institutions and alleviating poverty. If there is any single lesson to be gleaned from the experience of the past twenty years or so, it is that the United States cannot achieve lasting results with short-term interventions. Indeed, long-term U.S. engagement with Haiti in a supportive multilateral context will be required to move the country forward, and even then progress is likely to be uneven and expectations should remain modest.

Haiti's Political Context

Haiti's highly polarized politics has historically complicated efforts to address the country's deeply rooted development challenges. The country's weak national institutions have proved ill equipped to mitigate political conflict. Recent international efforts to move Haiti toward democracy have often focused on short-term election processes without sufficient emphasis on building democratic institutions capable of peacefully managing political competition. Haiti's profound levels of inequality, weak civil society, poorly articulated political party system, and structural class tensions have resulted in an extended period of low-intensity conflict that periodically sparks more widespread political upheaval. The 2004 uprising that forced the resignation of former President Jean-Bertrand Aristide and ushered in an interim regime was merely the most recent illustration of the divisive clash between four main forces in Haiti: the newly ascendant political classes elected by the poor in the 1990s (and renewed in the 2006 elections), the disbanded but influential ex-military, the traditional economic and business elites, and criminal and social gangs with strong roots in urban slums. The relationship among these groups is fluid and not mutually exclusive. The vast majority of Haitians do not fit into these categories, and are generally inhibited from having a voice in governance because of them.

The government of President Préval and Prime Minister Pierre-Louis now faces the constraints posed by Haiti's lack of stable institutions and democratic norms. Haiti needs sustained international attention for a state-building strategy that can develop functional government ministries, a workable legal and judicial system, and some form of democratic politics. However, the combination of Haiti's zero-sum politics and the episodic attention of the international community have made this difficult to put into practice. During the Obama administration, Haitian politics will continue to vacillate between two key dangers: capture by privileged elites who are harnessing government to protect their dominant position in society; or popular discontent so overwhelming that it seeks to eviscerate and redistribute the wealth of the country's dwindling productive classes. The potential reactivation of Haiti's armed actors for political purposes further exacerbates the risks for the Haitian government.

President Préval's record to date suggests that he is attempting to moderate the most noxious characteristics of the Haitian state without directly tackling the political interests that benefit from the status quo. Préval himself is a leader of limited vision, despite positive instincts toward compromise and moderation. He is seen as an honest man with democratic tendencies, but one who prefers to float above the fray and delegate to others rather than provide clear and directed leadership. Préval will need significant assistance from both his Haitian allies and the international community to achieve even modest aspects of his agenda. Until the outbreak of food riots in the spring of 2008, he appeared to be successfully balancing societal tensions by reaching out to the Haitian elites while signaling solidarity with the poor. However, this fragile consensus has become increasingly frayed and may unravel further, depending on how capably Haiti manages the social problems stemming from deep inequalities, rampant unemployment, population growth, and inadequate social services. Moreover, it remains to be seen whether Prime Minister Pierre-Louis will be any more successful in that post than her predecessor Jacques-Edouard Alexis—a former minister of education who served as prime minister from 1999 to 2001, during Préval's previous presidency—who is still nursing his wounds and may yet reappear on the political scene.

Still, Haiti is in somewhat better shape today than was the case just a few years ago. When President Aristide was driven from the country on February 29, 2004, following nearly a month of incursions by ex-military officers and a concurrent uprising of armed gangs, the country was a shambles. This implosion of Haiti's political system dealt a black eye to U.S. aspirations to build a viable, democratic state in Haiti, and little progress was made during the term of interim Prime Minister Gérard Latortue, who led Haiti's government from March 2004 to May 2006. (Former Supreme Court Chief Justice Boniface Alexandre served as president during this period, in accordance with the constitutionally mandated succession, but he was mainly a figurehead.) Latortue quickly assembled a cabinet of principally nonpartisan technocrats, although several opposition figures landed key posts, while Lavalas, the political organization founded by Aristide in 1991, went unrepresented. This unelected government largely derived its ability to govern from the support of the United States and other members of the international community, and its tenuous political legitimacy sprang from its rhetorical embrace of the mandate to organize a credible election and transition to a new government.

By the end of its mandate, however, the interim administration's technocratic credentials had become overshadowed by its penchant to become embroiled in messy political battles, such as sparring with member countries of the Caribbean Community, jailing dozens of prominent Lavalas supporters, and later jumping into the presidential contest to bar prominent Haitian-American candidates from participating. Latortue, lacking a strong political base within the country, was hesitant to alienate the rebel leaders and the opposition figures who had pushed for Aristide's ouster. Thus he was reluctant to challenge a campaign against Lavalas orchestrated by Justice Minister Bernard Gousse and other cabinet officials that cut deeply into the government's international legitimacy.

The interim government did have several key achievements. Its finance minister was widely respected and the Latortue administration was seen to have tighter fiscal controls and a greater emphasis on minimizing state corruption. In addition, the pledge taken by Latortue and his top ministers not to compete in the elections enhanced the political credibility of both the government and the election process as a whole. To its credit, the interim government never wavered in its support for Haiti's return to a democratically elected government, and it played a constructive role in the negotiations following the 2006 presidential elections. The Latortue government made little headway in promoting national dialogue and political reconciliation, but its political legacy was relatively benign.

Restarting Haiti's Democratic Process

In February 2006 Haiti renewed the process of establishing a democratic government through three rounds of elections, for presidential, parliamentary, and municipal seats. Since then the democratic process has faltered. For example, new elections planned for December 2007 to replace one-third of the senate (ten of the thirty seats) have been postponed until April 2009, underscoring Haiti's general inability to adhere to a regular election schedule. Furthermore, the Haitian constitution requires that the elected president (in this case Préval) appoint a prime minister to run governmental affairs, subject to approval by parliament. Préval once again selected Jacques-Edouard

Alexis. However, once Alexis was forced from office in April 2008, Haiti was left without a formal head of government for four months, until the Pierre-Louis appointment was finally ratified by parliament. This created a sense of drift that was further exacerbated by fallout from the hurricane damage.

Contrary to expectations, Haiti did not revert to a highly centralized presidential system following the 2006 elections, breaking a political pattern adhered to by Aristide and long evidenced in Haiti's decades of authoritarian rule. This is largely due to the quiet leadership style of Haiti's current president. During his first year in office, President Préval, in his self-effacing way, was showing signs of effective leadership. He appointed competent ministers in critical posts, and reached across party lines to bridge Haiti's historic political polarization. Préval forged alliances with moderate elements within Haiti's civil society, political parties, and business sectors, while holding on to support from the Haitian poor, and maintaining the backing of the international community. To date, Préval's instincts have generally been democratic and inclusive, and he has made tough choices, including the decision to green-light the UN peacekeeping force to confront the criminal gangs in Port-au-Prince. However, his understated approach to leadership has left him with declining political capital as he enters the third year of his presidency, and many Haitians judged his response to the spring 2008 food crisis to be well behind the curve, a factor that contributed to the recent instability. The government's lack of capacity to respond effectively to the hurricane damage in the fall of 2008, though unsurprising, further undercut its support and highlighted the degree to which the country has become dependent on the international community—especially the UN peacekeeping force—to fulfill basic state functions.

According to the constitution, parliament is supposed to play a crucial role in governing the country by confirming a prime minister, formulating the budget, and overseeing the operation of the ministries and the cabinet. In practice, however, the parliament lacks a working committee structure, a professional staff, or even adequate physical facilities. Haiti's legislative branch consists of two representative houses: the House of Deputies and the Senate. There are ninety-nine deputies and thirty senators in the parliamentary system. In 2008 the Haitian legislature was divided among several smaller parties with no one party holding a majority. President Préval's first-round presidential win did position him to secure a larger number of seats for candidates from his Lespwa Party (*lespwa* is the Haitian Creole version of the French *l'espoir,* "hope"), but its grassroots support was hardly overwhelming. The functioning of the parliament, however, has been further affected by the lack of adequate meeting space, the absence of trained professional staff, and the poorly developed institutional norms.

Local political institutions are nascent, but they do exist. In December 2006, voters filled 420 offices consisting of a mayor and two deputies for each municipality (that is, 140 mayors and 280 deputies in all) and 9,000 community officials, which according to the "bottom-up" approach designed in Haiti's constitution would provide the basis for selecting the permanent Haitian electoral council, the body that is supposed to be responsible for organizing democratic elections. Even with these local elected officials in place, though, Haiti continues to function with a provisional electoral council. Furthermore, the directors and staff of Haiti's provisional electoral council are frequently driven from the country following the election period, and the body's high levels of tension and turmoil are symptomatic of Haiti's larger institutional failings.

Similarly, Haiti's political party system remains highly fragmented, with few political forces articulated through regular party structures. During the past two decades the democratic process has been repeatedly interrupted and undermined, initially by remnants of the former Duvalier regime, later by conflicts among former democratic allies, and most recently again by armed groups of different political leanings. Haiti's political parties are generally small and narrowly based, led by figures of varying stature and charisma. Lack of trust, sparse resources, and underdeveloped civil society mechanisms have precluded the strengthening of the political system. The period from 2000 to 2004 was characterized by fitful and unproductive negotiations between President Aristide's Lavalas government and members of the opposition coalition that formed to protest irregularities stemming from the May 2000 elections. Key opposition leaders remained almost exclusively focused on their goal of unseating Aristide and never spent the time and resources to build a regional infrastructure or enhance their electoral competitiveness. As a result, most of these parties fared badly in the 2006 elections; their presidential candidates were relegated to single-digit support and only a small number of parties managed to claim a significant number of seats in parliament. The once-dominant Lavalas Party also suffered, leaving Aristide's influence over Haitian politics vastly reduced.

Insecurity and the Rule of Law

Haiti's security situation has deeply deteriorated and lacks easy remedies. The armed uprising of 2004 exacerbated trends that have been in evidence since the late 1990s, including the gradual disintegration of the Haitian police force, the prevalence of guns throughout the country, the absence of judicial institutions, and the violent activities of politically affiliated gangs. The return of former Haitian military officers (some credibly accused of terrible human rights abuses), the breakdown of the penal system and the release of many prisoners, and the apparent impunity for violence all mean that armed elements continue to be a powerful force for destabilization in Haiti. The potential for instability in Haiti is far greater today than in 1994, when it was occupied by a U.S.-led multinational force of 23,000 troops. Any efforts to restore security and the rule of law to Haiti will require a sustained international peacekeeping presence, the disarmament of militant groups, and the reconstitution of a national police.

International peacekeepers returned to Haiti in 2004 under the mandate of a UN Security Council Resolution that authorized the UN peacekeeping mission, led by Brazil. Following the 2006 electoral period, Haiti required an international peacekeeping presence of equivalent size, a force that will have to be maintained until a national police force can be established and made functional. This will require a decade at least, and possibly longer. Although Haiti's security situation has generally improved since 2006, largely attributable to better performance by the UN, it remains plagued by ongoing societal problems that pose a continued risk of renewed violence. On the positive side of the ledger is the more effective performance by the 9,100-troop-strong United Nations Stabilization Mission in Haiti (MINUSTAH), which entered the country in 2004. The UN Security Council has extended the mandate of the peacekeeping mission until October 15, 2009, with a total force of 7,060 military troops and 2,091 police officers. This one-year renewal marks MINUSTAH's longest extension since the mission began, and is a welcome sign of the international community's continued commitment to Haiti. Concurrently the Haitian National Police initiated a vetting process to examine officers' records in detail; hundreds suspected of corruption have been purged and new recruits have been selected and trained.

At the time of Aristide's ouster in 2004, it was clear that Haiti's 5,000-member police force was far too small to bring about order in a country of 8 million. An appropriate size would be closer to 20,000, which is substantially larger than what the international community has been willing to finance in the past. Building a new police force is possible—and indeed necessary—but this is a costly and time-consuming initiative and requires U.S. leadership and resources. The Haitian government's political will to tackle the gangs, combined with better cooperation between the UN and the Haitian National Police, has led to the capture or killing of major gang leaders and the reestablishment of a state presence in some of the country's most dangerous slums. This progress has restored the confidence of the Haitian population in the UN mission and increased support for the Haitian government as a whole. But the new calm in Haiti has proved tenuous and will be hard to sustain; any reduction in UN forces without a substantial increase in the Haitian police presence would lead to a return of violence. Moreover, currently Latin American countries continue to contribute the bulk of the UN troops, but many will eventually seek to shift their focus from peacekeeping to development. Haiti would benefit from a strategy to manage that process over the long term. Still, there is movement in the right direction. Today, the Haitian National Police comprises 7,000 policemen, and some 1,400 more completed training in 2008, but the force is still far from meeting its target of 15,000 officers.

What the United States Can Do

Haiti is likely to be plagued by familiar political instability during the next four years. The international development community, including the United States, will face an environment where no single action or set of actions can be guaranteed to put the country on the path toward long-term stability and economic progress. Efforts to encourage long-term policy planning by the Haitian government and improve donor coordination are valuable, but it will also be crucial to focus on generating tangible results for the Haitian poor in the short term.

The Obama administration could make a positive contribution to democratic governance and the rule of law in Haiti by using its leverage, both in Haiti and with the broader international community, in three discrete areas: facilitating elections, strengthening parliament and political parties, and embracing a pro-poor development agenda for Haiti.

Facilitating Elections

Haiti's political system is incapable of holding to its constitutionally mandated electoral timetable without international support, making it crucial to establish and finance a mechanism for regular elections. The electoral schedule is legally the responsibility of the Haitian provisional electoral council (given that no permanent council has yet been named), but the basic tasks of logistics, security, and maintaining and updating the civil registry are almost entirely in the hands of the international community, and upwards of $15 million in international funds are required to hold each election. This patch-work system has resulted in a situation where elections are perennially held late and at great expense. Moreover, when the terms of Haitian legislators expire and no new elections are held to replace them, large swaths of parliament are left vacant: for example, the ten senate seats that expired in January 2008 remained empty for more than a year due to a delay in holding new elections. Haiti simply cannot be expected to move toward democratic stability if it lacks the capacity to hold regular elections, maintain a viable civil registry, and verify the eligibility of political candidates. The United States, working with Haitian authorities and international partners, should seek to establish and finance a UN-supervised election mechanism so that Haiti can hold regular elections without constantly scrambling for cash and missing key deadlines.

Strengthening Parliament and Political Parties

Haiti's parliament is still far from fulfilling its role of providing advice and consent as a coequal branch of government, as outlined in the country's constitution. Efforts to assist parliament could take two forms. First, the United States could play a role in improving the institutional infrastructure of the Haitian parliament, including restoration of physical facilities, providing support for training programs, and enhancing the ability of the parliament to work effectively as a deliberative body. A second effort to strengthen parliament could entail developing better linkages between members of the legislature and their own constituents.

Strengthening political parties will be an important component of increasing legislator responsiveness. Haiti's legislators have traditionally had a poor record in tending to constituent concerns, yet they remain the most direct link between the government and the Haitian poor. By facilitating legislators' capacity to remain in touch with the localities they represent (such as by sponsoring legislative forums, encouraging resident offices in the provinces and departments, or even indirectly, by improving communication and travel infrastructure within Haiti), the United States could help to ensure a louder voice for the poor in the policymaking process. Many of Haiti's political parties would also benefit from expanded leadership training and working to deepen the connection between the Haitian people and their political representatives. Achieving the right balance of institutional capacity and attentiveness to constituent concerns will be essential to consolidate parliament as a viable democratic body, and political parties can play an important role in this process.

Embracing a Pro-Poor Development Agenda

The United States has a mixed track record in supporting pro-poor policies in developing countries: Washington typically favors strategies that focus largely on enhancing trade and expanding the private sector, a formula that does not necessarily fit all national contexts. In Haiti, for example, the formal private sector is primarily based in Port-au-Prince and has failed to generate much employment, and the informal private sector is not positioned to take advantage of new trade initiatives.

Other development actors in Haiti and abroad do often focus on the need for a "pro-poor social contract," and this concept is extremely relevant to Haiti. This is true despite the fact that concepts such as a "new social contract" are politically loaded and often manipulated for the benefit of certain parties. The "winner-take-all" nature of the Haitian electoral system can be expected to result in extreme reluctance on the part of potentially threatened classes to accept new policies that may restrict their range of action in the future. Instead, the United States should focus on concrete pro-poor social policies targeted at strengthening the social safety net, increasing access to education and health care, and bringing the informal market economy into the formal economy. The United States could also be a much more forceful advocate for Haiti in the context of international financial institutions such as the IMF, the World Bank, and the Inter-American Development Bank. Promoting a more progressive tax system, expanding the network of education and health services available to the poor, and extending infrastructure projects to underserved or forgotten areas can help to move the country incrementally toward greater political consensus by signaling that the Haitian poor are being given a rightful stake in their society. Haiti's effort to move toward democracy will rely on the development of a sustainable middle class, or the country will be subject to further backsliding. In the future, the U.S. strategy for Haiti should rely less on grand planning schemes delivered from the top down, and more on bottom-up development processes that can be incubated with international support and made self-sustaining over time.

seven

Responding to the Challenges in Haiti

Juan Gabriel Valdés

At the beginning of April 2008, as a result of the sudden rise in food prices, Haiti was engulfed by social unrest. By the end of October the country had been ravaged by three hurricanes that left hundreds dead and the city of Gonaïves completely covered by water and mud. The food crisis increased the suffering of the more than 6 million people who subsist on only two dollars a day, and the natural disasters once again pounded the morale of what are undoubtedly the people with the most tragic history in the Western Hemisphere. It is indeed unfortunate that the Caribbean nation has been hit by this series of catastrophes just when it was showing, for the first time in years, a reasonable degree of political cooperation between the main parties and the government; modest economic growth of 4.3 percent; a relatively better level of security as a result of the dismantling of gangs by UN peace-keepers and the local police; and above all, a cautious confidence within the elites and among international observers that the reforms the government was introducing to strengthen the rule of law would be implemented at last.

This welcome progress does not mean that President René Préval has managed to alter in any significant way the enormous precariousness of the Haitian state structure. Haiti continues to have very feeble institutions that do not possess the means and the resources necessary to organize and control the nation's territory. Its justice system is weak, dysfunctional, and often corrupt; and its police force is understaffed and underequipped. The country has a dangerously overcrowded prison system in which 90 percent of inmates have never been brought to trial. Haiti lacks social services: 70 percent of the population has no access to running water and lives on less than two dollars a day. Haitian society is threatened by drug trafficking and the criminal organizations that are sustained by it.

But President Préval has recognized the need to fight corruption and impunity. He introduced comprehensive judicial reforms, and three laws have already been approved by the Haitian Parliament and after being promulgated in December 2007 are now going through a phase of implementation. The government has also created a commission to reduce the arbitrariness of pretrial detentions. In a speech last January, the president declared the fight against corruption, drug trafficking, and impunity to be his first priority. Since then, several police officers involved in drug trafficking have been arrested, and some prominent businessmen have been convicted for banking fraud and tax evasion.

At the same time, with the support of the United Nations mission the electoral calendar has been properly followed. New electoral authorities were appointed and municipal elections took place in conditions of complete normalcy. In July 2007 Préval approved a program for the reform of the state judiciary, along with a vision for the reform of the administration and the decentralization of the country.

Yet the fragility of the institutional and economic situation continues to harm the possibility of a permanent stabilization of the country. The implementation of a reform of the judiciary remains a critical factor. "The dysfunctional state of Haiti's justice system has impeded the implementation of democratic reforms since the collapse of the Duvalier dictatorship," writes the International Crisis Group, correctly underlining what has been the main institutional factor in state failure in Haiti.[1] The ICG lists the characteristics of the current order of things in the judiciary as incompetence, poor case management, no criminal records, prolonged pretrial detentions, inadequate pay for judges, inadequate infrastructure and logistical support, lack of judicial independence, antiquated codes, and lack of defense counsels.

The Lessons Learned

Since 1993 the international community has promoted multiple programs of support to the Haitian judiciary and the police. By 2001 various governments, including France and Canada, and agencies, most prominently, the American Administration of Justice Program, had invested around $110 million in training and mentoring of the Haitian courts and in the reform of the police. In October 2000, however, the U.S. Government Accountability Office concluded "that millions of dollars had produced little or no progress in the justice and security sectors due to almost total lack of will in the Haitian government." It recommended the termination of the program and that future aid be given to NGOs.[2]

The lessons to be extracted from that experience were the subject of various discussions and analysis, both within the UN secretariat when it was planning the United Nations Stabilization Mission in Haiti (MINUSTAH), and within governmental and nongovernmental organizations involved in Haiti. The most often recurring explanations for the complete failure of these efforts were the lack of donor coordination, the lack of strategic planning, and the absence of civil society involvement. But less attention has been given to some political factors that might have been even more decisive. It should be remembered that the mistrust the main international actors felt toward the first Préval administration turned into overt hostility for the second Aristide government. Nationalism being the last and sometimes the only resource of Haitians, it was extremely unlikely that outsiders, who were perceived as potential enemies, could persuade Haitian authorities to embark on a reform of the state administration.

By the end of 2004, MINUSTAH once again launched a broad program to train the police and reform the justice system. Although gang violence and the opposition of judges to reform impeded visible progress in the period prior to the elections, the reestablishment of a constitutional government was a big step forward. As noted earlier, in December 2007 the Haitian parliament passed legislation establishing the independence of the judiciary and the status of magistrates, including creating the Superior Council for the judiciary and the School of Magistrates. During the same period—2005 to 2008—MINUSTAH was able to train 8,444 police officers and simultaneously introduce a process of individual vetting of candidates. Although the police force is still understaffed and underequipped, by 2011 it should maintain a force of a minimum of 14,000, marking the first time in many years, if ever, that Haiti would have a functioning police institution. Yet this young police corps will not be ready, now or in the near future, to confront the threats against stability brought about by drug lords and criminal gangs. And despite the genuine progress in its reform process, the Haitian justice system is not and will not for some years have the capacity to handle the wave of kidnappings and assaults that from time to time continue to engulf the capital.

What Can Be Done

How can these two efforts—training police and reforming the justice system—so critical to improving the prospects for an effective rule of law, be sustained over time? The first point to stress is that the international community must maintain its involvement in Haiti for the long run. MINUSTAH should stay in Haiti at least until 2012. Its presence is not simply a deterrence mechanism against internal violence and subversive adventures, but it also sends a strong political message to Haitians that the country's friends are determined to press for changes that can guarantee institutional stability and respect for the rule of law. As a peacekeeping operation, MINUSTAH's main role is to build with the Haitian authorities a common vision of democratic governance as well as to develop the political cooperation needed for a common selection of priorities and actions destined to stabilize the country. In recent months MINUSTAH has with the government agreed on benchmarks by which the emerging stability of the country can be measured:

—"Continued progress in the resolution of political differences through dialogue and the successful completion of the cycle of elections that culminates in the smooth installation of a democratically chosen President and legislature in 2011."

—"The establishment of a sustainable security structure that would enable Haiti to respond effectively to potential threats within the country and along its land and sea borders while respecting international standards and individual freedoms."

—"The establishment of an independent and credible judiciary and penal system that respects human rights and is accessible to all citizens."

—"The extension of State authority throughout the country through the establishment of legitimate, transparent and accountable State institutions."

After the next presidential election, in 2011, MINUSTAH should begin a gradual program of phasing its presence out while the international community at the same time sets up a robust program of assistance for national reconstruction. With Haitian government approval each year, this program should be supported by a technical task force, led by a permanent UN representative, endowed with an international police unit that continues the training and overseeing of the local police. The task force also should be able to coordinate the UN agencies and the financial institutions of the UN system. This structure should be actively supported by the Organization of American States and a core group of interested countries, including the United States, Canada, and Argentina, Brazil, and Chile (sometimes called the ABC). The role of the Latin Americans, most especially of the Brazilians, is extremely important for two reasons: they have a good grasp of development matters and the fight against poverty and also play a central role in a crucial aspect of Haitian development—the integration of the country into the Latin American and Caribbean community of nations.

A second precondition for maintaining the pace of reforms and stabilizing the country relates to development policies: the international community must reconsider its strategy for promoting development in the country. Today, as in the past, donor countries and organizations continue to oscillate between direct support to the Haitian state and donations to NGOs. This ambivalence does not improve the situation in a nation often described with the shallow concept "failed state." It is hard to imagine that Haitian institutions will find ways of their own to operate effectively if—as is now the case— about 60 percent of the government budget comes from foreign aid and 70 percent of that is channeled through NGOs or international organizations. This method of funding the rebuilding of education and health systems does not serve the goals of local ownership and political participation, which are indispensable for state reconstruction. Bypassing the government and continuing to treat state institutions as suspect does not serve anticorruption policies, because transparency cannot be demonstrated or proved wrongheaded in the absence of responsibilities. This criticism should not be read as an attack on NGOs. Some of them play an enormously positive role in the country. But their central function in channeling international assistance conspires against the rebuilding of state and local institutions. For example, it does not serve the cause of stability in Haiti to give the task of rebuilding Cité Soleil or other shantytowns in Port-au-Prince to a myriad of American NGOs instead of supporting the government's capacity to reach out and engage with these social sectors.

Internal civil society cannot be strengthened in the absence of a state structure. International efforts to promote a more active civil society in Haiti have too often ended up in creating further fragmentation of what initially looked like serious associations of citizens. It could even be argued that in some cases support was extended to NGOs only to steer clear of the complexities of Haitian politics. What MINUSTAH's experience shows is that it is essential in the political reconstruction effort to engage the Haitian elite and political class in a serious debate—on the future of the Haitian nation, on the need for internal dialogue and political cooperation, on the real priorities that should guide the orientation of the political debate, on the common effort against the threats to peace, and, last but not least, on the reality that the international community cannot sustain indefinitely the present state of affairs in Haiti. In 2005, the year before the last presidential election, a patient process of dialogue included representatives of many civil society organizations and party factions, who were presented at the same time with the concerns and priorities of the international community. Dozens of invitations to negotiating tables, political seminars, and agreement ceremonies were organized. Nobody was left out. In some cases MINUSTAH provided the scenarios and practical settings for the dialogue; in others the UN mission acted in close association with European NGOs playing an enormously constructive role.

This is why, under the conditions found in Haiti, supporting institution building demands not just a persistent involvement but also a direct presence of Haiti's friends on the ground. Aid conceded directly to the Haitian state requires the creation of control mechanisms, an attentive attitude from donors, as well as their full participation, along with the local authorities in the discussion and elaboration of the public policies to be supported. Up to now, coordination among donors has been difficult to achieve, yet coordination strengthens their capacity to influence governmental decisions, for it indicates political will and a turning away from technocratic and bureaucratic models, which often have the effect of weakening the pertinence and quality of development projects.

A critical point in the development of the country's future is its relationship with the Dominican Republic. The association between the two societies that share Kiskeya (the Taino Indian name for the island the Spanish called Hispaniola) is vital for the economic development of Haiti, for dealing with the security problems that threaten both nations, and for managing the environmental and migration problems that stymie progress at both ends of the island. Political difficulties in Haiti and the elections in the Dominican Republic have up to now prevented the two governments from making use of the goodwill between the two presidents and of Dominican investors, attracted to the Haitian market following the passage of a trade program, HOPE II, by the U.S. Congress, which is designed to facilitate Haitian exports into the United States. Various development projects that have been put forward by the European Union, the World Bank, and the Inter-American Development Bank to foster relations between the two countries should be integrated into a coordinated program of rapprochement and presented to the two governments with the full support of the international community. The two governments have agreed to the creation of a bilateral commission, but it has never been put in place. It is time to do so, particularly when the combined catastrophic impact of food and natural disaster crises might encourage further illegal migration into the Dominican Republic, leading to an eventual increase in tensions between the two governments.

The U.S. Role: A New Opportunity

The election of the first African American President in the history of the United States generates new opportunities for improved Haitian-American relations. There is a need for a new language in Washington that would restore the enormous symbolic meaning that Haiti has for people everywhere in the hemisphere, and most especially for black Americans. This new message, bluntly, should be that the present state of affairs in the Caribbean nation—so near the coast of Florida—is utterly unacceptable. The new administration should call without delay for an aid and investment conference on Haiti prompted both by the conviction that Haiti represents a development challenge much easier to confront than that of other "failed states," and the certainty that only direct foreign investment and a sustained policy of job creation can cure the present situation. Washington should take action under the premise that positive action for Haiti is not only an act of solidarity but also an act of calculated self-interest.

This call to action is even more important if one considers that since the devastating 2008 hurricanes and tropical storms, only 40 percent of the $107 million called for in the UN's Flash Appeal for humanitarian needs has been donated.[3] This is far less than the $800 million that the Haitian government, the UN, the World Bank, and the European Commission are requesting for a postdisaster needs assessment. The United Nations has recognized that aid to Haiti faces an uphill struggle in the face of the current global financial crisis, yet it is urgent to provide an increasingly desperate population with hope for the future if the hemisphere wants to avoid what President Préval has called a "social tsunami."[4]

President Barack Obama should review both the positive and negative aspects of previous U.S. policies toward Haiti but should also send a clear message of a change in direction in U.S.-Haitian policy. It is well known that the United States has tried since the overthrow of President Aristide to take a back seat in the Haitian arena. Its role, however, in inviting the Latin American countries to participate in MINUSTAH and in facilitating the multilateral effort both at the UN and the OAS was undoubtedly positive. The support given to the UN Mission and to the provisional government of Prime Minister Latortue was also decisive in the development of the electoral process and the success of the election. Yet in the one area where its involvement should have been greater, the war against drug trafficking, the big neighbor has shown a certain reluctance, which has puzzled not only the Haitian authorities but also some international observers. The United States has not done enough about this issue.

Some studies argue that the war in Iraq led to a reduction of U.S. military patrolling in the Caribbean and that this explains the increase in drug trafficking in the area. Whatever the reasons, the United States does not seem to be acting aggressively against drug lords in the Haitian capital who, though they may lack relevance in terms of their weight in the global business, certainly have a dangerous capacity to disrupt the peace process in Haiti. Most of the money funneled to gang leaders for weapons seems to originate in drug interests, and a large portion of these weapons come from United States territory. As a result, many of the sudden and unexpected explosions of violence that from time to time ravage Port-au-Prince are linked to the efforts by drug interests to prevent stabilization and maintain the measure of chaos necessary to keep their business thriving. Under these conditions, the United States would do well to make its presence felt in the capture and punishment of individual traffickers. Given the psychological profile of Haitians' relationship to the United States, a few arrests in Port-au-Prince with subsequent conviction and imprisonment in the United States would do more for Haitian security than a whole new MINUSTAH battalion on the field. A consistent policy should also put an end to the practice of the United States' returning to Haiti convicted criminals of Haitian origin. Exporting drug traffickers, kidnappers, and murderers from the United States to Haiti only increases the level of insecurity in Haiti and works against the efforts undertaken by the international community, most importantly the United States, to maintain order and peace in Port-au-Prince and other Haitian cities.

The new American administration should resist the linkage that some, particularly within the Haitian diaspora, will make between the change in administration and a demand for the immediate return to Haiti of former President Jean-Bertrand Aristide. President Préval has said that his government recognizes Aristide's constitutional right to return to his country whenever he wants. In response, Aristide in his usual convoluted way has called Préval "a traitor" and has chosen to remain in South Africa. Some of his former associates report that he fears for his security and is concerned with cases that could be brought against him in Haitian or Florida courts. Aristide is still a profoundly divisive figure in Haiti; although his Lavalas Party has been reduced in numbers through internal divisions and the political migration of his followers to other organizations, his popularity in Haiti's poorer areas seems to remain intact. The prospect of a U.S.-supported Aristide comeback could reproduce the situation of internal chaos that characterized the first months of 2004.

The United States should keep involved in and support the Haitian democratic process. The new prime minister, Michèle Pierre-Louis, deserves full support in her effort to bring together a majority government. Washington should avoid what is called in South America the Swiss Syndrome—that is, to demand institutional perfection when material conditions for it do not exist. It should also avoid "Haiti fatigue"—the tendency to become exhausted because of the pitfalls, grandiosity, and often byzantine character of the Haitian political debate. It should support the reorganization of a central Haitian state authority as well as the buildup of local power in the small towns, which are less politically tainted than Port-au-Prince. It should encourage the permanence of Latin American troops in MINUSTAH and the participation of Latin American governments in supporting Haitian development. It should promote Haitian participation in regional and subregional integration schemes, bearing in mind that the principal factor in Haiti's current backwardness was its isolation during the nineteenth and twentieth centuries. Washington should push not only for international donor coordination but also for integration of donor projects, merging into associated development operations between Haitians and the international community.

A Final Note

In late March 2008 the secretary general of the OAS led a mission of "Haiti's friends" to Port-au-Prince that included Assistant Secretary of State Thomas Shannon and officials from Canada, Brazil, and Argentina. The mission was prompted by international concern about the dramatic rise in food prices in Haiti and the violent riots that resulted, causing death and destruction in Port-au-Prince and other cities. (Ultimately the crisis resulted in the prime minister's resignation, after the parliament's no-confidence vote.) President Préval pulled no punches when he met with the group: dispensing with prefatory remarks and somewhat surprising his visitors, he stated his urgent request for immediate food relief: "Thirty thousand tons of rice; fifteen thousand tons of wheat; seven thousand tons of oil—this is what we need to survive."

The president's plea underlines a central characteristic of the Haitian dynamic that overshadows all efforts to stabilize the country: misery and inhuman conditions must be addressed first before there is any chance for development. These conditions make it necessary to provide assistance to Haiti on terms that respond to the country's emergency conditions. It is extremely difficult to build houses while earthquakes are occurring.

Haiti should receive international assistance on terms similar to those provided to countries after catastrophic events, when free market economic rules simply do not apply, when opposition to subsidies becomes academic, when formal principles of nonintervention have to be shelved. The U.S. Congress's decision to launch HOPE II, giving Haiti ten years of special tariff exemptions and easing the country's ability to use international fabrics in export clothes sewn by Haitian workers, is a clear step in this direction. HOPE II provides the best opportunity yet to provide jobs to the hundreds of thousands of Haitian youth who roam the streets of the two or three biggest towns in the country. The implementation of this and other such programs is extremely urgent. The present food crisis and the devastating effect of hurricanes and tropical storms could easily reverse all progress achieved in the last five years. It is up to the United States and the community of friends of Haiti to prevent this from happening.

Notes

1. International Crisis Group, Latin American/Caribbean Briefing No.14, Port au Prince/Brussels, January 31, 2007, p. 2.

2. U.S. Government Accountability Office, "Any Further Aid to Haitian Justice System Should Be Linked to Performance-Related Conditions," October 2000, p. 23, quoted in International Crisis Group, Latin American/Caribbean Briefing No.14, p. 6.

3. For more information, see UN, Consolidated Appeals Process, "Haïti Flash Appeal 2008" (http://ochaonline.un.org/cap2005/webpage.asp?Page=1695).

4. This remark by President Preval at a meeting with MINUSTAH officers was reported to me in a private letter.

eight

Cuba in Transition:
The Role of External Actors

Marifeli Pérez-Stable

For the first time in fifty years, Fidel Castro is not presiding over Cuba. On February 24, 2008, the National Assembly named his younger brother, Raúl Castro, then seventy-six, president of the Council of State and the Council of Ministers. Since July 2006 Raúl had held interim power. Now he was formally in charge, and for the most part substantively as well. As long as he is alive and mentally alert, however, Fidel—el Comandante—will remain a potent symbol and an influential voice.

Cuba is slowly starting down an uncharted path, not toward democracy but nonetheless toward something different from where it would have been had ill health not felled the elder Castro. Lacking his brother's charisma, Raúl must govern through institutions, especially the military and the Cuban Communist Party (Partido Comunista de Cuba, PCC). This is nothing new. In the 1970s and early 1980s, the younger Castro led efforts to institutionalize the political system and somewhat loosen central control of the economy. In the early 1990s, Raúl and the generals were likewise instrumental in the modest economic reforms enacted after Germans tore down the Berlin Wall. On both occasions el Comandante stopped the reforms at his whim.

Well before Fidel announced his retirement, on February 19, 2008, Raúl had disbanded the informal networks of loyalists his brother had used to keep tabs on the party and government bureaucracies. Institutions never stopped Fidel from setting and implementing policy as he saw fit, especially on economic and international matters. Since assuming the presidency, Raúl has emphasized the importance of *la institucionalidad*, the notion that decision-making flows through institutions. The first order of business is the economy. Although radical moves akin to China's or Vietnam's are not in the offing, even modest market openings constitute steps away from the *Fidelista* legacy. For Fidel, market socialism is just a notch or two less objectionable than outright capitalism.

For decades the character of Cuban politics—undemocratic, opaque, repressive—has been a concern for U.S. policymakers. Until the cold war ended, however, the United States never conditioned the normalization of relations to a democratic transition on the island. Now it does. Thus, the question "What is the current state of governance and the rule of law in Cuba?" lies at the core of current U.S. policy toward Cuba. There are two ways of answering. The first, hewing to the Helms-Burton Act of 1996—the Cuban Liberty and Democratic Solidarity (Libertad) Act—and thus to current U.S. policy toward Cuba, stands fast on maintaining the embargo until Havana takes meaningful steps toward democracy. Without a democratic rule of law, there can be no progress toward an understanding with Havana. The second, which marked U.S. policy under the Ford and Carter administrations in the 1970s and, intermittently, Clinton's in the 1990s, takes a realpolitik approach. Granting that a democratic Cuba should be the goal of U.S. policy, realism dictates that dialogue and engagement pave the way there.

The Helms-Burton Act is the law of the land in the United States, yet the Clinton and George W. Bush administrations sometimes looked beyond the law's seemingly inflexible margins. President Clinton, for example, emphasized people-to-people contacts, expanded academic exchanges, and authorized educational travel. In 2002 President Bush—perhaps in reaction to President Carter's successful trip to Havana that May and the Varela Project's petition to the National Assembly for a referendum to amend the constitution—mentioned the Popular Power elections in 2003 as an opportunity for Havana: "If Cuba's government takes all the necessary steps to ensure that the 2003 elections are certifiably free and fair and if Cuba also begins to adopt meaningful market-based reforms, then—and only then—I will work with the United States Congress to ease the ban on trade and travel between our two countries."[1] The president, in effect, accepted the Cuban constitution—which Helms-Burton does not—as the starting point for Havana to manifest a willingness to change and for the United States to respond in kind.

A realpolitik framework means a realistic dialogue: neither Cuba's commitment to a democratic transition nor a unilateral lifting of the U.S. embargo needs to happen before Washington and Havana start stepping back from the long-standing dead end. Without losing sight of the objective of a democratic Cuba, U.S. policy should take into full consideration the significance of the succession from Fidel to Raúl. Paralyzed since the late 1990s, official Cuba is now moving, albeit slowly. Under Raúl, turning back the clock from the current path could happen, though it will not happen suddenly. The Cuban government is set to be more predictable than it ever was under the larger-than-life Fidel Castro. U.S. policy should be more attuned to what is happening on the ground in Cuba, even if a democracy is not yet on the horizon.

The New Cuban Government

On February 24, 2008, Raúl named José Ramón Machado Ventura as first vice president of the Council of State instead of Carlos Lage, the then fifty-seven-year-old technocrat personally favored by the under-sixty generation. Machado is a hard-liner, one of Raúl's closest collaborators since the 1950s and the struggle against Fulgencio Batista. He is the Communist Party's long-standing fixer and ideological guardian. Yet one should not immediately conclude that his appointment sounds the death knell for reforms. The old guard may not be ready to give up power just yet, and may be banking on what they believe to be their legitimacy to bring changes while safeguarding the revolution. Given their advancing years, Cuba's ruling old men have a three- to five-year window to make their mark and leave the next generation a more orderly, less strapped country than the one el Comandante has left them. In 2013 the National Assembly will again elect the Council of State and the Council of Ministers. It is unlikely that Raúl and most of his cohorts would then remain at the helm.

Raúl's appointment of Machado is reminiscent of Moscow in the early 1980s. After Leonid Brezhnev's passing, two old men—first the more open-minded Yuri Andropov, then the mummified Konstantin Chernenko—ruled the Soviet Union. Not until 1985 did the youthful Mikhail Gorbachev take the Kremlin's reins. Is Raúl more akin to Andropov than to Chernenko? Although Gorbachev and China's Deng Xiaoping are often mentioned as two role models, the earlier Soviet pair may be a more apt analogy. But of Gorbachev and Deng Xiaoping, Deng is clearly the more attractive model for Raúl: the Communist Party still rules over China.

Economic Reforms in the Making

Even as interim president, Raúl was beginning to make his mark, calling for franker discussions, sidestepping the mass mobilizations that had been his brother's staple, and loosening some restrictions on the economy. His most noted statement was his speech on July 26, 2007, in which he called for "structural changes"; it was subsequently discussed in work and neighborhood assemblies throughout the island.[2] The reception of the assemblies themselves spanned a wide spectrum: "a national catharsis," "exhaustion and skepticism," "people couldn't stop talking," and "Cubans under forty were largely disengaged and uninterested."[3] Raúl raised popular expectations more than ever before, which carried considerable political risks if at least modest improvements in living standards didn't occur relatively quickly.

Since Raúl fully assumed the presidency, the Cuban government has taken some economic measures of note. In the mid-1990s Fidel had halted the modest market openings that he had initiated after the Soviet Union's collapse, and in 2003 he launched a partial retrenchment, back to greater state control over the economy. What is now in progress is a return to the economic ideas that el Comandante first proposed in the mid-nineties, then shelved in 2003, a cautious nod to markets and decentralization. This is an unspoken repudiation of the antimarket policies at the heart of Fidel's legacy. Improving food production is a matter of national security and thus of immediate urgency. Cuba is spending some $1.5 billion in food and agricultural imports, nearly $500 million of it from the United States.[4] That Cuba spends scarce hard currency on these imports can't but be an indictment of long-standing agricultural policies: el Comandante stood fast against markets and local control even as food production declined year after year. In 2008 nature dealt Cuba a heavy blow in the form of three major hurricanes—Gustav, Ike, and Paloma—which caused about $10 billion in damages, including crops for domestic consumption.[5]

Most of the following steps have been taken since Raúl came to power.

—*Agriculture.* The state has paid long-standing debts owed to agricultural cooperatives and independent peasants, increased prices for many agricultural products, and has begun selling agricultural tools and other inputs for CUCs (from peso *cubano convertible*), which, unlike ordinary pesos, are purchased with a hard currency such as U.S. dollars or euros. After Hurricanes Gustav and Ike, in mid-September, it also started leasing state-owned arable land, about 50 percent of which had been lying fallow, to cooperatives and peasants. The Agriculture Ministry has opened local municipal offices, which have the authority to make decisions affecting the sector in their jurisdictions.[6]

—*Consumer goods.* Since May 2007, the customs authority has allowed Cuban citizens to bring in limited quantities of video equipment and automobile parts at reduced duties. Since April 2008, special stores have opened to sell computers, cell phones, car alarms, microwave ovens, television sets, and other goods for CUCs. Internet access was still being restricted because of the U.S. embargo, which, the government claims, hinders quality connectivity.[7]

—*Foreigners-only establishments.* Cubans can now use hotels and super-markets that had been reserved for foreigners. Only CUCs are accepted for payment of goods and services.[8]

—*Homeownership.* Workers who have been renting their homes through their workplaces—in the military, the sugar industry, and others—are receiving property titles if they have lived in the units at least twenty years. With title in hand, they are now able to seek a government license to rent out rooms and include their homes in their wills.[9]

—*Wage ceilings lifted.* The Cuban government had long touted the ideal of equality in explaining why the narrow range of its wage scales and salaries had been capped for decades. Beginning in May 2008, however, salaries were no longer to be limited (because of the devastating hurricanes, enforcement of new salary measures was postponed until January 2009), and productivity is to be the sole determinant of wages. Workers in the courts and prosecutors' offices have received wage increases averaging 55 percent—judges and prosecutors are deemed central to the ongoing campaign against corruption.[10]

—*Foreign enterprises.* Cubans working in these enterprises are now allowed to receive their salaries in CUCs—a long-established under-the-table practice—but a 10 to 50 percent tax will be deducted.[11]

—*Social security and social welfare.* Retirees receiving pensions of up to 400 pesos and citizens on social assistance will receive a 20 percent increase in their stipends. Though all workers should be paying up to a 5 percent tax on their wages for social security, only those in the enterprise-management improvement system (*perfeccionamiento empresarial*) and the fishing fleet have had the deduction taken. Workers receiving salary increases will now have the tax deducted from their wages. A new social security law is in the works and will likely be enacted in 2009.[12]

Most of these measures are little more than window dressing, since average Cubans can't afford to spend their CUCs on consumer items or to stay in a hotel in Varadero on vacation. Basic necessities such as food take up whatever hard-currency funds they might have. Still, the psychological impact of potentially being a consumer should not be underestimated. There's no telling how many Cubans might now save some of their CUCs to celebrate a wedding anniversary at a nice hotel or to give a child a cell phone for his or her graduation. Viewed in the Cuban context, these changes are far from inconsequential.

Other changes could be more significant, especially if the momentum for reform should pick up. Even if only a start, the agricultural measures should yield higher outputs within a relatively short period of time. Success for cooperatives and peasant farmers would mean more food on the table for all Cubans. Increases in wages, pensions, and social welfare payments should give recipients more purchasing power or at least provide them with some relief from the higher cost of living. All the same, the hurricane season pushed forward into the future the time when the citizenry might find relief in their daily lives. And on July 26, 2008, well before the hurricanes hit, Raúl Castro had already signaled that reforms would slow down, referring to then rising costs of food and oil.[13] Cuba's gerontocracy prefers a slow rather than a bold pace.

Politics as Usual?

Under either Castro brother, Cuba is a dictatorship. Neither Castro brooks political opposition nor has anything but disdain for civil liberties. State security maintains a close check on ordinary Cubans, not just those in the opposition. Though officially condemned, the *doble moral*—saying one thing in public while actually thinking another—is well entrenched in the Cuban psyche. Civil liberties are the only antidote to this syndrome. In the meantime, the *doble moral* lives on, and citizens in peaceful pursuit of their own political or human-rights initiatives experience repression. On April 21, 2008, for instance, Raúl followed in Fidel's footsteps when he had ten members of the organization Ladies in White (*Damas de Blanco*)—women who, dressed in white, regularly protest the imprisonment of their loved ones—dragged from the Plaza of the Revolution. The women had intended to deliver a letter to the Interior Ministry demanding freedom for their husbands and sons. Since Raúl took over, opponents have faced arbitrary short-term arrests, though most have been released without being charged and tried.[14]

There were some noteworthy political developments in 2008. On February 28 Cuba signed the UN-sponsored International Covenant on Economic, Social, and Cultural Rights and the International Covenant on Civil and Political Rights. Although Cuba reserves the right to issue future "reservations or interpretive declarations," there is no denying the symbolism of the official signature or that the signing took place four days after Raúl formally assumed the presidency. Apparently, el Comandante disagreed. In December 2007 the Communist Party newspaper, *Granma,* published the transcript of an April 2001 interview with Fidel on *Mesa Redonda* (Round Table), a daily television program, in which he argued against Cuba's signing these treaties.[15]

A more substantive significance could develop later if, say, in a context of thawing relations with the United States Havana releases political prisoners or reforms the penal code to either eliminate the crime of dangerousness (*peligrosidad*)—a crime that covers whatever the government wants it to—or eases sanctions on those so charged.

In late February the Vatican's secretary of state, Tarcisio Cardinal Bertone, visited Havana. Building new churches, gaining regular access to the media, and establishing Catholic elementary schools are on the table. In early May Pope Benedict XVI himself called for the Church "to enjoy normal access to the social communications media" and for parents to exercise "their fundamental right to a religious and moral education for their children."[16] After the hurricanes, the Church and the government have engaged in a dialogue to find ways of cooperating in seeking humanitarian relief, though no agreement had been reached as of November 2008.

In early April 2008, the Cuban Writers and Artists Union (UNEAC) held its congress in Havana, whereby the media and the educational system came in for scathing criticism. When the education minister, a sixteen-year veteran, was sacked two weeks later, some attributed it to the UNEAC criticisms.[17]

Also in April 2008, the PCC's Central Committee met, and Raúl delivered the plenum's closing speech. Raúl declared an end to *la provisionalidad*, the government's provisional status, and announced the creation of a seven-person Politburo commission; in essence this puts an end to decades of de facto one-man rule. He also gave notice of a party congress in the second half of 2009, breaking a twelve-year hiatus.[18] In July Raúl delivered a speech to the National Assembly that differed markedly in substance and style from his older brother, particularly on the subject of egalitarianism and the need to reward workers on the basis of performance.[19]

U.S. Policy toward Cuba

Should U.S. policy toward Cuba change now that Raúl Castro is in charge? The cold war ended twenty years ago, yet Washington hasn't wandered far from a policy of confrontation. In the early 1990s, the Cuban Democracy Act, which tightened the U.S. embargo, made some sense. Without Soviet trade and subsidies, the embargo might have finally worked to significantly weaken Castro's regime. The Helms-Burton Act—enacted into law after Cuba's shootdown of two U.S. civilian aircraft in international waters over the Florida Straits, taking the lives of four people—tightened the embargo further. Yet the regime sailed on.

After Fidel's illness, some in the U.S. government, the exile community, and other quarters thought that the regime's days were numbered. Now the successors are planning to hold a Communist Party congress and have withstood the test of three natural disasters without major incidents. To be sure, U.S. policymakers, banking on the conviction that this time the end is really around the next bend—could leave the current policy in place. Which sounds an awful lot like what I heard the adults in my family say in the 1960s: "La próxima Nochebuena en La Habana"—"Next Christmas in Havana."

The Barack Obama administration needs a different road map, but to succeed it cannot start from scratch. Democratic governance and the robust rule of law in Cuba are goals the United States shares with the European Union and most of the nations of the Western Hemisphere. What has divided the United States from its allies is the means to get there: Washington has insisted on the embargo; the EU, Canada, and most of Latin America have opted for engagement. Neither policy has succeeded: Cuba is still a dictatorship. Not yet tried is for the United States and its allies to work together toward the shared goal. Hoping that U.S. allies will join forces with Washington on the embargo is delusional.

During the 1990s the United States succeeded in having Havana condemned at the old UN Commission on Human Rights in Geneva every year except 1998, when Pope John Paul II visited Cuba. That year Havana eased restrictions on the Catholic Church and released nearly two hundred political prisoners. Though the Clinton administration criticized the departure from what had become the norm, the commission wielded its vote to reward what most members perceived as moves in the right direction by Havana. In 1999 Cuba was again condemned. The National Assembly had enacted a law, Protection of National Sovereignty and the Economy, that imposed harsh sentences on citizens charged with giving what the government determined to be false information to foreign reporters.[20]

Until its dissolution in 2006, the UN Commission on Human Rights continued to denounce Cuba's record. Europe, Canada, and several Latin American countries almost always sided with the United States in criticizing Havana for violations of human rights. Little, however, was gained either in improving the situation on the island or establishing a human rights dialogue with the Cuban government. Still, the Geneva hearings brought to the world's attention Cuba's deplorable record, even if the resolutions mostly served political purposes. Washington blasted Havana on human rights, and Cuba denounced the U.S. embargo. It didn't help that the commission did not regularly condemn all governments that violated human rights.

Every year for the past two decades, the UN General Assembly has resoundingly approved a resolution calling upon the United States to end the embargo against Cuba. Year in and year out, almost all U.S. allies have voted for the resolution. The new U.S. administration faces the task of how best to engage the international community in support of a democratic transition in Cuba. As woeful as Havana's record is, the EU, Canada, and most Latin American countries do not consider the situation in Cuba so grave as to mount an international campaign against Raúl Castro's government. For the most part, Havana exercises low-intensity repression that cows ordinary Cubans into *la doble moral* while harassing peaceful opponents and sometimes condemning them to harsh prison sentences. Even though the EU imposed sanctions on Cuba for the Black Spring of 2003, when seventy-five citizens were rounded up for their peaceful activities, the European Union is now back to almost normal relations with Cuba, though only Spain and Belgium have economic cooperation agreements with Havana. Barring a Tiananmen Square–like massacre in Cuba, the kind of international outrage against the regime that the United States has long sought will simply not be forthcoming.

At the same time, Washington has an option that is not a sharp rupture from current policy: rescinding the travel and remittance restrictions that the Bush administration imposed in 2004. Until 2004, Cuban Americans could visit family in Cuba once a year and send them remittances, with family being defined broadly. Under the new guidelines, aunts, uncles, cousins, nieces, and nephews aren't considered family, so we cannot travel to see them nor send them remittances. Even travel to visit grandparents, parents, spouses, siblings, children, and grandchildren is allowed only once every three years. As far as I know, no special permissions have been granted in emergencies such as the imminent passing of a parent or sibling on the island. A bolder and preferable alternative would be lifting all restrictions on travel and remittances by Cuban Americans. That is, in fact, what candidate Obama said he would do in Miami on May 23, 2008: "I will immediately allow unlimited family travel and remittances to the island."[21] Keeping families apart—as Washington has done in the Cuban case—is unmistakably un-American. That Havana has exploited divided families for decades is no justification for the United States to do the same.

U.S. policy toward Cuba cannot change without some support in the Cuban American community. Clearly, Cuban Miami will more easily endorse the lifting of the 2004 restrictions or even what Obama proposed than a wholesale turn from current policy. In the 2007 Florida International University Cuba poll, conducted among Cuban Americans in South Florida since

1991, 55.2 percent of respondents agreed with the statement "The United States should allow unrestricted travel to Cuba." About 50 percent also agreed with ongoing U.S. sales of medicines and food to Cuba. Forty-two percent opposed the embargo outright, an increase of eight percentage points since the last survey in 2004.[22] Cuban American public opinion is clearly shifting toward easing travel restrictions, with a hefty minority then embracing the end of the embargo.

In 2008 the three Republican Cuban American members of Congress from South Florida—Lincoln Díaz-Balart, Mario Díaz-Balart, and Ileana Ros-Lehtinen—faced credible, well-funded Democratic challengers for the first time ever. The challengers—a former Hialeah mayor, Raúl Martínez (challenging Lincoln Díaz-Balart), a former executive director of the Cuban American National Foundation, Joe García (Mario Díaz-Balart); and a Colombian American businesswoman, Annette Taddeo (Ros-Lehtinen)—failed in their attempts to unseat the incumbents, Taddeo and Martínez losing by sixteen points and García by six. The meaning of these losses should be tempered by Obama's win in Florida: even though an estimated 65 percent of Cuban Americans in Miami-Dade County voted for John McCain, Obama won the county by a margin of 58–42, besting John Kerry's performance in 2004 by five points. An exit poll of voters in the 2008 general election showed movement in the Cuban American electorate, though not enough to move the three Republican districts into the Democratic camp. Some relevant statistics:

—Only 31 percent of those born in Cuba voted for the Democrats, whereas 61 percent of those born in the United States did.

—Sixty-five percent in the eighteen-to-twenty-nine age group preferred Obama.

—Cubans who arrived in the 1990s were split 49 percent for Obama and 51 percent for McCain, whereas those who arrived in the 2000s broke 58 percent for Obama.

—Post-1990 arrivals and U.S.-born Cuban Americans are trending toward the Democratic Party.

—Obama's 35 percent of the Cuban American vote is comparable to Bill Clinton's share in 1996, sixteen points better than Al Gore's in 2000, and ten points higher than Kerry's in 2004.[23]

Simply put, Cuban Miami is not what it used to be. A new 2008 Cuba/U.S. Transition Poll released on December 2, 2008, further highlights the community's evolving views: 67 percent favored unrestricted travel to Cuba and 55 percent opposed the U.S. embargo.[24] Democrats and those favoring eased sanctions against Havana have much to reap from the changing terrain in the Cuban American community.

The United States will not succeed in moving its allies toward a concerted approach absent a shift in U.S. Cuba policy. Even a small step such as rescinding the 2004 restrictions would earn the new U.S. administration international goodwill regarding Cuba. And if the U.S. government recognizes in 2009, however implicitly, that Cuba is on a different path under Raúl, opportunities may open up. For example, the new UN Human Rights Council (HRC) was set to evaluate Cuba in February 2009 as part of the new Universal Periodic Review mechanism, in which the human rights performance of all UN members, the United States included, are assessed. Countries under review are expected to cooperate with the HRC in the process of compiling the report, and Havana should not be an exception. Cuba never cooperated with the old commission. A less politicized process by the HRC and the ensuing report may carry greater credibility than the resolutions of the old Human Rights Commission. By the same token, a future HRC report on Cuba will at best bring only some respite on human rights violations. Not until civil liberties are guaranteed in the Cuban constitution will human rights be protected on the island. Still, the HRC provides a framework within which the international community can engage Havana on human rights issues. On a parallel front, Havana will continue drumming up the annual UN anti-embargo resolutions, though their resonance may diminish if U.S. policy changes somewhat.

The United States could give the green light (or at least look the other way) for the Organization of American States to test Havana's willingness to engage. Even though the Inter-American Democratic Charter, approved in Lima, Peru, in September 2001, reinforces the consensus in the Western Hemisphere on the primacy of democracy, a democratic government is not a prerequisite for the OAS to establish a dialogue with Cuba. Unraveling a fifty-year dictatorship will not happen overnight. If the Cuban economy truly opens up, the island would be moving toward protecting property rights and entrepreneurship, that is, an economic rule of law, which should be encouraged. Havana would then have greater incentives to engage with the world for economic reasons, not primarily for the political quests that always moved Fidel. The OAS could be instrumental in the gradual return of Cuba to the Western Hemisphere's community of nations as a relatively normal country, that is, one whose relations with the region are not primarily defined by the U.S. embargo or repression on the island.

The Ibero-American General Secretariat—headquartered in Madrid, with Enrique Iglesias of Uruguay, former president of the Inter-American Development Bank, at the helm—may offer an even better avenue to engage Cuba under Raúl. Its members are all the countries in Latin America plus Spain and Portugal, so Cuba is a member and the United States is not. Spain in particular can be a useful intermediary, and the United States needs to maintain regular lines of communication with Madrid regarding Cuba.

Even if U.S. policy remains unchanged, the European Union and most governments in the Western Hemisphere will increase their ties, or at least their communication, with Havana. The United States has two options in terms of its reaction: denunciation or encouragement.

Take relations between Brazil and Cuba. In January 2008 President Luiz Inácio "Lula" da Silva visited Havana. Though his meeting with el Comandante grabbed the headlines, Raúl and Lula spent four hours together and almost nothing has been leaked of their conversation. The two countries agreed to increase their economic cooperation, including the sugar and oil industries. Ethanol from sugar cane, which Fidel has decried, was not mentioned, but it didn't have to be: refined sugar is not where the profits are, and Brazil is the world's leading producer of cane-based ethanol. Cuba has offshore oil fields estimated at no less than five billion barrels, and Brazil's oil company, Petrobras, is among the foreign (private and state) companies cooperating with Havana.[25] Lula and Raúl may also have in common a certain antipathy to Hugo Chávez and Raúl may want to diversify Cuba's international partners to avoid overdependence on Venezuela. Thus, in May 2008 the Brazilian foreign minister, Celso Amorim, traveled to Cuba and expressed his government's desire that Brazil become Cuba's principal trading partner, and in November 2008 Lula again visited Havana. Shortly thereafter, the Rio Group, an organization of Latin American and Caribbean states, announced that Cuba was joining its ranks.[26]

Lessening Cuban dependence on Venezuela is in the national interests of Cuba, Brazil, and the United States. At the very least, the United States should continue to look the other way as Brazil engages Cuba—as did the U.S. administrations of the 1960s regarding Mexico's refusal to join all the other Latin American governments in breaking off relations with Havana. In the end, Mexico provided the United States with an important window into Cuba.

Since the end of the cold war, a democratic transition in Cuba—not always qualified by the adjective "peaceful"—has been front and center in U.S. policy. From 2001 to 2007 the United States Agency for International Development (USAID) and the National Endowment for Democracy (NED) spent

$70.5 million and $9.3 million, respectively, to promote democracy on the island.[27] In 2006 a U.S. Government Accountability Office report questioned the efficacy of the USAID programs, in no small measure because so much of the money stayed in Miami.[28] Better management and oversight are clearly in order, even if allocating funds to building Cuban democracy in the current state of U.S.-Cuba relations has not yielded results. There is no reason to think that renewing the program under different conditions—say, by funneling funds through European NGOs or foundations so that most goes to the opposition in Cuba—will fare any better.

It is useful to compare U.S. efforts to promote democracy in Cuba with those in China and Vietnam. In 2006 the NED awarded $5.6 million for projects directed at China and $300,000 for Vietnam. To be sure, neither Beijing nor Hanoi looks kindly on Washington's efforts, yet U.S. relations with China and Vietnam are on a normal track featuring diplomatic recognition, robust commerce, and innumerable people-to-people contacts. The Obama administration will have to decide whether, with Cuba, to stay a course that has not worked or to break new ground. By no means should Washington abandon the promotion of democracy, but his administration could take steps to liberalize travel and exchanges involving academics and even some Cuban officials. Academic exchanges could be resumed and expanded: in the 1990s Cuban professors, researchers, and students attended U.S. conferences and even U.S. universities, and U.S. counterparts did the same in Cuba. Even bolder would be to invite Cubans to participate in the Department of State's sponsored travel for foreigners to get to know the United States. Among the costs of current policy is that the United States has missed first-hand knowledge of a new generation of Cuban officials who will be players in Cuba, whether they are in a future government or in the opposition. Two tracks— one of supporting the opposition and the other of opening doors to official Cuba and those who are neither actively opposed nor fully supportive of the government—could be more fruitful for the future democratic Cuba than current policy.

No U.S. administration has ever come to terms with the extent to which its support for Cuban dissidents is a double-edged sword. The United States and Cuba have never had normal relations. Before 1959, the two countries had diplomatic relations but Washington often tended toward imperiousness. During the 1950s, the Eisenhower administration basically supported Batista's dictatorship. Fidel and the revolution tapped into the deep well of nationalist feelings in millions of Cubans, who responded to his powerful message of independence. Maintaining current policy while refusing to implicitly acknowledge the legitimate grievances that Cuban nationalists have against the United States has led nowhere. Most Cubans in the opposition reject the embargo and the heavy-handedness with which the U.S. Interests Section sometimes deals with them. On May 6, 2008, even Marta Beatriz Roque—the most pro-U.S., pro-embargo opposition figure—asked the Bush administration to ease restrictions on Cuban American travel and remittances.[29]

Even if normal U.S.-Cuba relations are not on the horizon, the United States would create a more challenging context for Havana if it eased the 2004 restrictions on travel and remittances or, better yet, ended them altogether. The Cuban government has always been more adroit at managing confrontation than engagement. Openness, in fact, may be the real hard line. Thirty years ago the Carter administration moved toward a rapprochement without forgoing U.S. commitment to human rights. A similar combination today is considerably more difficult: then, the United States did not seek regime change in Cuba, whereas now it does, but the Obama administration could consider making this goal implicit rather than continuing to loudly insist on it, which has wrought very little. Havana's incipient path away from Fidelismo could strengthen the economic rule of law and open other opportunities as yet unforeseen. A new policy that allows for some dialogue is in order if the United States is to take advantage of events already in process in Cuba.

In the end, democracy can only come to Cuba from within. Precisely because Cuba is at a critical crossroads, the Obama administration should look for common ground with its European and Western Hemisphere allies. To do so, it must enact modest changes in U.S. Cuba policy. An OAS that engages Cuba in some way and a European Union that completes the return to engagement would facilitate action and influence for all. By taking a new turn, Washington would also take some of the hot air out of Havana's imperialist-baiting balloon. In addition, engagement—ultimately impossible under Fidel—may well work with Raúl Castro's government. In the 1990s Cuba's shootdown of two U.S. civilian planes quickly dissipated the Clinton administration's efforts to either veto the Helms-Burton bill or pass a diluted version. After the incident, the harshest possible version of the Helms-Burton bill was signed into law by President Clinton.

On several occasions since the cold war, the United States tightened the embargo in the belief that the end of the Cuban regime was near. Instead, two decades after the cold war, another Castro presides over Cuba. Change may bring risks, but so does staying the course, a fact that the U.S. government has too often overlooked. A new U.S. policy toward Cuba is long overdue.

Notes

1. "President Bush Announces Initiative for a New Cuba," May 20, 2002 (www.state.gov/news/releases/2002/05/20020520-1.html).

2. Raúl Castro, "Trabajar con sentido crítico y creador, sin anquilosamiento ni esquematismos," *Granma*, July 27, 2007 (www.granma.cubaweb.cu).

3. Javier Mestre, "En torno a la encomiable tozudez del socialismo cubano," *Rebelión* (www.rebelion.org), August 27, 2007; Mauricio Vicent, "Cuba inicia el debate del cambio," *El País* (www.elpais.es), September 11, 2007; "Repiten consulta popular de los 90," *Reforma* (www.reforma.com), September 21, 2007; Rafael Alcídes, "Ideas sueltas en La Habana," *Encuentro en la red* (www.cubaencuentro.com), October 8, 2007; Pedro Campos, "Más socialización pidió el pueblo en el debate del discurso de Raúl," *Kaos en la red* (www.kaosenlared.net), October 16, 2007.

4. Patricia Grogg, "Challenges 2007–2008: Cuban Economy in Need of Nourishment," Inter Press Service (www.ipsnews.net), January 4, 2008; Wilfredo Cancio Isla, "Ventas de alimento de Estados Unidos a Cuba escalan a cifra récord," *El Nuevo Herald*, June 16, 2008 (www.elnuevoherald.com).

5. Gerardo Arreola, "Daños hasta por 10 mil mdd calculan que provocaron *Gustav* e *Ike* en Cuba," *La Jornada* (www.jornada.unam.mx), September 14, 2008; "Información oficial de datos preliminares sobre los daños ocasionados por los huracanes Gustav e Ike," *Granma*, September 16, 2008 (www.elnuevoherald.com).

6. "El gobierno comienza a vender insumos en pesos convertibles a los campesinos," *Encuentro en la red*, March 18, 2008; "Decreto-Ley No. 259 sobre la entrega de tierras ociosas en usufructo," *Granma*, July 18, 2008; "Se inicia proceso de entrega de tierras estatales ociosas en usufructo para incrementar la producción de alimentos," *Granma*, September 15, 2008.

7. "Nuevas regulaciones aduaneras," *Encuentro en la red*, May 11, 2007; "Nota informativa de la Empresa de Telecomunicaciones de Cuba," *Juventud Rebelde* (www.juventudrebelde.cu), April 12, 2008; Mauricio Vicent, "Cuba se acerca al vértigo del consumo," *El País*, April 13, 2008; Rigoberto Díaz, "Las computadoras regresan a las tiendas de La Habana," *Agence France-Presse* (www.afp.com), May 1, 2008; "Cuba descarta acceso a internet para particulares," *El Nuevo Herald*, May 13, 2008.

8. Pablo Bachelet and Frances Robles, "Cuba Lifts Ban on Locals Staying at Hotels," *Miami Herald*, March 31, 2008.

9. Will Weissert, "Raúl's Cuba Tweaks Housing, Wage Rules," Associated Press, April 12, 2008.

10. Marc Frank, "Cuba Removes Wage Limits in Latest Reforms," Reuters, April 10, 2008; Lourdes Pérez Navarro, "Nuevo sistema de pagos por resultados," *Granma*, June 11, 2008; "El sistema de 'pagos por resultados' deberá esperar hasta enero," *Encuentro en la red*, October 28, 2008 (www.miamiherald.com).

11. At a meeting in Havana's National Theater, employees in mixed Cuban-foreign enterprises loudly protested the announced taxes. Mauricio Vicent, "Los cubanos alzan la voz," *El País,* February 1, 2008. I haven't found subsequent references to these taxes.

12. "Decide el gobierno revolucionario el incremento de las pensiones de la Seguridad y la Asistencia Social," *Juventud Rebelde,* April 27, 2008; Alfredo Morales Cartaya, "Acerca de la necesidad de modificar la ley de seguridad social," *Granma,* July 13, 2008.

13. Raúl Castro, "Nuestra batalla de hoy es la misma iniciada el 26 de julio de 1953," *Granma,* July 27, 2008.

14. Marc Frank, "Cuba Breaks Up Sit-in, Arrests Women Dissidents," Reuters, April 21, 2008; Frances Robles, "Wave of Arrests Targets Cuban Activists," *Miami Herald,* July 18, 2008.

15. "La historia dirá quién tiene la razón," *Granma,* December 14, 2007.

16. "Address of His Holiness Benedict XVI to the Bishops of Cuba on Their 'Ad Limina' Visit," *Vatican News* (www.vatican.va), May 2, 2008.

17. "Raúl Castro acepta reclamos de intelectuales," *El Nuevo Herald,* April 5, 2008; "Cuba destituyó ministro de educación," Reuters, April 22, 2008.

18. Raúl Castro, "Si se ha trabajado fuerte en estos últimos meses, habrá que hacerlo mucho más en los que están por delante," *Granma,* April 29, 2008.

19. Fidel announced his "political will and testament" in a speech at the University of Havana on November 17, 2005, where he sounded the alarm on the revolution's possible reversal if revolutionaries abandoned their vigilance. "Discurso pronunciado por Fidel Castro Ruz, Presidente de la República de Cuba, en el acto por el aniversario 60 de su ingreso a la universidad, efectuado en el Aula Magna de la Universidad de La Habana, el 17 de noviembre de 2005" (www.cuba.cu/gobierno/discursos/2005/esp/f171105e.html); Raúl Castro, "Socialismo significa justicia social e igualdad, pero igualdad no es igualitarismo," *Granma,* July 13, 2008.

20. "Ley 88 de Protección de la Independencia Nacional y de la Economía de Cuba," *Trabajadores,* March 8, 1999, p. 4.

21. "Text of Obama Speech," *Miami Herald,* May 23, 2008. Obama spoke at a luncheon sponsored by the Cuban American National Foundation.

22. Institute for Public Opinion Research and Cuban Research Institute, Florida International University, 2007 FIU Cuba Poll (www.fiu.edu/~ipor/cuba8/).

23. Bendixen and Associates, "The Miami-Dade County Electorate: An Exit Poll Study of 2008 General Election Voters" (Miami: November 13, 2008).

24. Institute for Public Opinion Research, Brookings Institution, and Cuba Study Group, 2008 Cuba/U.S. Transition Poll (www.fiu.edu/~ipor/cuba-t/Cuba-T.pdf).

25. Jeff Franks, "Cuba Oil Claims Raise Eyebrow in Energy World," Reuters, October 24, 2008. Cuba announced that the offshore fields could contain 20 billion barrels, a figure oil experts considered "hard to believe but not out of the realm of possibility."

26. "Ingresa Cuba al Grupo Río," *Granma,* November 14, 2008.

27. "Cuba: Issues for the 110th Congress," report, Congressional Research Service (Washington: February 29, 2008) (www.fas.org/sgp/crs/row/RL33819.pdf).

28. U.S. Government Accountability Office, "Foreign Assistance: U.S. Democracy Assistance for Cuba Needs Better Management and Oversight," publication GAO-07-147 (Washington: November 15, 2006) (www.gao.gov/products/GAO-07-147).

29. Jennifer Loven, "Bush Criticizes New Cuban Leadership," Associated Press, May 8, 2008.

nine

Turning the Symbol Around: Returning Guantánamo Bay to Cuba

Bert Hoffmann

As one of his very first steps in office, President Obama signed an executive order to close the detention center at the U.S. naval base at Guantánamo Bay in Cuba within one year's time. Shutting the infamous facility is a crucial first step toward the restoration of the moral credibility of the United States: the use of the base as an extralegal detention center has made it a symbol of disrespect for the rule of law and the rights of detainees. But righting the wrongs represented by the U.S. presence at Guantánamo should not end there. The political symbolism of the U.S. naval base on Cuban soil predates its post-9/11 uses and is embedded in its very origin. By returning Guantánamo Bay to Cuba it can be transformed from a symbol of what has been wrong with U.S. foreign policy into a symbol of a new and positive policy outlook. Initiating the voluntary devolution of the naval base to Cuba could become a key step in a longer-term repositioning of U.S. standing in the region.

Since 1903, when the Cuban government felt obliged to lease the Guantánamo Bay naval base to the United States in order to gain formal independence, the base has been a symbol of overbearing U.S. power in the hemisphere. Returning it to Cuba would convert it into a symbol showing that the Obama presidency marks "a defining moment in history." The repercussions of such an initiative would be felt not only in U.S. relations with Cuba but throughout the Americas, and indeed throughout the world.

The U.S. military presence on Cuban soil is a direct result of the 1898 conflict that in Spanish and U.S. schoolbooks is called the Spanish-American War but that, from a Latin American perspective, was Cuba's aborted war of independence. As a result of that war, the island switched from Spanish colonial rule to U.S. dependence. At the beginning of the twentieth century, Cuban politicians were given to understand that incorporating the so-called Platt Amendment into the Cuban constitution was a precondition for the country to be granted formal independence after two and a half years of U.S. military occupation. The Platt Amendment, drafted in Washington and enshrined in the 1901 Cuban constitution, gave the United States the explicit right to intervene unilaterally on the island. In addition, paragraph VII of the amendment included the lease in perpetuity of a naval base to the United States. This was later enshrined in the Guantánamo Bay Lease Agreement, signed by Cuba and the United States in 1903.

As a result, for nationalists in Cuba and in much of Latin America, the Platt Amendment became emblematic of U.S. infringement on the sovereignty of the nations to its south. Therefore, when Franklin D. Roosevelt in 1933 proclaimed his Good Neighbor policy toward Latin America, his approach to Cuba came to highlight the new foreign policy spirit of his administration. FDR's policy signaled a shift in Washington from a reliance on hard power to the exercise of soft power, as previous U.S. interventionism had proved costly and counterproductive. The United States needed to extricate itself from political and military commitments and rebuild its relations with Latin America along more pan-American lines. To this end, the Roosevelt administration moved quickly to abrogate the infamous Platt Amendment in 1934. However, within the framework of the termination of the Platt Amendment, a new treaty was signed and ratified whereby the United States retained an indefinite lease on the Guantánamo Bay naval base, to be ended only by mutual agreement. Thus, "Gitmo," as the U.S. base is called in military jargon, is not the product of the cold war, nor of the Cuban revolution, but is rather a relic of the gunboat diplomacy of the late nineteenth and early twentieth century.

Seventy-five years after FDR's derogation of the Platt Amendment, Cuba once again presents an opportunity to become Washington's showcase for a new U.S. foreign policy in this hemisphere and beyond. Since 9/11 the United States has used the U.S. naval base at Guantánamo Bay, located at the southeastern tip of Cuba, as an extraterritorial detention and interrogation facility in the course of the war in Afghanistan and the "war on terror" against al Qaeda. Because the base lies beyond U.S. jurisdiction, it could be used to deliberately hold detainees in a legal limbo, where they are deprived of access to due process, which includes being charged for a crime, having access to legal representation, and being brought to trial in a court of law.

During the 2008 presidential campaign, Senators Barack Obama and John McCain both pledged to close the camp and transfer the detainees to regular facilities on U.S. territory under U.S. jurisdiction or to third parties. This step would be applauded internationally, but it would be seen as just a first step toward restoring the foreign policy credibility of the United States. It would put an end to what will be remembered as a lamentable episode, but it would not by itself signal a new foreign policy approach. If the Obama administration is to pursue a more audacious foreign policy, it must consider taking additional steps.

In his victory speech on election night, Barack Obama proclaimed a "new dawn of American leadership" based on the belief "that the true strength of our nation comes not from the might of our arms . . . but from the enduring power of our ideals." It is hard to see how the U.S. naval base in Cuba, given its historic origin, could play a positive role in a U.S. policy guided by such ideals unless the new administration were to take a bold initiative to return the naval base to Cuba, making Guantánamo Bay the foremost example of a new U.S. policy based on the "power of ideals" rather than the "might of arms."

Certainly the return of Guantánamo Bay would be a surprising move: debate on the status of the naval base is rarely heard in the United States, and although the detention camp has been a cause of international concern and has generated powerful demands to close this facility, there is no global pressure on the United States to return the territory to Cuba. Neither has a forceful legal case been presented in any international forum demanding U.S. withdrawal.[1] Politically, however, it is precisely the absence of external pressure that would make the return of Guantánamo Bay to Cuba such a powerful move for the U.S. administration.

The U.S. administration would, of course, have to consider military aspects. Since 2005 the U.S. Base Realignment and Closure Commission (BRAC) has scaled down or closed numerous overseas bases that have become costly and militarily obsolete. It is hard to see why Guantánamo Bay should be an exception: it is also costly and the base's use as a refugee and detention camp over the past few years certainly suggests a relative lack of relevance in purely military terms. While the U.S. military keeps using "Gitmo" as a logistics, storage, and refueling site as well as a naval training base, it should be possible to transfer these functions to other locations with little strategic loss. Moreover, there is an underlying understanding in military circles that "Gitmo" is not a U.S. facility unlimited in time, and that some day—usually thought of as after Cuban democratization—it will be returned to Cuba. Such a perception has effects already today, and will lead to rather low proclivity to undertake major long-term investments on the premises. However, the author of these lines is in no position to fully assess these aspects. Before putting the naval base issue on the international political agenda, the U.S. administration would be wise to set up a civilian-military commission to provide for a comprehensive assessment. With this important caveat in place, this proposal parts from the assumption that the presence of a U.S. naval base on Cuban soil in the twenty-first century is much less a military requirement than a political issue.

Returning the Guantánamo Bay base would have enormous political impact on Cuba. For the five decades since the Cuban revolution in 1959, the leadership in Havana has portrayed the United States as antagonistic toward Cuban national sovereignty. In the past, U.S. policy has time and again contributed to the plausibility of this claim. For instance, the Helms-Burton Act of 1996 (the Cuban Liberty and Democratic Solidarity [Libertad] Act), particularly its section II, contains echoes of the Platt Amendment that are unpalatable even to some Cubans and Cuban Americans most resolutely opposed to Castro, on and off the island.[2] In this way, U.S. policy has been most helpful for regime stability in Cuba, because defending the nation's independence remains one of the key elements of the regime's legitimacy. There would be no more effective way to challenge Cuban state propaganda regarding the annexationist ambitions of U.S. imperialists than if Washington were voluntarily to announce its intention to restore Cuban national sovereignty over Guantánamo Bay's approximately forty-five square miles.

There is a strong argument in some American circles against policy changes of any sort, namely, that current policies are working well. Within the most intransigent sector of the Cuban American community there are some who can be expected to argue that, after years of U.S. pressure, the Cuban regime is finally on the brink of collapse. Changing course now, goes this argument, would constitute a betrayal of all that has been done to bring about Castro's demise. But the empirical evidence for this view of conditions in Cuba is weak. Notwithstanding the formal end of Fidel Castro's prolonged tenure in February 2008, and despite severe economic problems, recently aggravated by the destruction wrought by Hurricanes Ike, Gustav, and Paloma, there is little indication that regime collapse is likely to occur anytime soon. Moreover, an uncontrolled and potentially violent regime change on the island—while unlikely at present—could put at risk U.S. interests in the Caribbean region and trigger a major migration crisis.

The U.S. presidential elections showed that the Cuban American community is far less homogeneous than often assumed. Instead, a differentiated debate about constructive policies, such as fostering people-to-people contacts as advocated by Barack Obama, has taken hold. The proposal to return Guantánamo Bay to Cuba would move that debate one step further. It is fair to assume (though survey data are lacking) that there is broad agreement among Cubans and Cuban Americans of whatever political orientation that Cuban sovereignty should extend over the whole territory of the island. Objections to the devolution of Guantánamo Bay would most likely turn on timing and process rather than on the validity of the proposal itself, and some would argue that it should not be done as long as a Communist Party–run government remains in power. But there is little to suggest that the devolution of Guantánamo Bay would increase the scope for the present regime in Havana to extend or consolidate its hold on power. Indeed, the opposite could be true. The return of the base, rather than "rewarding" the Castro government, would actually challenge its nationalist legitimacy and free Washington from a historical legacy that has become burdensome, obsolete, and politically counterproductive.

Consider, too, that no military base can be closed overnight. Returning Guantánamo Bay cannot be achieved by a stroke of a pen, as it would entail the normal process of revision by the U.S. Base Realignment and Closure Commission. In addition, the 1934 treaty states that the lease can be terminated by mutual agreement only, making moot the possibility of unilateral U.S. action. What the new U.S. administration can do immediately is state its intent to restore sovereignty to Cuba when a mutually acceptable agreement is reached and invite the Cuban government to negotiate the terms of that restoration. The political impact would be immediate, even though actual devolution inevitably would be a gradual and probably prolonged process. Although the process likely would not take as long as the return of the Canal Zone to Panama (it was negotiated in 1977 and completed only in 2000), it is by no means certain that the leaders who initiate the process will still be in power to oversee its completion—and this applies to Havana as much as to Washington.

The U.S. stance on human rights in Cuba would not be forfeited if the new U.S. administration were to invite the Cuban government to negotiate a timetable and modalities of devolution. Rather, such talks would open an entirely new field in relations with Havana. Such a shift would be all the more advantageous in light of the fact that President Obama might find only limited room for maneuver on the embargo, which has been a centerpiece of U.S.-Cuba policy for decades.

President Obama is likely to lift restrictions on remittances and family visits as he advocated during his campaign. He may also take steps to ensure that other measures become more flexible in order to promote, rather than prevent, people-to-people contacts of emigrants with the island, and between scholars, artists, and others. However, the embargo has been codified by the wording of the Helms-Burton Act, which means that putting an end to that policy cannot be done by executive decision but will require complex negotiations in Congress. Moreover, Obama endorsed the embargo during his campaign. So, although more exceptions to the embargo and prohibition on traveling to Cuba may be in store—along the lines of those Congress granted in 2000, by means of the Trade Sanctions Reform and Export Enhancement Act, to agricultural exports from the United States to Cuba—a sweeping turnaround on the embargo seems unlikely unless there were substantive political change in Cuba.

A new initiative in U.S.-Cuba relations is also necessary because the embargo, as codified by the Helms-Burton Act, keeps U.S. policy deadlocked on nothing less than full-fledged regime change in Havana as its foreign policy goal. However, it is unlikely that the present sanctions policy will be able to bring this about. Not only did it fail to produce the desired results in the past, but international experience also shows that economic sanctions of the type applied by the United States to Cuba rarely constitute a life-or-death threat to a regime and that they are therefore unlikely to force regimes to make concessions the latter view as terminal. Take the case of South Africa, the most often cited showcase for effective sanctions: if President Frederik de Klerk and his colleagues in the apartheid regime had believed that they would be put on trial for human rights violations after power slipped from their hands, no amount of economic sanctions would have made acceptable negotiated elections culminating in an African National Congress victory.

Notably, Cuban state propaganda and U.S. government representatives agree that the resignation of Fidel Castro as Cuba's supreme leader did not represent any meaningful political change on the island. But this assessment seems inadequate to the actual post-Fidel situation: To be sure, the brotherly succession was not legitimated by a pluralist election, Raúl Castro continues to rule out democratization in a Western sense, and reform policies have thus far failed to meet the expectations raised by Raúl Castro's initial announcement of "structural changes" and by his call for a societal debate "free of fear of any type." Nevertheless, Cuba has entered the post-Fidel era, and this means a sea change in political expectations in Cuba. The shift from Fidel's highly personalist leadership to a far more bureaucratic brand of "socialism" is bound to reshape the perspectives of all actors on the island. Although it is impossible to assess such recalibrations in detail, it seems safe to say that the situation has become much more uncertain and thus potentially more open-ended than it was under Fidel's almost fifty-year tenure. Working against this possibility for new openings, however, the United States' current all-or-nothing stance tends to cripple whatever ideas for reform might otherwise evolve within the Cuban establishment or outside of it.

The United States readily accepts that working to advance policy goals below the threshold of regime change in other countries that are not governed by Western democratic standards is not synonymous with reneging on the commitment to universal democratic values. This is also the view underpinning policies pursued by Canada, the European Union, and many Latin American countries with respect to Cuba. While U.S. rhetoric regarding Cuba has long catered to those who denounce such policies as "collaboration with the dictatorship," in practice Washington has long taken the same approach to Cuba when it comes to specific policy areas such as migration control or drug interdiction.

The devolution proposal could extend this logic to the broader foreign policy and security arena. The Raúl Castro government probably has most clearly departed from Fidel Castro's policy course with regard to Cuba's international profile. The new Cuban leader has worked consciously to pull Cuba back from its overcommitment in world politics by scaling down the provocative rhetoric and the emphatic international projection that was the hallmark of Fidel Castro's foreign policy. Raúl portrays himself as the country's top administrative authority, and has allowed Hugo Chávez to take on Fidel's mantle as Latin America's anti-imperialist leader. Whereas the alliance with Chávez and Venezuela was enthusiastically ramped up under Fidel, Raúl is much more pragmatic and has made major efforts to diversify Cuba's international partners to prevent excessive dependency.

If the devolution of Guantánamo Bay is to be successful, negotiations should focus only on the fate of the naval base itself and not be weighed down by political conditions. Any linkage with broader political demands would only invite Havana's hard-liners to denounce it as just another trick of U.S. imperialists. Nor would conditionality serve U.S. interests: it would undercut the clarity of the message of voluntarily returning Guantánamo Bay as a historical legacy the new U.S. administration wishes to overcome.

It should be noted, too, that under Raúl Castro's leadership Cuba has displayed an ability to engage in some skillful indirect diplomacy, the aim of which has been to ensure that regime moves are not interpreted as "concessions" to external pressure. When the new government signed two major UN human rights treaties shortly after taking power in February 2008—a move Fidel had long rejected—this was presented as an autonomous gesture rather than as a fulfillment of an externally set precondition, but the move did help to pave the way for the EU-Cuba cooperation agreement of October 2008. Similarly, while Cuba's Latin American neighbors never formulated such a demand, the announcement by the Cuban foreign minister during a visit to Moscow that no Russian missiles would be stationed on the island certainly was much appreciated and taken into account when Cuba was admitted to the Rio Group in November 2008. With this indirect diplomacy there are no concrete assurances as to outcomes, but it is likely to be the most effective type of diplomacy when more formalized quid pro quo arrangements are politically unviable.

If the issue of Guantánamo Bay is essentially about political symbols, the question inevitably arises as to the fate of the base after devolution. For obvious reasons, the call to turn the base into a demilitarized zone should meet with broad support. Abraham Lowenthal has suggested that it could become the site for a joint U.S.-Cuban project, for instance a research center on tropical diseases, the environment, or on educational technology.[3] Alternatively the site, with its airstrip, port, housing, and storage facilities would be ideally suited to house a Caribbean center for hurricane and disaster relief operations, an area in which Cuba has shown particular strengths and which would require cooperation not only of Cuba and the United States, but of all the states of the region. Working toward a project of this type would enhance the public appeal of the devolution proposal, as it would provide tangible positive results for the entire region. If, in the case of Hong Kong, China's communists had no problem in accepting a broad political autonomy status for the former British colony, the Cuban government certainly should be able to see Cuban sovereignty as fully compatible with the development of a commonly agreed upon joint project at the Guantánamo Bay site.

President Barack Obama has turned the enormous energy, public attention, and economic resources devoted to this long electoral campaign into an investment in soft-power capital. This is the foundation of his quest to relegitimate U.S. international leadership. Even though the president's soft-power appeal has gained much global backing in the wake of his historic election, the idea of soft power must be converted into concrete political initiatives in the months and years ahead. The campaign slogan of change will, in Cuba policy as in other fields, almost inevitably translate into incremental measures rather than sweeping turnarounds. And this is precisely why symbolic gestures are so crucial: they signal that small and gradual changes are part of a pattern of broader historic change.

Notes

1. It is not the purpose of this chapter to join the legal debate concerning the status of Guantánamo Bay and the validity of the 1903 and 1934 treaties, as these have been discussed elsewhere from different perspectives, by writers possessing extensive legal expertise. While the Cuban government questions the validity of the 1903 and 1934 treaties and has not cashed in the rent checks sent by the United States since 1960, it did cash in one check in the first year after Revolution—an act that, according to the U.S. government, constituted an official validation of the lease treaty.

2. One Bay of Pigs veteran, Alfredo Durán, in his testimony to the U.S. Senate on June 14, 1995, stated: "Under Helms-Burton, Cuba would pass from the dictatorship of Fidel Castro to the tutelage of the U.S. Congress. The specifications in the proposed Act . . . establish parameters for democracy in Cuba that are unequivocally the prerogative of the Cuban people" (see Alfredo Durán, "Testimony to the U.S. Senate," *Cuban Affairs/Asuntos Cubanos* 2, no. 1–2, 1995).

3. See Abraham Lowenthal, "A New U.S. Approach to Cuba," Pacific Council on International Policy, July 23, 2008 (www.pacificcouncil.org /pdfs/Lowenthal_oped_072308.pdf).

ten

Engaging Venezuela: 2009 and Beyond

Jennifer McCoy

Since his election in 1998, President Hugo Chávez of Venezuela has taken on the mantle of creating a new model of independent politics and economics, and of challenging U.S. dominance in the region and the world. Utilizing a strategy of intense confrontation with adversaries at home and abroad, combined with new foreign alliances globally and integrationist schemes regionally, the Chávez administration seeks to redistribute power and resources both domestically and internationally. In so doing, it has vexed the United States, exasperated neighboring Colombia, befuddled Latin American and European governments, and attracted support from those who feel exploited, marginalized, or impotent in the face of capitalist markets or U.S. unilateralism.

U.S. foreign policy interests make imperative an attempt to find a modus vivendi with Venezuela in order to cooperate on issues of mutual interest and coexist on issues of disagreement. As a major energy producer and a competitor in the marketplace of ideas, Venezuela should command respectful attention from Washington. The mutual dependence on the oil trade—the United States buys about 55 percent of Venezuelan oil exports and Venezuela provides between 11 and 14 percent of U.S. imported oil—keeps the antagonism within bounds and has not been interrupted even when diplomatic relations have fractured. Narcotics transshipments, Chávez's support of Cuba, and growing ties with Russia, China, and Iran are also issues of concern expressed in Washington. Venezuela's early strategy of revitalizing OPEC and emphasizing production cuts and higher prices over increased market share provided abundant revenues to fuel Venezuela's traditional petrodiplomacy in recent years. Simultaneously, the lack of U.S. attention to Latin America since 2001 has provided a vacuum into which Chávez has enthusiastically stepped to offer ideas that are alternatives to the liberal democratic market model embraced by the United States. Nevertheless, the late 2008 downturn in oil prices may diminish the sustainability of the current strategy of petrodiplomacy. And the extreme concentration of power that is accompanying Venezuela's model of participatory democracy risks a return of deep polarization, destabilization, and violence that could spill over to Venezuela's neighbors and trade partners.

Chávez's Venezuela

With the election of Hugo Chávez in 1998, Venezuela was the first of several governments—followed by Bolivia, Ecuador, and Paraguay—elected to bring about fundamental change through constitutional "re-founding" and the inclusion of previously excluded groups in the distribution of power and resources.[1] Simultaneously, another group of countries—including Chile, Brazil, and Uruguay—elected center-left governments to address through more gradual reforms the frustrated expectations arising from the transitions to democracy and open markets in the 1980s and 1990s.

Venezuela's own political dynamics must be evaluated in the context of the demand for radical change expressed by the voters in the 1998 election. A near tripling of poverty rates from the 1970s to the 1990s produced a serious social dislocation, and a rejection of the traditional political elites led to the collapse of what had been considered one of the strongest political party systems in the region. Venezuela's political regime today remains in a transitory state, as one political system was dismantled and another is still being created. The constitutional "re-founding," or rewriting, promised by Hugo Chávez in his 1998 campaign initiated a process of elite displacement, redistribution of economic and political resources, concentration of power, and experimentation with new forms of participatory democracy. It included a new constitution written by a popularly elected constituent assembly and approved by Venezuelan voters in 1999. The process has been conflictive, including mass protests with occasional violence, an attempted coup in 2002, a two-month petroleum strike in late 2002 and early 2003, and a presidential recall referendum in 2004. Although President Chávez survived each attempt to remove him from power and subsequently consolidated his power, the country has not yet achieved a new social contract including all sectors of the society, and the society remains polarized.

The 1999 constitution did not radically change the constitutional foundations of the state; it essentially followed the statist approach of the 1961 constitution, protecting private property while giving the state responsibility for social welfare, but also rolling back some of the liberalizing reforms in the labor market and in pensions. The constitution deepened human rights and citizen participation mechanisms, but also strengthened an already centralized, presidentialist system, weakening the 1989 reforms aimed at decentralization.[2]

The process referred to as the Bolivarian Revolution actually retains many of the basic traits of Punto Fijo politics (1959–98): dependence on oil revenues; highly centralized decisionmaking structures, with a new set of privileged actors displacing the traditional elites; reliance on the distribution of oil rents; and failure to strengthen the regulative and administrative capacities of the state (though there is increased tax collection capability).[3] The changes lie in the centralization of decisionmaking in one person (Chávez) rather than two hierarchical political parties; emphasis on class divisions rather than cross-class alliances; emphasis on confrontation and elimination of opponents to achieve change rather than consensus seeking to achieve stability; dismantling of traditional representative institutions and erosion of the separation of powers in favor of new forms of participatory democracy and accountability; change in petroleum policy from one of increasing market share to one of controlling production in order to raise prices; and a shift from market capitalism to "twenty-first-century socialism."

In broad terms, the Bolivarian Revolution is an attempt to reformulate the political economy to be more inclusive of those who perceived themselves to be excluded in the latter half of the Punto Fijo period (which included large numbers of the urban poor, middle-class civil society organizations, intellectuals, and junior ranks of the military). It is full of contradictions: nationalistic and integrationist, top-down and bottom-up change, centralized and participatory. It seeks to move beyond representative, liberal democracy to achieve a new form of participatory democracy, which in its utopian form allows for empowered citizens to hold the state accountable without intermediary institutions, through recall of elected officials, legislative referenda, and citizen participation in local decisionmaking. Inspired by the South American liberator Simón Bolívar, it incorporates both a Latin American integrationist dream and a centralization of domestic power. Foreign policy is fundamental to Chávez's vision; his goal is to counterbalance U.S. global and regional hegemony with a more multipolar world. Like domestic policy, Venezuela's foreign policy is confrontational and conflictive.

Chávez's reelection with 63 percent of the vote in 2006 encouraged him to propose even more radical change in a second constitutional proposal in 2007, which was ultimately rejected by the voters in a close vote. Institutionally, the failed 2007 constitutional reforms would have deepened the executive control of the political system, concentrating power to an extraordinary degree. The reforms would have created a system of direct executive-community relationships and new regional vice presidencies parallel to, and thus having the effect of weakening, popularly elected regional and local officials. They would have given the executive further control over the Central Bank, weakened due process under states of emergency, and allowed a president to serve unlimited consecutive terms (the current maximum is two six-year terms).

After that first electoral defeat, the president reached out to dissidents within his own movement; reshuffled his cabinet to attempt to address severe problems in government services, crime, and inflation; and restored relations with neighboring Colombia while calling on the FARC (Fuerzas Armadas Revolucionarias de Colombia) to end kidnapping and unilaterally release hostages. He campaigned heavily for his party's candidates for the November 2008 mayoral and gubernatorial elections, charging the people to vote for "the revolution" and casting the elections as a plebiscite on his rule. With a 60 percent presidential approval rate, such a strategy was reasonable. Opposition parties, on the other hand, united in order to field single candidates in many of the races, and focused their campaign on the problems of governance rather than the person of Hugo Chávez. This shift in strategy won them the mayorship of the metropolitan area of Caracas, plus five of the twenty-two governorships—in five populous states that represent 45 percent of the population, including the oil-rich state of Zulia and the state encompassing the capital city.

Although the electoral results revived political pluralism in Venezuela for the first time in five years, they are unlikely to mean that the government or the president will abandon the goals of "twenty-first-century socialism." Indeed, early reactions to the vote indicated that the government intended to intensify confrontation with the newly elected opposition officials, rather than seek mechanisms to work with them. President Chávez almost immediately announced his intention once again to present to the people his proposal for continuous presidential reelection in a referendum as early as February 2009. Venezuela thus has yet to agree on a national vision, with the government continuing to espouse radical change with little compromise and the opposition struggling to articulate a coherent alternative vision that will resonate with a majority of the population.

The State of Democracy in the Bolivarian Revolution

Formally, Venezuela is a constitutional democracy whose citizens have the right to change their government peacefully through regular elections based on universal suffrage. Democratic legitimacy in Venezuela is based on electoral legitimacy and popular participatory mechanisms. The concern with the current state of democracy in Venezuela is the erosion of separation of powers and weakened mechanisms of horizontal accountability (checks and balances), and the dominance of the governing party in representative institutions.

The Chávez administration has accepted elections as a mechanism for citizen participation and choice, and the electoral process will continue to provide the best opportunity to achieve pluralistic representation at local, regional, and national levels. A dozen elections and referenda were conducted in the first ten years of the Chávez administration, 1998 to 2008. The president himself consistently won between 56 percent and 63 percent of the popular vote in every election in which he participated. Nevertheless, early on in the Chávez administration, the electoral authorities became politicized, public confidence eroded, and the opposition moved to a strategy of abstentionism and boycotts in late 2004 and 2005. Subsequent efforts by the electoral authorities to gain opposition participation in new, extensive audit procedures increased public confidence in the electoral process, which includes one of the most advanced automated voting systems in the world, and all candidates accepted the results of elections in 2006, 2007, and 2008.

The implosion of the traditional parties after 1998, and the discouragement of opposition voters to participate in electoral processes in 2004 and 2005 in response to opposition leaders' allegations of fraud led to the dominance of all elected positions by the government coalition and resulted in its ability to control other major institutions. By 2006 the opposition was maturing and for the first time the presidential contender immediately acknowledged his electoral defeat, instead of alleging fraud. For the 2008 regional elections, opposition parties united in many of the races and shifted their campaign message to focus on policy issues and government performance deficits, rather than the earlier focus simply on removing the president.

The perceptions of social inclusion, political representation, and personal empowerment and hope provided by Hugo Chávez to the impoverished majority of citizens are a powerful factor often ignored in external evaluations of Venezuelan democracy. Direct democracy mechanisms and experimental community-based political organization provide opportunities for citizen participation and empowerment, but have mixed reviews to date. The 1999 constitution was written in a sociopolitical context in which political parties were completely discredited and social inclusion was a priority. The constitution thus does not contain the term "political party" and instead promotes citizen initiative through recall and legislative referenda; civil society participation in the nomination of important positions, including all positions embodying the mechanisms of accountability (electoral council, comptroller, attorney general, ombudsman); and the nomination of candidates for elected office by individuals and associations, as opposed to parties.

One of the hallmarks of the Bolivarian Revolution has been the experimentation with various forms of citizen organization and community-based political organization, from the early Bolivarian Circles to the Election Battle Units to local Water Committees to the more recent Community Councils (now estimated to number about 30,000). The president himself has proposed many of the organizational forms for community-based political movements, and some of these have been linked to more autonomous, organic movements (many with historical roots) within the barrios (poor urban neighborhoods). Although more systematic evaluation is needed, preliminary studies of the effectiveness of these experiments in terms of bringing citizen empowerment, technical expertise, autonomy, and sustainability, and their ability to hold the government accountable, show mixed results. Grassroots social movements within the barrios have attained a certain autonomy, even while remaining dependent on state resources to function. Citizens, especially in poor neighborhoods, do appear to feel empowered by such mechanisms, and in many instances have effectively used the community councils to bring state resources for needed neighborhood projects. Challenges by local groups to the government party's imposition of electoral candidates and criticism of the government's failure to meet community needs lends credence to the optimistic view about the empowerment of local citizens.

On the other hand, the fact that the organizational ideas have often come directly from the president, and that the organizations themselves often depend on state resources controlled at the executive level, have led to questions about the ability of these organizations to be truly autonomous of the state, to be able to hold the government accountable, and to avoid clientelist practices of resources being awarded on the basis of political loyalty and partisanship. In addition, delays in receiving the funds and mixed reports about oversight of the funds give some indication of inefficiency and corruption.

The recomposition of the political party system, after the collapse of the Punto Fijo party system in the 1990s, is another challenge for Venezuelan democracy. The ability of the small, new opposition parties to challenge the hegemonic position of the governing party, the United Socialist Party of Venezuela (PSUV), in the 2008 regional elections, as well as dissidence within the governing party, indicate the potential for a growing pluralism in Venezuela.

Chávez's electoral vehicle started as a clandestine movement within the military, then morphed into a political-electoral movement, then into a political party within a coalition. Finally, in 2007, the government launched the PSUV in an attempt to create a unified government party. Chávez was initially distrustful of political parties and bureaucracies, and after his election in 1998 he empowered the military to handle public revenues at the regional level, carry out development activities, and play an active role in his cabinet and in elected positions. The need for a party in order to participate in elections led to the creation, in 1998, of the Movement of the Fifth Republic (Movimiento V [Quinta] República, or MVR),[4] but political ambitions of its members as well as coalition members distressed the president and he moved in 2007 to create a single socialist party more under his control. That attempt failed when several coalition parties refused to join and one openly opposed his constitutional reforms. After a year's delay, the March 2008 election of the national directorship of the PSUV surprised many, as delegates rejected the military men who had been part of Chávez's inner circle and elected traditional leftist politicians and media personalities.

The opposition is now led by three principal parties: Primero Justicia, a relatively new party most of whose members are young professionals; Un Nuevo Tiempo (A New Time), with its base of support in Zulia state and led by Manuel Rosales, Zulia's former governor and a 2006 presidential candidate; and the Movement for Socialism (Movimiento al Socialismo, or MAS), one of the few remaining parties from the Punto Fijo years. The two dominant parties of the Punto Fijo period, Acción Democrática and Copei, have virtually disappeared. In addition, Podemos (meaning "we can"), a division of the MAS that joined the president's coalition early in the Bolivarian Revolution, carved out a new role for itself as a potential center party between the government and the opposition, when it refused to join the PSUV and opposed the constitutional reforms in 2007. Despite the number of parties, party identification remains low: only 17 percent of citizens identify with the opposition parties, 30 percent identify with the government's party, and almost half of the population call themselves independents.[5]

The State of Rule of Law

Traditional mechanisms of horizontal accountability under liberal democracy—the separation of powers and independent organs of control such as comptroller general and ombudsman—are largely absent in Venezuela today. Because of the electoral weakness of the opposition and its decision to boycott the 2005 National Assembly elections, the government coalition controlled 100 percent of the legislative seats and the vast majority of the elected gubernatorial and mayoral posts in 2008. The National Assembly appoints officials of three other branches: the Supreme Court, the National Electoral Council, and the Citizen's Power (Poder Ciudadano); the Poder Ciudadano comprises the ombudsman, the attorney general, and the comptroller general. All of these institutions are perceived to be partisan and to favor the government and ruling party. The ability of democratic institutions to protect individual civil and human rights and provide equality before the law has thus been thrown into question.

The government generally respects most civil liberties, though there are some concerns about infringements on the rights of assembly, political dissent, and free speech. One recent concern was the attempt by the government to introduce legislation requiring the registration of NGOs and the regulation of their foreign funding. A similar provision was included in the defeated constitutional reforms of 2007.

The issue of perhaps greatest debate is the degree of freedom of speech and independence of the media from government control. Venezuelan media have long been politicized, but with the polarization and conflict that began to take hold in 2002, both private and public media, especially television, took on overt political roles. Two opposing realities were presented in the media, and the opposition and the president engaged in public discourse and mutual accusations through the airwaves. After the 2004 recall referendum, several changes occurred: the government opened several new television stations and sponsored hundreds of community radio programs, changing the balance between opposition- and government-controlled media from overwhelmingly oppositionist to a majority of official broadcast media. The National Assembly passed the Social Media Responsibility Law to regulate violence and pornography during prime-time television; and some media decided to make peace with the government and take on a less political role.

There is still vigorous criticism of the government and the president in the privately owned media, and there is no formal censorship. Nonetheless, legal, economic, and regulatory mechanisms create a climate of self-censorship.

The state-owned media are strongly politicized and pro-government, while the private media continue to be antigovernment. Owners of private media complain that they are denied equal and full access to government facilities and official events. Perhaps even more worrisome, reforms to the criminal code in March 2005 increased the penalties for libel and defamation of public officials from a maximum of thirty months to four years in prison, directly counter to the direction of most of the rest of the region and the rulings of the Inter-American Court of Human Rights. Nevertheless, two international watchdog groups, Committee to Protect Journalists and Reporters Without Frontiers, report that from 2002 to 2006 only two Venezuelan journalists were reported killed while working, and none were imprisoned or reported missing, a considerably better record than those of two of Venezuela's neighbors, Colombia and Brazil.

The government also places restrictions on the media through its administration of broadcasting licenses; renewals appear at times to be motivated by political concerns. In May 2007 the government declined to renew the broadcasting license of the country's oldest commercial network and most vocal critic, Radio Caracas Television, for allegedly supporting the 2002 coup and violating broadcast norms. In addition, under the Law of Social Responsibility in Radio and Television, media outlets that fail to comply with regulations can be heavily fined and risk having their broadcast licenses suspended.

The 1999 constitution provides strong protections for human rights, but major challenges continue to plague Venezuela: low personal security, poor prison conditions, and police abuse. Overcrowded and dangerous jails, pretrial detentions, and high crime rates have long been a problem in Venezuela, and the national homicide rate as reported in government statistics has more than doubled during the Chávez administration, from twenty to forty-five per 100,000 inhabitants—one of the highest in the world. The homicide rate in Caracas is a staggering 130 per 100,000 inhabitants.[6] Personal insecurity is now the number one problem in the country, according to opinion polls. Police forces receive the lowest confidence levels from the public of any other public institution, no doubt reflecting the high crime rate, the heavy-handed approach of the police, and the lack of investigation of and convictions for police abuse. There has been some progress, though. In 2006, the president named a national commission on which human rights organizations were represented to make recommendations for police reform, and the April 2008 Organic Law on the Police Service adopted many of the recommendations regarding reporting on and improving police behavior to bring them into line with human rights norms.

With regard to access to justice, complaints are often heard about delayed justice, impunity for violent acts, a politicized judiciary, and inconsistent application of the law. Some positive reforms are being initiated. One ongoing problem is the high rate of provisionally appointed judges, which affects judges' independence. In addition, the threat of trial, or continually postponed trials, is used to intimidate government opponents or restrict their international travel.

Corruption—a problem that is notoriously difficult to measure—is related to access to justice. It has long been recognized in Venezuela that corruption increases directly with petroleum booms, and the Chávez government is no exception. Lack of independent oversight and audit mechanisms hamper the control of corruption. A further circumstance creating opportunities for corruption is the dual exchange rate system, whereby access to U.S. dollars is restricted at the official rate, and an unofficial black market sells dollars at almost double the price of the official rate. (This system is reminiscent of the Recadi multiple exchange rate system of the 1980s, which generated large-scale corruption and abuses.)

State of Governance

Weak state capacity, long-deteriorating public services, political instability, and a continuous mode of campaigning during the dozen elections in ten years plague the government's ability to respond to the needs of the populace through effective governance. Venezuela's public services have been deteriorating since the 1970s, a prime cause of much of the dissatisfaction with the prior Punto Fijo regime and increasingly with the current regime. Both regimes have relied on external petroleum rents to finance a distributive policy and have failed to develop effective regulatory policies. Venezuela's oil booms have historically fueled a paternalistic state as well as a foreign policy characterized by petrodiplomacy; the criticism of Chávez's programs as unsustainable populist giveaways have been directed to past governments as well. So far, however, no serious international attempt to assess and measure the effectiveness of the extensive social programs called *misiones*, missions, has been conducted, in contrast to the studied (and lauded) conditional cash transfer programs in Brazil and Mexico.[7] The Chávez administration has been effective in increasing tax collection capacity, and impressive economic growth rates stem not only from the oil economy but, importantly, from the non-oil economy, too.

The government gained greater political control over the petroleum industry in 2003 after a strike by managers and workers in the oil industry who opposed the government, from December 2002 to February 2003, and it has since used the rise in oil prices to fund many of the newly created *misiones*. The impact of this spending is hotly debated among scholars and policy agencies. There is a general consensus that rates of poverty and unemployment have decreased, and access to drinking water and school enrollments has improved. On the other hand, the impact of the adult literacy mission and a program whereby Cuban doctors are available in the neighborhoods is difficult to measure and is a subject of debate. Housing shortages continue to be a major problem. Conclusions one can draw concerning the impact of the social programs on income inequality depend on which statistical source one uses. The rise in social spending has also contributed to inflation rates of 25 to 30 percent annually. A truly adequate evaluation of the impact of Venezuela's social programs requires transparent data with consistent measures, which so far are lacking.

In addition to personal insecurity and unemployment, a new pressing problem emerged in public opinion polls in 2007 and 2008: food shortages. A combination of foreign exchange controls, price controls, rising consumer demand, and lack of producer confidence resulted in serious shortages of milk, oil, sugar, eggs, and meat. With worldwide demand and food prices rising, Venezuela's traditional reliance on imported food became a real vulnerability for the government.

Despite the issues discussed here, perhaps surprisingly, satisfaction with democracy in Venezuela has risen consistently since 2002 and at 59 percent was the second highest in Latin America in 2007; the regional average was 37 percent.[8] In addition, Venezuelans also gave a higher ranking of the "democratic-ness" of their country, which was defined primarily in terms of liberty, than did the citizens of any other country in the region.[9] These numbers reveal that Venezuelans have a generally more positive perception of their democratic system than do citizens of the rest of the region.

Vulnerabilities abound, however. Chávez's drive to deepen the revolution through an accelerated process of change after his 2006 election victory put tremendous pressure on the public bureaucracy, which lacked the capacity to implement his directives to improve government services and expand the *misiones*. His personalization of power means that he is increasingly being held responsible for problems of governance. Chávez himself interpreted his defeat in the 2007 constitutional referendum as an expression of discontent with government performance, and he started 2008 with a commitment to focus on policy implementation and improved governance.

Nevertheless, the potential for any renegotiated social contract based on compromise, pluralism, and coexistence faces an important obstacle: the competing visions for how to accomplish change in Venezuela. The willingness of so many citizens to accept some authoritarian traits in exchange for the empowerment they feel from the president's recognition of them and his giving them visibility, as well as the material benefits they are receiving, illustrates the deep desire for political change over the last decade. The problem lies in Chávez's view that change is possible only through confrontation and by displacing the traditional elites, while the traditional elites have come to believe that coexistence with Chávez is not possible.

These views have created a deep-seated polarization and fear throughout society on both sides. With some justification, those who oppose the government fear recrimination and retaliation, as reported by people who signed petitions for the recall of Chávez in 2004. Likewise, many *chavistas* fear retribution if they were to lose power, in part because of the arrests and persecution during the short-lived Carmona government in April 2002, when a coup removed Chávez from office for forty-eight hours and then a countercoup returned him to office. Therefore, citizen perceptions and memories of persecution haunt both sides, and the views of political elites on both sides that it is not possible to coexist and compromise with the other provide the greatest challenge to an inclusive, peaceful, pluralist, and democratic Venezuela in the near future.

International Engagement with Venezuela—2009 and Beyond

Engagement with Venezuela in 2009 and beyond will take place in an international context very different from that of the previous five years. The election of Barack Obama, the international financial crisis, and volatile oil prices all constrain Venezuela's room to maneuver on the global stage. Inside Venezuela, the 2007 and 2008 election results combined with shrinking oil revenues demonstrate vulnerabilities of the administration.

The election in the United States of Barack Obama removes the primary target of Chávez's anti-imperialist rhetoric of recent years, which focused personally on President George W. Bush. Representing hope for millions of Americans previously discriminated against or fighting for social change, Barack Obama will not be the foil that George Bush was for President Chávez. In addition, the slowdown in demand for oil in the midst of an international financial crisis makes Venezuela even more vulnerable to its dependence on oil revenues. Taking office at the bottom of oil prices in 1998, when Venezuelan oil sold for $7 per barrel, Hugo Chávez has ridden a rollercoaster as prices zoomed up to $150 per barrel in mid-2008 and back down to $50 per barrel a few months later. The 2009 government budget is based on a price of $65 per barrel, a level that would necessarily cause a curtailment of spending plans. Indeed, the government had already announced delays in planned refinery projects with Nicaragua and Ecuador in late 2008.

Nevertheless, growing economic ties with Russia, Iran, and China are evident. All three have been increasing their presence in Latin America. For Russia, Venezuela is proving to be a significant arms purchaser, as the government attempts to reestablish parity with Colombia after a decade of significant U.S. military aid to that country. Iran and Venezuela have a long-standing relationship as co-founders of OPEC, and more recently a common foreign policy goal of curtailing U.S. influence unites them further. Iranian commercial ventures in Venezuela are increasing and there are now direct flights daily between the two countries. Meanwhile, Chávez continues to seek to diversify Venezuela's oil market to China by jointly developing new refineries in China and Venezuela that can handle Venezuela's heavy crude.

Domestically, growing dissatisfaction with government performance was reflected in the narrow defeat of the 2007 constitutional referendum and the governing party's loss of the largest states and cities in the 2008 regional elections. The most striking results were in the Caracas urban areas, where the official candidates lost the race for mayor of the greater metropolitan area as well as mayor of the eastern half of Caracas, which includes the largest poor neighborhood in the country. This was the first time since 1998 **that** the government had lost these votes, and it came despite the fact that some of the president's closest confidants were candidates and the president campaigned personally on their behalf. Though not necessarily a rejection of Chávez personally, the vote reflected the frustration of the people with the inability of the government to solve the pressing problems of soaring crime rates, lack of water and paved roads, unemployment, and inflation. Analysts had been asking since the beginning of the Chávez electoral movement how long the honeymoon would last, with voters prioritizing their personal support for the president over accountability for poor government service. A decade later, the president's coattails failed to carry his candidates, and declining oil prices indicated even more pressure on government services.

At the same time, the failure of dissident candidates within the government's political alliance to garner significant support reflected the difficulty still of creating "*chavismo* without Chávez," that is, the radical change represented by Chávez's movement without Chávez himself.[10] It also indicated continued polarization of the population. Nationwide, the popular vote totals represented 52 percent for the PSUV, 43 percent for the opposition parties, and only 4 percent for dissidents within the government's political alliance.[11]

A third implication of the regional elections concerns the potential for the opposition victors to deliver better government services and thus launch competitive bids for national-level offices. Unfortunately, their ability to perform is largely dependent on national revenue sharing and the cooperation of the federal government. The Chávez administration had already rolled back some of the decentralization reforms of the previous decade and has decreased the autonomy of municipal and state governments, which reduces the power of those in opposition who won these seats. In addition, the proposal to create another layer of government with presidentially appointed vice presidents running newly created geographic regions, which was defeated in the constitutional referendum of 2007, could be reintroduced; if approved, it would weaken the elected governors and mayors. The announcement soon after the vote that a number of public spaces and buildings in the cities won by the opposition would be transferred to central government authority further reflected the administration's drive to curtail the opposition's current and future political power.

Finally, the president asked the National Assembly to reintroduce a constitutional amendment for indefinite reelection (defeated in 2007). Though the November 2008 elections provided a weaker mandate than he had hoped for, after the vote the president indicated his desire to hold a referendum to approve such an amendment early in 2009, well in time for the 2012 presidential election, and perhaps an attempt to gain approval before dissatisfaction with government services grows in the wake of declining oil prices.

U.S.-Venezuela Relations in the New Context

Given this new context, the United States should seek to engage Venezuela rather than isolate or confront it, with three objectives in mind. First, the U.S. has real strategic interests in Venezuela. as described earlier: oil, drugs, and security. Second, Venezuela's participatory democracy experiment is developing concomitantly an overconcentration of power, risking a return of extreme polarization, destabilization, and violence that should be avoided. Third, defusing the rancorous standoff between the United States and Venezuela would open the door to more cooperative relationships and problem solving with other countries in the region.

Past U.S. policies seeking to isolate or confront Venezuela have been counterproductive. In recent years the United States and Venezuela seem to have been engaging in a Western Hemisphere "cold war," a competition over financial and political influence in other countries that they are attempting to get on their side. U.S. attempts to isolate Venezuela in hemispheric arenas have failed miserably, as shown in the drawn-out affair to elect a new secretary general of the Organization of American States in 2005. In that incident, the United States proposed and backed two different candidates before the Venezuela-backed candidate finally won the vote. Latin governments do not want to be forced to choose between the United States and Venezuela, and they resent it when hemispheric politics is held hostage to the two countries' competition.

In the realm of democracy promotion, the United States lost its moral authority in the region with its welcoming of the 2002 coup against Chávez, and more broadly with its unilateral policy on Iraq where "regime change" became rationalized as democracy promotion. The strong-arming of Chile and Mexico in the UN Security Council to vote for the invasion of Iraq was also resented, and failed to achieve its aim.

Within Venezuela, the clumsy U.S. opening of the Office of Transition Initiatives in 2003 created the impression in the Venezuelan government that the United States expected to see, or was going to engineer, a regime transition. The Chávez government cited U.S. assistance for democracy promotion to opposition civil society organizations (NGOs, labor unions, and private sector organizations) prior to the 2002 coup in alleging that the U.S. was funding a conspiracy against the government. Many NGOs have since decided to stop accepting U.S. funding in the wake of strong government criticism. The Office of Transition Initiatives nevertheless continues a vigorous program of assistance to Venezuelan NGOs.[12]

By refusing to engage in confrontation with Venezuela, the United States can defuse that destructive relationship and more effectively work to create cooperative relationships with other Latin American countries to further U.S. interests. As discussed in other chapters of this volume (see chapters 1, 3, and 13), the most important factor to change the negative dynamic will be a change in style and attitude by the United States, a turn toward greater multilateralism, consultation, and respect. Chávez's anti-Americanism resonates at home and abroad because of general antipathy toward U.S. unilateral actions and perceived bullying. The new nationalism led by Hugo Chávez and joined by other Latin American countries seeks to assert greater independence of U.S.-dominated multilateral organizations such as the International Monetary Fund and the World Bank, and greater control of and equity in their own natural resources (reflected in the renegotiation of contracts and increases in royalty and tax payments for extractive industries). A more consultative American foreign policy that also addresses the agenda of Latin America will ameliorate the negative attitudes toward the United States and open the door to greater receptivity of U.S. ideas and assistance in Venezuela and elsewhere.

There is a possibility for limited engagement with Venezuela on issues of mutual concern. However, we should not expect major change in the relationship, given the fundamental foreign policy goals of the Chávez administration and the Bolivarian Revolution: to increase Venezuela's national autonomy, to increase the global South's autonomy vis-à-vis the North, and to lessen U.S. dominance in the region and the world. Therefore, Venezuela will continue its attempts to diversify its oil export markets and to build coalitions to create a more multipolar world and a better integrated South.

Nevertheless, a new administration should start with positive signals and focus on pragmatic concerns of interest to both countries. The United States should make clear that it respects the sovereign right of the Venezuelan people to choose their leadership (as they have done consistently in voting for Hugo Chávez) and that the U.S. has no intent to engineer regime change in Venezuela. In the past different offices of the U.S. executive branch have sent conflicting signals, as the Pentagon broadcast negative descriptions of the Chávez administration while the State Department tried to moderate its rhetoric. A more consistent policy across the executive branch would help to reinforce the message of respect for Venezuelan sovereignty.

Anyone analyzing Venezuelan democracy must take into account the social roots of the political change happening in Venezuela and Latin America, and must acknowledge the pressing demand for jobs and personal safety, for poverty reduction, and for closing the huge income gap. Populations marginalized from economic and political power have a strong hunger for recognition and inclusion. Procedural democracy is not a priority for many in this situation; having greater control and participation in the forces that determine their daily lives is.

Likewise, judgments about the Chávez administration's social policy should be based on sound empirical evidence. Though the Chávez administration falls prey to the same easy-oil-money trap as every other Venezuelan administration—distributing money to ease social tensions and build political support while ignoring the more mundane tasks of maintaining crucial infrastructure and building human capital—the notion that this administration is simply conducting an irresponsible populist policy should be questioned. There may be political bias in the distribution of benefits, and some of the programs may have a short-term horizon, yet what the Chávez administration has achieved must be acknowledged: There has been significant investment in education and health, including adult education programs, new integral schools, and medical clinics in the barrios. The most important achievement, however, and the least understood by Chávez's foreign and domestic opponents, is the sense of human dignity that Chávez's leadership and social missions have conferred on the poor and marginalized. Until his challengers understand this key point, there will be no credible alternative.

Enhancing Democratic Governance and Rule of Law

The United States has only very limited direct influence, and even less leverage, over Venezuela, as a result of U.S. tacit approval of the 2002 coup attempt against Chávez, both countries' dependence on the oil trade, and Venezuela's status as a resource-rich state that is not dependent on international or American aid. To the extent that the United States provides democracy assistance, it should be all-inclusive, striving to increase the democratic capacities of newly emerging power centers rather than simply aiding traditional opposition ones. Assisting many diverse groups seeking to open political space and increase tolerance can also help to reduce political polarization. In the past, U.S.-funded democracy assistance through the National Endowment for Democracy and its affiliated organizations focused on civil society groups who came to form the core of political opposition to the Chávez administration (labor unions, the business sector, selected NGOs, and opposition political parties). Although *chavista* organizations are less interested in democracy assistance from the United States, attempts to offer assistance to multiple groups is important in overcoming the perceptions that U.S. democracy promotion is aimed at undermining the government.

A more fruitful approach than U.S.-provided democracy assistance, however, would be for the United States to refrain from direct democracy promotion and instead work through multilateral forums and broader regional networks of NGOs to support democratic spaces and mechanisms for the Venezuelan people to determine their own direction. The international community can best contribute to enhancing democratic governance and rule of law in Venezuela by engaging the Venezuelan government and its citizens in multilateral mutual review mechanisms, and offering the flexibility to recognize and explore new forms of democratic participation. In other words, Venezuela needs to be engaged on its own terms.

The international community should continue with its obligations to monitor member-state commitments to international treaties and principles, which may require punitive responses, but should also engage with the country in a positive way, recognizing where it is in terms of its own political evolution. The United States in particular will gain credibility in the realm of human rights and rule of law only when it addresses its own shortcomings with regard to torture, restrictions on civil liberties, and lack of due process for detainees resulting from the "war on terror."

Venezuela has ambitions to be a regional leader and has used its own wealth to advance a petrodiplomacy to win friends and allies in the region. Some reports estimate that Venezuela's own forms of foreign aid (discounted oil, purchase of bonds, joint energy ventures, barter trade) may well be the equivalent of total U.S. aid to the region since 1999, or perhaps even more. Latin American neighbors' commercial and investment interests in Venezuela usually supersede democracy concerns. Nevertheless, regional institutions, including the OAS and Mercosur (of which Venezuela is an aspiring member), have democracy clauses. The European Union and the United Nations have programs within Venezuela. These provide some opportunities for strengthening Venezuelan democratic governance and rule of law. Multilateral organizations and networks of NGOs could take the following steps:

Use universal international monitoring mechanisms. Venezuela is a party to many international treaties on human rights, democracy, and anti-corruption. Focusing on review mechanisms that are reciprocal and universal (such as United Nations protocols and treaty review mechanisms) is likely to be more effective than unilateral U.S. certifications (such as human trafficking, counternarcotics, and so on). Venezuela insists on reciprocity and mutual review and has refused to abide by U.S. unilateral requirements (for example, on human trafficking), leading the U.S. to issue reports and sanctions on the basis of lack of reporting rather than evidence of wrongdoing, in several instances.

Be sensitive to regional monitoring mechanisms. The Inter-American Commission on Human Rights, the Inter-American Court on Human Rights, and OAS conventions and charters provide additional resources. However, the perception that the United States dominates the OAS and is using these instruments to punish Venezuela makes Venezuela particularly resistant to any OAS oversight. (This was the case during the drafting of the Inter-American Democratic Charter.) In addition, the failure of the United States to be a party to the Inter-American Court on Human Rights and its refusal to sign many international human rights treaties weakens its own moral authority to judge others' compliance with these norms.

Encourage space for dialogue to combat polarization. Public opinion polls indicate that the populace is tired of confrontation and political struggle. They are likely to welcome dialogue opportunities that can help to reduce the physical segregation in the cities, misperceptions and misinformation among different sectors, and the accompanying fear of "the other." Such dialogue opportunities should focus on tolerance, mutual respect, common problem solving, and national identity and pride.

Focus on security issues. Venezuelans in all classes and areas own guns. This fact, plus poorly trained and heavy-handed police, contributes to extremely high homicide rates as well as extrajudicial executions. Encouragement of a citizen disarmament law (which was discussed but never accomplished during the 2002 turmoil), control of gun imports and sales (and control of U.S. gun exports), and police training and monitoring would contribute to improving this situation.

Encourage transparency in government spending and the right to public access to information. The relative opaqueness of government decisions and especially revenue collection and spending is an obstacle to improved bureaucratic performance and citizen accountability mechanisms. Encouraging Venezuela to provide a leadership role in these areas would be extremely beneficial. For example, Venezuela could be invited to join the Extractive Industry Transparency Initiative (EITI) and develop a model for state-owned petroleum industries to make transparent their income and spending decisions. International oil companies operating in Venezuela should be invited as well to join the EITI. Venezuela's constitutional right of citizens to have access to public information needs to be enshrined in national legislation.

Encourage competitive electoral conditions. Assuring competitive elections is the most important element in providing the opportunity for pluralist decisionmaking and representation. Venezuela has made great strides since 2005 in regaining citizens' confidence in the fairness of electoral processes, but more remains to be done, particularly in campaign finance and equitable campaign conditions. Support of domestic monitoring groups is important as well. Venezuela is a world leader in the development and use of electronic voting systems, which have sparked controversy in the United States and Venezuela alike. Venezuela could be invited to participate in or host forums on best practices in improving the accountability of such voting systems, to demonstrate its own lessons learned, and to help ensure transparency and confidence in such systems in the future.

Encourage independent national or international monitoring of prison conditions and protect human rights defenders. The deplorable prison conditions are recognized by the Chávez government and efforts are being made to improve them. Supporting national monitoring groups and proposing international monitoring could help to spur such reforms, and to encourage the protection of human rights defenders.

If Venezuela moves in the direction of seeking accommodation among the various political factions and visions to provide mutual guarantees of safety and respect for agreed-upon rules of the game, the international community will need only to respond to any specific requests for assistance and generally applaud the efforts. If, however, the government moves in the direction of curtailing the authority of elected officials—as it has tried to do with the recently elected governors and mayors—or otherwise disrespects the will of the people as expressed through votes and referenda, the international community has a responsibility to act collectively to defend democratic principles. Likewise, if extreme factions opposing the government use extraconstitutional measures (as in 2002) or foment violence, the international community has the duty to condemn such actions.

The attitude of Venezuela's neighbors is vital regarding standards of democracy, governance, and rule of law. Reliance on Venezuelan largesse in its petrodiplomacy, commercial interests in Venezuela, and a general desire not to interfere in each other's internal affairs (or to judge others, for fear of being judged oneself) constrain Venezuela's neighbors from criticizing its political behavior. But the hemisphere needs to identify the lines that cannot be crossed, in terms of human rights, lack of protection of minority rights, and concentration of power, as a basis for building regional consensus to collectively protect democracy. Identifying and developing a consensus on indicators of violations of the Inter-American Democratic Charter would be a first step toward identifying that line, and toward galvanizing the region collectively to promote and protect democracy.

Notes

1. These governments proposed to restructure political and economic relations in their countries through constituent assemblies elected to write new constitutions, thus "refounding" the state more than simply modifying the constitution. The proposals to rewrite the constitutions were symbolic of a desire for fundamental political change, even where the resultant constitutions did not differ radically from their predecessors.

2. Venezuela moved to popularly elected governors and mayors in 1989; the new constitution retained these posts but also created new mechanisms, bolstered by Chávez administration policies, to reduce the local government controls over revenue.

3. The Bolivarian Revolution is named after Simón Bolívar (1783–1830), one of the most important leaders of South America's struggle for independence from Spain. Born in Venezuela, he was known as The Liberator and became the first president of

Gran Colombia (Colombia, Venezuela, Panama, and Ecuador). He dreamed of a federation of South American states, based on a liberal philosophy of governance, but in later years advocated centralized power to control the internal bickering in Gran Colombia. Chávez claims Bolívar as one of his central inspirations. The Punto Fijo period of Venezuelan politics refers to the democratic political system established in 1959 as the result of a power-sharing agreement known as the Punto Fijo Pact that ended the military dictatorship of General Pérez Jiménez.

4. The Fifth Republic refers to the fifth constitution of Venezuela, which was promoted in Chávez's political campaign and came to fruition in 1999. The new constitution renamed the country the Bolivarian Republic of Venezuela, among other changes.

5. Escenarios Datanalisis: Informe Quincenal, Segunda Quincena, Julio 2008 (Caracas: Datanalisis).

6. "Death in Venezuela: Deadly Massage," *The Economist,* July 17, 2008. See also Derechos Humanos [Human Rights] PROVEA, "Informe Anual Octubre 2006/Septiembre 2007: Situación de los derechos humanos en Venezuela," report, October 2007 (www.derechos.org.ve/publicaciones/infanual/2006_07/index.html [accessed on March 26, 2008]).

7. The Venezuelan programs use a mixture of cash transfers, general subsidies, block grants to neighborhoods, and technical assistance to individuals and groups, in addition to providing services in health, education, and vocational training.

8. Latinobarómetro, cited in *The Economist,* "A Warning for Reformers," November 15, 2007 (www.economist.com/world/la/displaystory.cfm?story_id=10136464 [accessed April 2008]).

9. Latinobarómetro, "Informe de Prensa 2005" [Press Report 2005] (Santiago de Chile: Corporación Latinobarómetro), states that the three primary meanings of democracy for Latin Americans are liberty, elections, and an economic system that provides a dignified income, though the relative weight of each of these factors varies by country. For example, in Brazil, a dignified income ranks the highest, whereas in Venezuela liberty ranks the highest, followed by elections. To download the report (in Spanish) go to www.latinobarometro.org, click on "Informes" link, and then download "Informe de Prensa 2005."

10. When several coalition partners refused to join the PSUV, Chávez allowed his party to enter into negotiations with them to seek unity candidates for each position. But in some cases the negotiations broke down and smaller coalition parties ran their own candidates, becoming "dissidents" in Chávez's view.

11. I am indebted to Ana Maria San Juan for these statistics and their implications.

12. USAID's Office of Transition Initiatives budgeted $6 million in 2004 and $4.5 million in 2005 to assist primarily opposition civil society groups. The National Endowment for Democracy provided another $1.7 million in 2004–2005 and by 2007

was still providing nearly $1 million to Venezuelan and U.S. NGOs for democracy assistance (see Jennifer McCoy, "International Response to Democratic Crisis in Venezuela," in *Defending the Gain*, edited by Esther Brimmer [Washington: Center for Transatlantic Relations, 2007], pp. 119–32, and "Grants: Latin America and the Caribbean Program 2007," at the National Endowment for Democracy website [www.ned.org/grants/07programs/grants-lac07.html#venezuela]).

eleven

The United States and Bolivia: Test Case for Change

George Gray Molina

For more than a decade, U.S. engagement in the Andean region has concentrated on security and counter-narcotics issues and favored unilateral over multilateral intervention. In recent years the rise of Hugo Chávez in Venezuela, Evo Morales in Bolivia, and, to a lesser degree, Rafael Correa in Ecuador has tested this approach. In the final months of the George W. Bush administration, U.S. relations with these countries, and especially with Bolivia, have gone from bad to worse. Developments at the end of 2008 included Bolivia's expulsion of the U.S. ambassador, the tit-for-tat expulsion of the Bolivian ambassador from the United States, and then Bolivia's announcement that the U.S. Drug Enforcement Administration would not be allowed to operate in Bolivia.

The crisis of late 2008 is only the most recent episode of an unraveling relationship. Despite all this hostility, however, there are some lessons to be learned from the current crisis, and there is some indication that U.S.-Bolivia relations might make a relatively hopeful test case for a different kind of diplomacy in the future, if the incoming Obama administration is open to a new approach. There is general agreement that Washington has more pressing priorities than Bolivia, and the present climate in La Paz offers no guarantee that conciliatory overtures from the Obama administration would immediately be reciprocated. However, Bolivia's democracy remains quite open, and the political balance there is still fairly fluid. Public opinion continues to count and may well prove receptive to a suitable U.S. overture; the economic logic also favors renewed cooperation. So Bolivia offers an appropriate setting for a "thought experiment" about what it might take to shift course from confrontation to a restoration of partnership. This chapter is such an exercise, and makes the case for such a change.

This chapter rests on the assumption that both sides could benefit from repairing this damaged bilateral relationship and that an early effort to do so is warranted. But before I develop that case, an alternative perspective needs to be acknowledged. U.S.-Bolivia interactions are to the highest degree asymmetrical. Whatever their objectives, political actors in La Paz are obliged to follow with the closest attention any developments in Washington that could have an impact upon their country and its prospects. Almost the opposite is true in Washington. U.S. relations with Bolivia rank far down in the hierarchy of foreign policy concerns, in a capital that has to manage bilateral relations with almost two hundred other states. During the cold war Bolivia had at least some limited and theoretical leverage, based on the remote possibility that La Paz might switch sides in that bilateral confrontation. But in the "war on terror" Bolivia has no place, and even in the "war on drugs" it is a second-rank player. Beyond such international alignments something quite drastic—an urban insurrection, a credible threat of civil war—would be required to attract Washington's attention to Bolivia. If the Morales administration now chooses to escalate its disagreements with Washington, why should any but the most specialized U.S. foreign policymakers care? Surely it is the people of Bolivia who will bear all the costs of an unnecessary confrontation brought on them by their own government, while the incoming U.S. administration remains free to concentrate its attention on the far more significant challenges it faces elsewhere.

This perspective contains a powerful element of realism. However, this essay, written from a Bolivian standpoint, argues that the Obama administration would be well advised to analyze how the bilateral relationship deteriorated to this point, and to consider a change of course.

Five Reasons for a Fresh Start with Evo's Bolivia

First, U.S. foreign policy does sometimes get embroiled with distant and asymmetrical conflicts that could have turned out better if they had not been allowed to fester. At present Bolivia can probably be broadly bracketed with such distant (and also landlocked) nations as Mongolia, Nepal, and Zambia, all of whose policy problems are of very little interest to Washington power brokers. But the same was once true of Afghanistan, Kosovo, and Rwanda, three other landlocked states that now present the United States with much more insoluble problems than those emerging from Bolivia. Prudent realism could therefore counsel against allowing any distant conflicts to escalate through unnecessary neglect.

Second, a brief review of the history of the interactions between Washington and La Paz could uncover some lessons of wider utility to the U.S. foreign policy establishment. Although when viewed in isolation this relationship may seem very marginal, some of the patterns observable there are liable to recur wherever there is acute asymmetry. For example, in the 1990s a forceful Bolivian leader did all he could to position his country and his government at the forefront of Washington's approval. President Gonzalo Sanchez de Lozada aimed to capture U.S. attention by embracing the political and economic reforms associated with the Clinton administration more vigorously than his neighbors. He was so successful in securing endorsements in North America that, arguably, he became overconfident of his external support and therefore ceased to attend to the beliefs and expectations of his home population—until his domestic power base abruptly collapsed, in 2003. Perhaps there is a more general lesson here for Washington policymakers, if they care to reflect upon it. Similarly, after 2005, a related domestic dynamic may help to explain escalating confrontation between President Morales and the U.S. government. Provoking retaliation from Washington has the undoubted drawback that some established Bolivian interests will get hurt. But an administration in La Paz that has no hope of securing particularly warm relations with Washington may well gain domestic political capital from pursuing the opposite course, since one result can be to cast rival political parties and candidates in the role of disloyal instruments of an overbearing foreign power. This, too, is a logic that can be encountered far beyond Bolivia, and that can take far more dangerous and perverse forms elsewhere. If a more healthy and constructive pattern of interactions can be achieved in this case, the resulting lessons could be of more general utility to the new administration.

Third, although just at present the Morales administration may seem out on a limb, and therefore of trivial interest to Washington power brokers, Bolivia is in fact located at the center of a still-volatile region. For example, it was only by a narrow margin that voters in Peru rejected a more intractably radical and nationalist candidate for their presidency in 2006. Ecuador, Nicaragua, and Paraguay all subsequently elected presidents of a general outlook similar to Evo's. Although this chapter is concerned with the United States and Bolivia, when that bilateral relationship sours, the consequences can easily become regional. This might not matter much if Washington's ties with the major Andean states were secure. But, as shown in the chapters on Colombia and Venezuela in this volume, Washington faces graver problems elsewhere in the Andes, and this underlines the expediency of exploring the scope for some détente with La Paz.

Fourth, some of the current troubles with Bolivia arise from congressionally mandated programs of certification and sanctions that have also caused friction and resentment in various other more important bilateral relationships. Such programs may be overdue for an overhaul independent of the Bolivian case. Benefiting from the enhanced Democratic majority in Congress and the desire of many U.S. allies to develop more multilateral alternatives to this pattern of mechanistic unilateralism, the Obama administration might derive some lessons from the failed history of Drug Enforcement Administration operations in Bolivia that could be of more general applicability.

Finally, as the Obama administration struggles to reestablish Washington's eroded international "soft power" and to repair its damaged reputation as a benevolent regional hegemon, it is worth recalling that President Morales also possesses assets of this kind. He has a strong and authentically democratic mandate from the Bolivian electorate. His status as a self-educated leader of popular and indigenous extraction gives him a legitimacy similar to that of President "Lula" da Silva in Brazil. Although some of his policy choices may prove misguided or even counterproductive, his administration is still widely viewed in Bolivia and in the Andes as the best chance for overcoming the huge handicaps of exclusion and discrimination that have held back Bolivian society for so long. U.S. policy measures designed to discipline his government's conduct are more likely to stiffen its resistance and to hurt the Bolivian people by further reducing their long-postponed hopes of social progress. Precisely because Bolivia is not a security threat, and is indeed of general low salience in Washington, there may be little to lose from allowing an experiment to see whether the United States can achieve better results by adopting a less intrusive and punitive approach.

These are the reasons for claiming that despite its many other higher priorities, the Obama administration should take an interest in exploring the scope for a different approach to its relations with Bolivia. Obviously this would compete with more urgent claims, and it would take time; it could come about only through the efforts of some intermediary officials with delegated powers. The authorities in La Paz would need to grasp the opportunity, and various third parties would have to lend support. Furthermore, for new relations to develop, some long-standing political obstacles would need to be dealt with. None of this is easy, but neither is any of it impossible.

The next part of this chapter focuses on how U.S.-Bolivia relations deteriorated, in both the long run (with the unraveling of a unilateral counternarcotics policy) and the short (as a result of intense domestic political conflict). The closing section looks at steps that could be taken to reestablish U.S.-Bolivia relations on a sounder footing. These include advancing toward the establishment of a multilateral counter-narcotics policy, and changing drug policy and the way that aid, trade, and democracy promotion policies are delivered. From a comparative perspective, there are policy experiments that might be easier to make with Bolivia than with a number of other countries in the region.

Behind the Diplomatic Breakdown

How can the downturn in U.S.-Bolivia relations over the past few years be explained? The version receiving the most international attention has been that the United States meddled in domestic politics at the time when political instability was at its highest in Bolivia, but closer analysis indicates that the downturn was mainly a product of longer-term tensions arising from the way U.S. foreign policy has been conducted in Bolivia, rather than from the more immediate political context. These tensions gained salience with the election of Evo Morales in Bolivia, and were aggravated by domestic political conflict between the government and the opposition. Three types of tensions underlie the current impasse.

The Long Run: The Ups and Downs of Unilateralism

The United States has a long history of unilateral engagement in Bolivia.[1] In the 1950s—when the country was in the throes of land reform and industrial nationalization and was governed by populist politics—President Eisenhower took the unprecedented step of recognizing the Bolivian National Revolution as a "third way" between capitalism and Communism. In a series of overtures to the leaders of the Bolivian revolution, U.S. policymakers sought to dissuade revolutionary factions from shifting into the pro-Cuba camp in the 1960s or from reverting to the fascistic tendencies prevalent in the early 1940s. In 1956, an economic mission, called the Stabilization Commission and presided over by George Eder, introduced the first "stabilization" package, during the presidency of Hernan Siles Suazo.[2] By the early 1960s, President Kennedy had engaged the leaders of the Bolivian revolution with the Alliance for Progress and the Peace Corps and had provided generous financing of what eventually became the first roads integrating the eastern and western regions of the country, running through what is now the coca-growing province of Chapare.

In the wake of a series of military governments in Bolivia, the Carter administration played a role in supporting pro-democracy social movements, aiding Domitila Chungara's compelling hunger strike, which later set the stage for a protracted and ultimately successful democratic transition in the 1980s. Clearly, it has been no easy task to build democratic rule of law, consolidate free and fair elections, and bolster the legitimacy of democratic institutions. However, the overall record is robust. Despite different periods of social upheaval and political polarization, Bolivia has experienced uninterrupted democratic rule since 1982. Morales, a member of the MAS (Movimiento al Socialismo), won the presidency in December 2005. His landslide electoral victory was a result of pulling together a broad coalition of social and indigenous movements as well as left-wing academics and NGOs under the umbrella of the MAS.

Reforms that bolstered democratic participation in the 1990s, such as Popular Participation and Administrative Decentralization, account for the emergence of both an energized social grassroots movement at the local level and stronger regional politicization in the eastern departments of Santa Cruz and Beni and in the southern department of Tarija. Local and regional politics were transformed over a twenty-year period, and continue to play a crucial role in some of the country's most pressing unresolved tensions over indigenous rights, land rights, natural resources, and regional autonomy.[3]

Despite deep political polarization in 2003 and 2005, the expansion of democratic legitimacy in Bolivia deepened with the election of Evo Morales, the country's first indigenous national leader, in December 2005. Today, the challenge of democratic rule is about institution building and promoting effective governance and the rule of law rather than bolstering the legitimacy of democracy. U.S. involvement has been long-standing, but has too often been framed in unilateral terms, in contrast with the multilateralization of other efforts to assist Bolivian democracy, including those promoted by UNASUR (Unión de Naciones Suramericanas, Union of South American Nations), the OAS (Organization of American States), and others framed by different regional agreements.

Counter-Narcotics Policy

Counter-narcotics policy has been the driving force in U.S.-Bolivian relations since the 1990s; it plays a critical role in determining where the Bolivian government stands today and how relations might improve in the future. Morales is president of Bolivia as much because of his defiance of drug policy in the 1980s in his home province of Chapare as for his success in gaining power in local and later national elections in the 1990s and 2000s. During the 2002 presidential election, the U.S. ambassador in Bolivia remarked that he "would like to remind the Bolivian electorate that if they want Bolivia to return to being an important cocaine-exporting country, this result would put U.S. aid in danger in the future." This is a vivid reminder of how intrusive U.S. involvement in domestic affairs has affected the political career of Evo Morales, both threatening him and ultimately boosting his patriotic credentials.[4] It should be remembered that the coca leaf is a legitimate traditional stimulant within Bolivia, and the coca growers (led by Evo Morales) expect their democratic politicians to protect their interests, much as some U.S. politicians defended the tobacco interest. It is only when heavily processed that coca becomes the dangerous drug cocaine.

President Morales has been careful to broaden his political appeal beyond the narcotics issue, despite having his political base in the Chapare region—indeed, perhaps because of it—and in doing so he has tried to reassure the popular and middle classes that he "will not run a narco-state in Bolivia."[5] In fact, however, his administration's support for worldwide depenalization of the coca leaf as a narcotic substance has been relatively unsuccessful, and his administration has also been relatively ineffective at engaging credibly with multilateral counter-narcotics initiatives in order to craft joint eradication, interdiction, and alternative development policies for the future.

However, U.S. counter-narcotics policies have not been very effective either. Many analysts point to the weakness of supply-side controls.[6] Patterns of coca cultivation and smuggling and the availability of low-priced cocaine in consumer markets suggest that the narcotics issue has reached an impasse, and that a different approach could be worth attempting.

Three main trends need to be taken into account in the design of an anti-narcotics strategy. First, in the entire Andean region the coca-leaf-production trend is relatively stable, occupying between 200,000 and 250,000 hectares (556,000 to 618,000 acres) over the past twenty years. This pattern has endured in spite of eradication efforts covering hundreds of thousands of acres and a relatively aggressive policy at the ground level over the past decade. According to the UN Office on Drugs and Crime, in 2007 Bolivian coca-leaf production increased by about 5 percent for the second year in a row (to 28,900 hectares, or 71,383 acres), and potential cocaine production increased by a similar percentage, to 104 metric tons (114 short tons) of cocaine. Nevertheless, the relative share of Bolivia in the hemispheric drug trade has declined, with most new additional crops and potential drug production emerging in Colombia, despite huge U.S. efforts to curtail drug trafficking there.[7]

Second, Bolivia's patterns of production and smuggling have also shifted over the past decade. On the producer side, new crop cultivation has shifted from the Chapare to the Yungas region, with a higher rate of net eradication in the Chapare. A significant feature of the current situation in Bolivia is that President Morales himself presides over the country's coca union system, and has the formal responsibility to negotiate quota and alternative development compensation agreements. On the smuggling side, Bolivian cocaine is being smuggled increasingly through European trading routes via Brazil and western Africa. Although the UN data are imprecise on the degree of movement from the U.S. to the European route, Brazil is clearly concerned with promoting greater joint action to reverse this trend.

Third, on the demand side, the easy availability and low price of the drug suggest that the current policy is not having a significant impact on consumer markets. Contrary to the hoped-for effects of supply-reduction policies, the street price of cocaine has fallen substantially over the past thirty years.

The Short Run: Domestic Conflict

In addition to the tensions over counter-narcotics policy, short-term factors precipitated the most recent diplomatic crisis between the United States and Bolivia. The expulsion of the U.S. ambassador in La Paz, Phil Goldberg, on September 11, 2008, occurred weeks after a recall referendum and days before the outburst of violence in the northern region of Pando, an opposition stronghold in northern Bolivia, which led to the deaths of fifteen to twenty people. Within a few weeks the Drug Enforcement Administration (DEA) decertified Bolivian drug eradication efforts, USAID suspended operations in Bolivia, the Peace Corps pulled out of the country, and ATPDEA (Andean Trade Promotion and Drug Eradication Act) trade preferences were suspended by executive order of President George W. Bush.

Then, on October 21, 2008, the Bolivian government and the congressional opposition reached a fragile agreement for a new draft constitution and dates for referenda and general elections.[8] That agreement came about as a result of backlash in response to the violence in Pando, but it has not settled all the contentious issues and therefore offers no guarantee that conflict will not reemerge.

Close to 140 amendments were made to the 411-article constitution, many of them on substantive dimensions of political disagreement. The amendments made it possible to establish new procedural rules for new appointments to the judiciary and electoral court. It was also agreed that there should be a referendum to approve the constitutional amendments in January 2009, and that new general elections should be held in December 2009. Other agreements on indigenous rights, regional autonomy, and land issues were also reached.

These agreements set the stage for future diplomatic talks between the United States and Bolivia. The Morales administration is in a better position to revisit its foreign policy decisions from a posture of domestic political strength. Clearly, the government of President Morales has gained renewed impetus as a result of the agreements, since the new constitution is likely to be approved and because the compromise that broke the impasse is seen as a victory for all moderate forces in the political arena. Bolivia remains a genuine electoral democracy.[9] President Morales won 67 percent of the vote in the recall referendum of August 2008, and his political party emerged the winner in 95 of Bolivia's 112 provinces, including nearly half of the opposition's strongholds in Santa Cruz, Beni, Tarija, and Pando. Congressional moderates of the opposition parties—PODEMOS (Poder Democrático y Social, Social and Democratic Power; "podemos" means "we can"), UN (Frente de Unidad Nacional, National Unity Front), and MNR (Movimiento Nacionalista Revolucionario, Revolutionary Nationalist Movement)—emerged strengthened by the agreements, which catapulted a number of potential presidential candidates to the fore. The main losers in the agreements were the radical left, campesino leaders who opposed modifications to the constitution, and the radical right, mostly concentrated in the regional civic committees of the so-called Media Luna (the half-moon-shaped entity formed by the departments of Pando, Beni, Santa Cruz, Chuquisaca, and Tarija).

Until the January 2009 referendum on the constitution and the end-of-2009 general elections take place, Bolivia's immediate political future will remain quite uncertain. The first and most likely scenario is that Morales wins the elections with a divided regional and congressional opposition, giving him a stronger hold on Congress and allowing the MAS to make inroads in regions currently dominated by the opposition. In a second scenario,

Morales faces a united opposition that balances power regionally and challenges the center and center-left urban vote through a broad coalition. This would lead to strengthened opposition in Congress and more negotiating power for the regions on the issues of regional autonomy and decentralization. This scenario is unlikely because of the highly fragmented nature of regional and opposition politics and the absence of a popular opposition leader with national stature. A third, but also unlikely, scenario involves more conflict and violence like that which occurred before the agreements, ending in a legitimacy crisis over the rules of the game and the electoral calendar. Neither the Obama administration nor UNASUR wants to see the third option come to pass, but only a Brazil-led coalition would have much chance of preventing this. And any attempt by external actors to sway the balance between the first and second outcomes would be likely to backfire.

In the short term it is likely that polarization will decline, although pockets of regional discontent, electoral boycotts, and contained social conflict may persist. Two of the three scenarios described feature majority support for Evo Morales, which may increase his room to maneuver on domestic and foreign policy and result in relatively pragmatic alliances. The renewed impetus gained by President Morales as a result of the agreements, together with the current global economic crisis, could lead to more moderate domestic and foreign policies, a trend that might be reinforced by new U.S. policies aimed at multilateralism and rapprochement.

Future Diplomatic Talks

Bolivia's foreign policy has been pragmatic in the country's negotiations with Chile, Brazil, and Argentina and relatively ideological in relations with the United States and the European Union, in which the focus has been on drugs and free trade. The existence of a pragmatic streak in Bolivia's foreign policy bodes well for a gradual rapprochement between Bolivia and the United States. The election of Barack Obama in November was welcomed by the Morales administration and is seen as heralding a relatively comprehensive change in political outlook in the United States.

From the Bolivian perspective, the period between the constitutional referendum in January and the presidential elections in December 2009 will represent an opportunity to forge more positive ties with the United States. From the U.S. perspective, a window of opportunity is opening for innovations of the type explored in this chapter as a result of the inauguration of Barack Obama and the change in top U.S. State Department officials.

Participants in renewed talks should explicitly contemplate the establishment of a road map that can help to change the tone of relations between the two countries. Three issues are likely to dominate discussions between the two countries: drug policy, aid and trade, and democracy and human rights promotion.

Drug Policy: A Move to Multilateralism

For two decades the United States played a leading role in counter-narcotics policy in Bolivia and in other Andean countries. It is time to evaluate the achievements and shortcomings of that policy. Beyond assessing the impact of U.S. drug policy in Bolivia, now is also the time to reassess whether unilateral U.S. leadership is still useful and effective.

Two pieces of evidence suggest that U.S. drug policy in Bolivia is not working. First, despite a decade of coca-leaf eradication programs in the Chapare and Yungas regions, the level of coca-leaf production has either remained the same or increased over the years. This means coca eradication and alternative development are not reducing the supply of coca-leaf on the ground. Second, the prices for retail sales of cocaine have changed little over the past few years. This suggests that drugs are plentiful on U.S. streets, meaning demand-side interdiction policies are not effective either.

Both the European Union and the UN Office on Drugs and Crime (UNDOC) have gradually increased their presence in Bolivia. At the end of 2008 the Bolivian government asked the Brazilian anti-narcotics agency to join a broader alliance to address what has increasingly become an interdiction problem involving Bolivia, Brazil, the West Africa Coast, and the European Union.[10] Although these initiatives clearly need to be scaled up if they are to begin to fill the void left by U.S. alternative development and interdiction activities, they show evidence of an international disposition to develop approaches that are more multilateral and that could therefore enlist stronger Bolivian cooperation.

There are at least two other reasons for testing a multilateral counter-narcotics approach in Bolivia. First, Bolivia has not experienced the levels of violence that have affected other countries involved in the Latin American drug trade. This can be explained in part by the position of Bolivian coca production in global drug markets. Most coca leaves produced within Bolivia are processed into drugs outside Bolivia, and the trade is controlled by more powerful and sophisticated drug networks outside the country. In addition, coca-leaf production in Bolivia is organized within a campesino union system, rather than by a drug cartel. The union system acts as a countervailing power to the establishment of a sprawling drug trade at the supply source. Second, Bolivian drug-smuggling target areas have shifted from the United States to Europe over the past five years. This suggests that the U.S. market is mostly supplied via the northern smuggling routes, which start in Colombia and Peru and go through Mexico. This does not mean that counter-narcotics policy is not important in Bolivia; rather, it suggests that it could be timely to explore a different policy approach.

How to move on the multilateral front? Both the European Union and the UNDOC have gradually increased their presence in Bolivia. In December 2008 the Bolivian government reached an agreement with the European Union to scale up operations over five years, until 2013.[11] This includes pursuing a closer partnership with the Brazilian government to stem drug flows to Europe. A new compact on drug policy between Bolivia and a multilateral coalition would still need the support of the United States, but this might be best achieved by means of a broad partnership with other agencies. The Bolivian government would welcome a shift in policy whereby U.S. counter-narcotics agencies contribute to rather than lead the design and implementation of policies. The U.S. government will find that greater multilateral involvement in drug policy would encourage a more constructive Bolivian disposition to develop cooperative relationships on other fronts, notably the environment, and trade, aid, and energy policy.

Beyond Drugs: A New Deal on Trade and Aid

At present, U.S. trade preferences in the Andean region are tied to drug reduction commitments, as framed by the Andean Trade Preferences and Drug Enforcement Act (ATPDEA). Preferences were extended for the Andean region, but suspended for Bolivia after December 15, 2008. The impact of trade preferences on the Bolivian export economy has been significant, increasing both the volume of trade and also the diversity of products exported to the U.S. market.[12] After annual exports to the United States worth less than $100 million obtained for nearly a decade, today the figure is over $400 million, concentrated mostly in textiles, leather, jewelry, furniture, and products of organic agriculture. Between 30,000 and 50,000 jobs just in one city, El Alto (not far from La Paz), depend on access to the U.S. market, and these jobs in turn have an impact on the rest of the economy.

Today, Bolivia is an odd case in Latin America because economic growth has not translated into less poverty. In fact, poverty has increased in absolute terms over the past few years. The exceptions to this pattern are concentrated in the export sector linked to U.S. trade preferences—labor-intensive sectors such as textiles, leather accessories, gold jewelry, and organic agricultural products that have higher labor and environmental standards than other sectors of the economy. This may be the pocket of growth that could contribute most to a "win-win" U.S.-Bolivia trade scenario. The Bolivian government seeks a different relationship on trade, less focused on conventional free trade and concentrating more on "fair trade" and on using different benchmarks to judge performance.

There is a good case for testing a new trade approach with Bolivia, and a new approach could set a new precedent for collaborative policymaking. Bolivia is the poorest country in the hemisphere with the exception of Haiti, but unlike Haiti, Bolivia has a workable administration and is a sovereign constitutional democracy. Thus, new, enlightened trade policies would also show the region that the United States has not written off Latin America when it comes to economic growth, trade, and development. There is a mutual interest in enhancing labor and environmental standards, and maintaining reciprocal market access. The Obama administration should upgrade the status of development goals in the foreign policy agenda and set out clear objectives to engage the developing world. Again, Bolivia is well placed to build on successful past experience with USAID initiatives and to revise less successful programs and projects.

Democracy and Human Rights: A Pending Challenge

The Morales administration charges that U.S.-backed democracy promotion programs have catered to opposition interests and meddled in internal affairs. This accusation followed a similar claim by President Chávez concerning democracy promotion programs in Venezuela.

However one evaluates these charges, it can be seen that after a decade of work to support democratic elections, promote the rule of law, and build institutions in Latin America, the results are in, and at best they are mixed, as can be seen in other chapters of this book. The Obama administration may therefore wish to reflect on the strengths and weaknesses of U.S. programs.

In the case of Bolivia, democracy promotion, conflict prevention, and human rights advocacy are clearly necessary. Both the government and the opposition are responsible for the recent violence, ongoing human rights violations, and instances of authoritarianism. But if Washington is to play a constructive role in the future, it is more likely to exercise influence in La Paz through multilateral rather than primarily through bilateral action. Indeed, only by backing away from intrusive unilateralism can the United States hope to regain credibility and perhaps leverage as a moderating influence working in partnership with UNASUR and like-minded regional entities.

The October agreement process, which was mediated and overseen by UNASUR, the OAS, the EU, and the UN, is an excellent example of what multilateralism can achieve. The UNASUR mission in particular is credited with providing much-needed support to both the government and the opposition. It was established after a crisis summit at the behest of President Inácio "Lula" da Silva of Brazil and Chile's President Michele Bachelet. Although the first round of meetings with the opposition, in Cochabamba, failed to produce an accord, concessions were made in La Paz to the benefit of opposition groups in Congress. Most analysts concur that Morales would not have pursued amendments to the constitution in the absence of external observers and domestic pressure for oversight.

Recently, two missions, one fielded by the UN High Commission on Human Rights and one by UNASUR, examined the violence in Pando, and established the terms for a future evidence-gathering mission. Although multilateral actions have not always been successful in the past decade, these episodes have reinforced the case that a "new Latin American multilateralism" is necessary to tackle some of the intractable democracy and human rights issues in the Southern Hemisphere. The Bolivian government has been open and supportive of multilateral organizations, and will come under pressure from its neighbors to be receptive to multinational collaboration in the future.

Conclusion: Testing a New Approach

U.S.-Bolivia relations are at a low point, but a changing hemispheric context is likely to open a new era in U.S.–Latin American relations. Bolivia could be a test case for a new style of U.S. engagement with the region. There are policy options that could be jointly implemented with the Bolivian authorities that would do no harm to others in the region. The most important is a shift in counter-narcotics policy. U.S. policy toward Bolivia has been dominated by the drug issue and usually has been handled in a rigidly bilateral manner, without giving enough consideration to other dimensions of mutual policy interest, including economic growth, poverty reduction, energy, trade, and aid.

Rather than wait for a comprehensive new U.S. approach to the Americas to be developed on multiple policy fronts, this chapter outlines the case for an early and low-cost experiment, a pilot study that could help Washington policymakers explore the practicalities of a change of course. Four actions could frame a new and more positive approach to U.S.-Bolivia relations in the near future.

First, evaluate U.S. counter-narcotics policy in Bolivia and move toward multilateralism over the next twelve months; this also calls for EU and UNDOC leadership on drug interdiction and alternative development in Bolivia.

Second, consider special treatment for Bolivia on trade and aid that is geared toward growth and poverty reduction rather than on nondevelopment objectives (current U.S. aid and trade policies are explicitly conditioned on coca-leaf eradication in Bolivia). This should substitute for the APTDEA initiative until a new trade framework is in place in the hemisphere.

A third area for action is human rights and democracy promotion. There is a clear need to upgrade the role played by third countries in democracy promotion and human rights in the region. Organizations such as the OAS, the Inter-American Human Rights Office, and UNASUR need to be strengthened if a viable hemispheric partnership is to prove resilient over time.

Fourth and finally, there is scope to help Evo's Bolivia engage with the region and the world on new terms, by reestablishing normal diplomatic relations, sending an ambassador to La Paz, and resuming other programs currently suspended. Political isolation pushes Bolivia deeper into regional polarization and internal conflict. The country has so far avoided massive violence and institutional collapse, but more external support is needed to underpin this relative peace and order.

How can new U.S.-Bolivia relations strengthen the democratizing dimensions of social and regional change in Bolivia? Much of the challenge lies in "doing no harm" in Bolivia and in moving toward a multilateral counter-narcotics policy. The move from drugs to development—more specifically, to economic growth and poverty reduction—would be welcome precisely because these policy aims have been absent in U.S.-Latin America relations over the past decade. The global financial crisis adds dimensions of urgency to an already ailing economy. Both the political changes in the United States and the economic changes worldwide are causing a shifting of gears in Latin America. With recent U.S.-Bolivia relations at a historic low, the Obama administration could simply allow this legacy of the Bush administration's stewardship to fester. There is certainly no compelling reason for the new administration to give its relations with Bolivia a high priority. However, this chapter has set out the rationale for a different and more constructive approach, one in keeping with the Obama administration's declared objectives, and one strikingly different from the outlook of his predecessor. At no great cost to the United States, the incoming administration has scope to explore new and more acceptable ways to support democracy, strengthen the rule of law, and build a long-lasting partnership to reduce poverty in one of the hemisphere's poorest countries.

Notes

1. See James Dunkerley, *Rebellion in the Veins: Political Struggle in Bolivia, 1952–1982* (London: Verso, 1984).

2. George Eder, *Inflation and Development in Latin America: A Case History of Inflation and Stabilization in Bolivia* (University of Michigan, Bureau of Business Research, Graduate School of Business Administration, 1960), p. 479.

3. George Gray Molina, "The Politics of Popular Participation in Bolivia, 1994–1999," Ph.D. dissertation, Nuffield College, University of Oxford, 2003.

4. "EEUU suspendería ayuda si Evo es presidente," *Correo del Sur,* June 27, 2002.

5. "Evo hizo un llamamiento a hacer un pacto contra el narcotráfico," *Europress,* March 11, 2006.

6. UN Office on Drugs and Crime, *Coca Cultivation in the Andean Region: A Survey of Bolivia, Colombia, and Peru* (New York: 2008).

7. UN Office on Drugs and Crime, *World Drug Report 2008* (New York: 2008).

8. George Gray Molina, "El acuerdo boliviano," *Argumentos* (Lima: Instituto de Estudios Peruanos, 2008).

9. George Gray Molina, "Bolivia's Long and Winding Road," IAD Working Paper (Washington: Inter-American Dialogue, 2008).

10. "Nueva política antidrogas en preparación," *La Razón,* November 15, 2008.

11. Ibid.

12. Freddy Ehlers, "The Andean Trade Promotion and Drug Eradication Act: Impact on the U.S. and Andean Economies," testimony at the U.S. International Trade Commission, Washington, July 22, 2008.

twelve

The Rule of Law in Mexico: Challenges for the Obama Administration

Carlos Elizondo and Ana Laura Magaloni

How should the Obama administration first assess, and then respond to, the evidently worsening crisis of governance, lawlessness, and large-scale criminal violence that has been gathering momentum in Mexico throughout 2008? This is shaping up to become possibly the most urgent policy challenge Washington faces in the Western Hemisphere in 2009. Given the extent of U.S.-Mexico interconnections on so many fronts—migration, trade, investment, energy security, environment, as well as cross-border illegal transactions of all sorts—the apparent disintegration of the rule of law is one challenge that cannot be postponed or sidestepped. Already, certain quarters of the U.S. press and public opinion are becoming increasingly agitated about this issue, and it would be easy for the new team to respond too impulsively to such pressures.

The situation is indeed urgent, but it also requires a measured assessment. The new administration would do best to evaluate the immediate problems with an eye to the longer-term health of U.S.-Mexico relations as a whole, and with a clear understanding of the broader historical and institutional context. Today's dramas have been in gestation for a considerable period, and they will require sophisticated and coordinated long-term management. They are the product of complex interactions between U.S. and Mexican institutions

The authors would like to thank Laurence Whitehead for his invaluable contribution to this chapter.

in general, and between their justice systems in particular. Lessons can be learned and better relationships can be forged, but it must be understood that the most important reforms in this area will take considerable time. Short-term responses need to be harmonized with this longer-term logic.

Just how serious is the present violent-crime problem? On the one hand, newspaper headlines in both countries reflect a gruesome reality. On the other hand, U.S. decisionmakers should always bear in mind that Mexico is a sprawling and complex society with a large modern economy and highly elaborated structures of governance. There were times in the not so distant past when considerable areas in large U.S. cities such as New York and Washington were also severely afflicted by frightening levels of criminality. Yet it was always understood that this was just one aspect of a far more complex U.S. reality, and that in any case it could only be corrected by reforms introduced from within. Despite the temptation to view Mexico's current crime problems as much more overwhelming of domestic law enforcement capabilities, the same basic principles still apply there as well.

From a Washington perspective, the big policy options can be broadly divided into two categories: measures that reinforce the U.S. capacity to insulate itself from southern instabilities ("quarantining" the problems by, for example, building a higher wall, issuing more tourist warnings, directing more aggressive U.S. law enforcement against Mexican nationals), and those that seek to reinforce the Mexican state's capacity to deliver security to its citizens and enhance rule-of-law protections and guarantees. Although there may still be some limited scope for further measures in the first, "quarantining," category, our focus in this chapter is the second alternative. This is mainly because we think responses of the first kind have already been pursued to the point of diminishing returns, and indeed may now start becoming counterproductive. Furthermore, it can be argued at a deeper level that the "quarantining" response reflects a false diagnosis of the dynamics of the problem. If Mexico's current crime problems arise from interaction effects between the two societies, then longer-term remedies will require corrective measures coordinated from both sides.

Mexican Democracy and the United States

Mexico's new democracy is struggling, and its future stability cannot be taken as given. The "breakthrough" elections of 1997 and 2000 (when the PRI [Partido Revolucionario Institucional], which had governed Mexico for almost seven decades, peacefully lost first the chamber of deputies and then, in 2000, the presidency) created illusions of easy progress. But the problems in enacting needed reforms, mainly as a result of the resistance of the PRI and the PRD (Partido de la Revolución Democrática), and then the close-fought 2006 presidential contest, showed that the results of the elections would be contested again at the street level by the defeated party and that the credibility of the elections was very low among nearly one-third of the electorate. There is a real danger that drug money could begin to taint the midterm congressional elections of 2009 and that the presidential election of 2012 could accentuate rather than alleviate the negative tendencies.

The erosion of confidence in the Mexican state's capacity to confront international crime is also generating risks and dangers for our major partners. Some emergency measures may be required to cope with cross-border illegality and criminality between 2008 and 2012—the remainder of President Felipe Calderón's single six-year term and President Barack Obama's first term.

Although these are only negative tendencies and not by any means inevitable progressions, they are intensifying and could come to a head during the Obama administration. So the incoming team in Washington would be well advised to take a hard look at the adequacy of recent and current policies toward Mexico and to prepare itself for the possibility of harder times ahead.

A number of high-profile U.S. policy domains merit reassessment: the unintended consequences of ongoing immigration and border controls; the unsatisfactory state of the NAFTA agreement (different sources of dissatisfaction on the two sides of the Rio Grande suggest that renegotiating NAFTA could prove highly polarizing); the medium-term prospects for North American energy security if neither government improves its current policies; and the public security crisis arising from current cross-border trafficking incentives (drugs and undocumented migrants flowing north and high-caliber weapons and laundered funds flowing south).

If the new U.S. administration intends to be taken more seriously than the Bush administration as a supporter and promoter of democracy in the rest of the world, there is no more critical testing ground of what this means than in its relations with its neighbor to its immediate south. In particular, if the United States decides to project its soft power to recover lost influence in those parts of the world that were not persuaded by "war on terror" unilateralism, Mexico again is a crucial arena. Mexico is of far greater significance to the United States than any other country of Latin America. It is also a relatively sympathetic and promising partner, at least by comparison with most alternatives in the region and in the rest of the world.

A Mexican Perspective

In this chapter, while taking all of these interconnected issues into account, we focus specifically on the rule-of-law challenges facing Mexico and on ways U.S.-Mexico cooperation could be improved to strengthen the rule of law and democracy in Mexico. We turn first to the deeply embedded problem of Mexico's legal system and identify the long-run changes that will help the country move toward a more reliable democratic rule-of-law legal structure.

Strengthening Mexico's democracy requires improvements on other fronts, but we believe it is especially important to focus on the rule-of-law dimension. An absolutely critical component of a high-quality democratic regime, it has not received the same attention as other Mexican political institutions and practices.

Recently, the justice system underwent some reforms that attracted external interest and, indeed, support—notably the switch to oral criminal proceedings to speed up court procedures and improve due process standards, and enhanced cooperation in the fight against drug trafficking and organized crime. Yet our view is that Mexico's rule-of-law weaknesses are long-standing and systemic. Partial fixes, however necessary, are unlikely to deliver the required improvements and may even be counterproductive.

Durable reforms require an accurate diagnosis of core systemic dysfunctions, and responses to problem areas come largely from within and take time to mature. The origin of Mexico's rule-of-law problems is domestic, rooted in the legacies of the old authoritarian political system. Despite democratization, the old model of relations between political authority and pressure groups has not been superseded.

This issue is central, lying at the heart of the sustainability of Mexican democracy. Since Mexico's independence, in 1810, the Mexican justice system has always been an institutional weak point within the Mexican state. There can be no escaping the evidence that the current deficiencies of Mexico's justice system pose a serious threat to our democratic institutions. The current upsurge of violent criminality (much of it drug-related) is exposing it to unprecedented strains, as it is proving to be ineffective and perhaps is infiltrated by criminal gangs. This carries the risk of fueling growing demands for reversing the decentralization of power that occurred with the establishment of democracy, and strengthened local governments, which have very strong constitutional powers and are responsible for administering justice locally. The recentralization of power could be perceived as a mechanism to restore a sense of firm government—without too fine a regard for democratic niceties, including strengthening the rule of law.

A process of North American integration that takes into account existing institutional asymmetries can help to build a Mexican democracy with stronger institutions. But in the interim, Mexico's partners will need patience and understanding. They can usually offer encouragement and transmit "best practices" from elsewhere, but they need to bear in mind that our country's legal and judicial institutions are among the most ancient and embedded in the democratic world. So, as in other Latin American countries and even in older democracies, there is great institutional inertia and internal resistance to changes in the status quo on the part of those whom it advantages.

Tensions are likely to arise as a result of, on the one hand, the glacial time scale required for internally driven structural reform and, on the other, the much more short-term pressures deriving from the upsurge in drugs and arms trafficking and associated violence. An added short-term source of tension is the migratory flows that could be prompted by an imminent severe economic downturn across North America.

Background to the Rule of Law in Mexico

One cannot understand the challenges to strengthening the rule of law in Mexico without understanding certain peculiarities of Mexican institutions.

The Law as a Mechanism of Authoritarian Control

Mexico's institutions were created to accommodate a model of development and control that treated different actors according to their capacity to exert pressure on and negotiate with the regime. This was a corporate structure that was not based on economic or political competence.

Entrepreneurs, workers, and peasants were organized from above so that they might be controlled politically. In exchange for showing political loyalty, entrepreneurs benefited from trade protection, subsidies, and low taxes, and workers, and especially official trade unions, benefited from key labor rights, financial resources, and autonomy for union leaders. For public sector workers, particularly those in central government institutions, job security was virtually guaranteed and payoffs for political loyalty—growing social security contributions and pensions in particular—became an increasing burden on the public purse.

Governments had less scope to manage these interests than is normally believed. Rather than a dictatorial system, there was a complex balancing of powers at the top. Discipline might be enforced when a direct challenge was mounted against the regime, but the norm was to negotiate and ensure power-sharing arrangements among the various players.

In contrast with other countries at a similar level of development in the region, this system ensured a notable degree of political stability. However, the system was based on its ability to distribute income discretionally, on the negotiation of norms, and on a closed economy that protected uncompetitive businesses.

The Effects of Trade Liberalization on Democracy and the Rule of Law

Democratization became possible because of the 1982 economic crisis that led to the breakdown of this model of exchange. With trade liberalization, some of the control mechanisms became more complex or simply ceased to exist. This was particularly difficult to accommodate, as North American market integration (unlike European integration) did not include mechanisms to develop strong and modern institutions to accompany liberalization. Democratization only shifted one of the pieces of the machine: control over the vote. This was the only arena that was opened up for the development of solid institutions capable of guaranteeing compliance with the law. The belief was that the free vote and equal competition for the vote would suffice to establish a new political system. But by leaving all other institutions intact, Mexico's democracy inherited a logic of exchange based on inequality before the law, only now without the disciplinary power of the presidency over the various players, and without a dense institutional framework.

The limits of this strategy have become clear. In the absence of a social pact based on equality before the law and respect for the rule of law, it is not possible to consolidate democracy or to improve economic growth rates. But the solution does not lie simply in passing new laws; it is necessary to forge a social pact for cooperation based on equality before the law for all actors.

The nature of Mexican ties with the United States has not helped to forge this shared foundation. Trade between the two countries has rewarded some types of investment and generated better-paid jobs in some parts of the country. However, because of the absence of compensation mechanisms to protect the most vulnerable sectors, the number of "winning" groups has been limited. What is more, the illegal markets in drugs and firearms have strengthened the culture of illegality, which also erodes the capacity to build a state based on rule-of-law governance.

The Courts as Triggers of Legal Asymmetries

Judiciaries can play a central role in resolving key social asymmetries, as shown by the experiences of the post–World War II European constitutional courts and of the U.S. Supreme Court up until the end of the 1970s. For example, the U.S. Supreme Court played a pivotal role in the early stages of the dismantling of racial segregation of American schools.

Unlike in the United States and or Europe, Mexico's courts have done little to resolve deep-rooted social asymmetries and to protect constitutional rights. On the contrary, the Mexican Supreme Court is still often allied to powerful groups and does not see itself as mandated to protect the constitutional rights of the most vulnerable groups in society.

An analysis of the role of the *juicio de amparo* (literally writ of protection, similar to habeas corpus, which gives citizens the right to gain the protection of the courts when their constitutional rights are violated by any authority) in the fiscal and penal domains shows that, contrary to what one would hope, the Supreme Court and the federal courts have tended to reinforce regimes of privilege and existing social asymmetries. The *juicio de amparo* is not an efficient instrument to protect constitutional rights; on the contrary, it has been used to limit government action in areas that are rightfully within the domain of democratic administrative and legislative authorities.

In the fiscal arena, Mexican taxpayers enjoy unusually broad constitutional protections when compared with most other countries, through the *amparo*. This allows the taxpayer to seek the protection of the courts in order to avoid paying taxes that are believed to violate the Constitution. It is, however, an onerous mechanism, and it only makes sense for major taxpayers to resort to it. For smaller taxpayers, the investment of time, effort, and money to avail themselves of the *amparo* does not pay off, as the cost of the legal services can be higher that the taxes they may recoup. Thus, the government is constrained by a minority of powerful taxpayers, and tends to exert abusive and discretionary authority over the rest of the taxpaying population. The constant intervention of the Supreme Court in fiscal matters has accentuated inequalities among taxpayers and limited the tax-collecting capacities of the state.

In criminal cases as well the constitutional rights of the accused are systematically violated because here, too, the protection of the law offered by the *amparo* is largely ineffective. The court has failed to exert the necessary strict constitutional controls to guarantee the constitutional rights of the accused and thereby to modify authoritarian practices. One study on constitutional case law regarding the right of the accused to "adequate" legal representation during detention and in court shows that the *amparo* continues to operate as it did during the authoritarian period.[1] The Mexican procedural norm is that statements made by the accused during pretrial detention are admissible in court, whether or not a judge has verified that the statement was obtained legally; and constitutional case law holds that statements made under early detention are to be regarded as more trustworthy because they are more "spontaneous" than later statements. So it is hardly surprising that 96 percent of the cases presented by the attorney general of the Federal District (Mexico City) end in a guilty verdict.[2] According to data from the prosecutor (*consejería jurídica*) of the Federal District, there were only 318 public defenders in 2007 to deal with 46,816 criminal, family, and civil law cases. Despite this workload, a public defender only earns a thousand dollars per month.

The effect of all this is the reinforcement of inequality before the law and of social asymmetries. Access to justice is strongly conditioned by who one is, how much one earns, and whom one knows. So far, the Supreme Court has lost the opportunity to redefine the role of the *amparo* and establish the foundation for a new constitutional democratic justice characterized by respect for the constitutional rights of the minorities that are systematically excluded from the political agenda.

How to Strengthen the Rule of Law in Mexico

There is a growing consensus that institutional development is the key variable for the establishment of the rule of law. The level of trust of social agents depends on the existence of legitimate and efficient institutions that increase predictability and stabilize social relations. Social cooperation becomes impossible when there is no certainty about the rules, or when social agents are not all bound by the same set of norms.

The task is to build a state with the power and ability to regulate and administer conflict and to impose laws that are in the public interest, and a system that imposes equality before the law, to prevent the systematic abuse of the rights of some groups in favor of others.

Bringing about such a transformation in Mexico is a medium- to long-term task. In the meantime, the executive branch urgently needs to modify the perception that some people are immune to the law because of their economic and political power. Constructing well-founded prosecutions and promoting the trial of exemplary cases of corruption among trade union leaders or monopolistic firms would help to modify the widespread perception that laws are applied to some but not to others. To do this, in the short term the executive would have to make a significant effort to limit de jure and de facto regimes of privilege that were established under authoritarian rule. This is a basic necessity if Mexico is to cultivate a climate of voluntary compliance with the law.

Steps Mexico Can Take to Promote Rule-of-Law Governance

There are measures that can be undertaken immediately to ensure that rule-of-law government is strengthened in Mexico.

First, the *amparo* should be redefined. Federal judges must rigorously control the constitutionality of government decisions that violate constitutional rights, particularly when it comes to the principle of equality before the law for vulnerable groups and minorities. Constitutional judges must defer to legislators and to the executive when it comes to public policy.

Second, the efficacy of the courts must be measured not only by what they do but also by what they do not do. Effective judicial decisions and authority should provide clear incentives for individuals to refrain from negative behaviors that undermine the idea of rule of law. For example, even though 90 percent of creditors win in court, practically none manage to collect the money owed to them. This problem of lack of enforcement of judicial decisions needs to be solved.[3]

Third, judges' decisions should educate the population about the role of law. Good decisions show that the law is not simply a question of who has power; they can be provide persuasive rhetoric and illustrate the rationale underlying existing laws. The quality of judicial reasoning in Mexico must be improved and this goal should be a focus of judicial reform.

Fourth, it must be clear that new legal frameworks cannot suffice to change social realities. There can be no progress if it is not understood that reform is largely about management and administration. Incentives, the management of cases, judicial statistics, performance indicators, and judicial careers, among other issues, are all indispensable ingredients of any judicial reform.

Fifth, it is necessary to overcome resistance to change in Mexico's rigid judicial bureaucracy, one lacking a strong system of accountability. Despite some recent efforts by the Supreme Court to reject *amparos* in tax cases, bureaucratic resistance explains the continued distorted application of the *amparo* to defend large firms against the tax authority, even while the worst off are denied protection of their constitutional rights. Judicial reform must include mechanisms to develop new criteria—a new vision of what it means to be a judge—to appoint judges that embody the new vision, and to provide incentives to ensure that constitutional case law changes to meet the needs of Mexico's new democratic political and social context.

Sixth, asymmetries between the U.S. and Mexican legal systems must be eliminated. A legal system cannot be built in isolation from the rest of the world. The asymmetry between Mexico and the United States is the source of many beneficial exchanges but also of complex institutional arbitration. Because the possibility of resorting to U.S. courts is available where large businesses and commercial transactions are concerned (contracts between parties often state that any conflicts will be resolved in a U.S. court, and company executives often relocate to San Diego to sign contracts there), Mexico has done less than it might to reform its institutions. At the same time, activities that are unlawful in the United States can legally be undertaken with impunity by simply crossing the border into Mexico. Rectifying this situation calls for much greater cooperation between responsible agencies on both sides of the border.

The role played by the European Union in the consolidation of rule-of-law governance in its region is an example to be followed. The European Union emphasized the need for norm convergence in trade and for judicial cooperation and convergence more broadly. It helps, of course, that the European Union is founded on principles of legal equality and reciprocity between member states, which generate a much closer degree of institutional convergence than does NAFTA. The European experience shows that the carrot is much more effective than the stick in establishing fair legal norms.

The Current Situation in Mexico

It is no easy task to build a state that operates according to the rule of law. It cannot be taken for granted even in the regions of the world where the rule of law has been established, nor should one believe that legal models can be exported, or that one country's rule-of-law model is the best for others.

The long-established democracies do not all practice the rule of law in the same way, so if they are to strengthen the rule of law in other democracies it must be with considerable tolerance for diversity of traditions, and with a firm commitment to pluralism of forms and even values. There are limits to the special pleading that can be accepted from the new democratic regimes (or indeed, the old ones): there are some rule-of-law systems that, though imperfect, carry the broad promise of justice for all, and others that cannot be condoned because of deep procedural flaws or because they violate basic rights.

Mexico's democracy has inherited fragile institutions, because the authoritarian system was based on the power of the presidency, not on the rule of law. Therefore, it cannot simply adopt the best public policies to broaden social benefits; it must also build a rule-of-law state in a context further complicated by a plurality of competing political agendas and the decentralization of power, which gives governors and municipal presidents broad powers to manage local police forces.

The task has been made even more complex by the rise in violent crime partly caused by the sale of illegal drugs. Strong demand for drugs in the United States is one of the mainstays of organized crime in Mexico, and thus is a key contributor to the erosion of the rule of law. The link between illegal drugs and illegal firearms coupled with the existence of an extended and geographically complex border makes this a problem unique to the United States and Mexico. The main source of the firepower of Mexican criminal organizations is the steady flow of firearms across the U.S.-Mexico border, which in turn is made possible because of permissive U.S. laws on the sale of high-caliber firearms.

Like no other president before him, President Felipe Calderón has made a commitment to invest human, financial, and political resources in the fight against organized crime. The opportunity to build security institutions can be maximized through strong ties with a U.S. administration that understands the challenges that Mexico faces and that opts for cooperation rather than confrontation (for example, in issues related to tax avoidance).

How the Obama Administration Can Promote Democracy and the Rule of Law

A crucial ingredient in any review of overall U.S. policy toward Mexico concerns Washington's understanding of and attitude toward the strains facing Mexican democracy. How that part of the bilateral complex is handled will strongly affect how the other policy domains are tackled and how Washington's stance is viewed: whether as integrated, constructive, and proactive policy or as fragmentary, unilateral, and reactive crisis management.

There is opportunity for the United States here, as well as some risks. Mexico is an unavoidable U.S. policy priority, yet many recent and current Washington policymakers and opinion formers may not see the need to make any substantial changes in existing policies. There has been an American tendency to take Mexico's cooperation and its troubled but still broadly acceptable political arrangements for granted. NAFTA underwrote the stabilization of the economy after the 1994 crisis, both by providing the crucial credit to avoid the meltdown of the financial system and by opening up markets for a growing export sector. If Calderón's opponent in the 2006 presidential election, Andres Manuel López Obrador, the PRD candidate, had been the choice of the Mexican electorate, the Bush administration would have been prepared to work with him. The Mérida Initiative is an American bipartisan effort to shore up the Mexican state's capacity to confront the drug cartels. It has a long-term focus, and has been crafted to take into account Mexican domestic political sensibilities.

What more than this should be demanded of an Obama administration that is facing severe domestic stresses of its own and that has overarching global security responsibilities? The Obama administration can increase the chances of cooperation across the full range of sensitive bilateral issues and recover some lost goodwill if it undertakes a long-term commitment to work more closely with what has been a trusted neighbor; if the relationship is framed in terms of multilateral cooperation rather than bilateral imposition (Canada could be important here, both as an example of how to manage the relationship with a neighbor and as a partner of NAFTA); and if policy is crafted in a spirit of willingness to listen as well as to instruct.

A more integrated and proactive supportive stance for Mexican democracy would also improve the chances of securing Mexican assistance in promoting democracy elsewhere in Latin America and the world.

The current escalation of resentment between the United States and the elected presidents of Bolivia, Nicaragua, and Venezuela illustrates the kind of dynamics that need to be avoided. Were such a standoff to develop following a Mexican presidential election, the repercussions would be much more dangerous.

Washington is no more responsible when political demagogues seek electoral advantage by resorting to anti-American sloganeering than Mexico is when U.S. candidates seek advantage by invoking anti-Mexican sentiment. In open democracies there is no way of avoiding this kind of political campaigning when voters are willing to condone it. But to contain the potential damage to bilateral relations and North American democratic solidarity, it is important for the governing authorities on both sides to establish protocols and transmit signals of reassurance limiting the fallout from such electoral-gesture politics. The United States has not as yet developed such protocols for Mexico in the way that it has for Canada and the United Kingdom, and this needs to be worked on if NAFTA is not to erode.

Mexican Institutions under Strain

Like many other new democracies, Mexico is encumbered by troubling legacies from its authoritarian past. It takes a generation or longer for participants in the political system to fully internalize the new rules of the game. Those rules are not always immediately available: in Latin America, Chile had to undergo painfully cumulative processes of "democratic state crafting" from the 1990s onward. Even in the best-case scenario those processes are subject to setbacks. In Bolivia, the attempt to democratize by bringing in excluded social groups and by rewriting old constitutions and electoral rules has disseminated instability and conflict.

Within this comparative framework, Mexico presents a number of advantages, but it is by no means free of such problems. Its 1917 constitution and its rigid electoral calendar provide elements of stability that are lacking elsewhere. There have been some promising attempts at state crafting, but authoritarian legacies and suspicions undermine public trust in these advances, and may even put them in jeopardy.[4]

There is a cost to making incremental adjustments to the existing rules of the game instead of more sweeping changes, as many key players may continue to operate according to tacit pre-democratic assumptions. For example, the oil industry is governed by rigid constitutional rules that make it very difficult to run the sector, as everything is overregulated and there is virtually no space for the private sector. Yet these circumstances are considered virtually untouchable by some. There are even key areas—such as civilian control over the military—where long-standing institutional rules may be weakening, to the dismay of democratic observers.

Experience from elsewhere indicates that new democracies facing such challenges can be materially reinforced and supported by regional structures and communities of democratic states that engage with these issues in a non-intrusive manner.

The European Union helped to stabilize the new southern democracies of Greece, Portugal, and Spain, partly through economic incentives and the benefits of regional integration, but also through legal and political arrangements that helped the main parties in contention to cooperate and to craft better political institutions. Unfortunately, there is no directly equivalent dynamic for the Mexican case. The United States Supreme Court, far from reinforcing the rule of law in Mexico, has issued a series of decisions—on the extradition of Mexicans to the United States; on death sentences for Mexicans in the

United States without access to their consular officials; and on the extraterritorial reach of U.S. law enforcement—that tend in the opposite direction.

A converging community of democracies should be able to devise substitute arrangements that can help Mexico address its own issues, such as its weak judicial system, by providing a framework that is perceived as legitimate. NAFTA is a major regional structure intended to protect private property rights and promote other features of a liberal society, but promoting democracy is not one of its stated goals. There ought to be scope for a new U.S. administration to work with its partners in NAFTA, and with its allies in the Americas and the European Union to provide as much support for the Mexican people's aspirations for political democracy as the treaty currently extends to private investment and commerce.

To be credible and durable such multilateral arrangements need to be broad-based, long-term, and reliable. It is not realistic to expect immediate compliance or unquestioning conformity. However, the United States has a very long-term national interest in encouraging a thriving rule of law and political democracy south of the Rio Grande. The economic and social integration of North America has now progressed so far that cross-frontier political influences are bound to follow, no matter how strenuously the United States strives to "control its borders." Whether democratic or crisis-torn, the southern neighbor will not go away! Attempts to insulate the United States from the bad effects of failure in Mexico are likely to prove ineffective and perhaps even counterproductive.

In any case, the potential for gently tilting Mexico's development in a more congenial direction is high—far higher than the potential for democratizing Iraq and Afghanistan, not to mention Cuba. And Washington's success (or failure) in Mexico will have demonstration effects that are likely to extend far beyond the immediate vicinity.

Conclusion: The Immediate Dangers Ahead

It is quite feasible for serious worst-case contingencies to arise in Mexico within the four-year term of the Obama administration if no steps are made to improve the situation. The militarization of the war on drugs could so corrupt and entangle the Mexican armed forces that a "Colombia in the 1980s" scenario, where organized crime controlled vast segments of the territory and assassinated several important politicians, is possible.[5]

Immigration controls in a context of rising unemployment could force Mexico's electoral leaders to pursue a more defensive and nationalist course than they would otherwise wish, which could provoke more anti-Mexico pressures in the United States. Food and energy security conflicts could intensify. If this were to happen, it would surely create problems within the Hispanic community inside the United States and would also make Mexico's democratization process more unstable, and therefore more of a risk to U.S. security.

These possibilities are genuine, and could materialize surprisingly fast. Indeed, according to media reports, the number of violent deaths in Mexico attributable to drug-related criminality approximately doubled between 2007 and 2008. The grisly nature of many of these crimes has shocked public opinion.

The Calderón administration is adamant that the current violence is evidence of the headway it is making in curtailing the trafficking, dismantling the big cartels, and capturing and extraditing their key operatives. It points to record seizures of drugs and money and also to increased confiscation of weapons and vehicles.[6]

The counterargument to this assertion of government effectiveness is that many of these successes may have come through anonymous tip-offs from rival gangs rather than from the internal intelligence available to the Mexican security forces—although having the capacity to react to such tip-offs is also to be counted as a genuine success, given the fact of a bureaucracy seriously corrupted by drug money. Indeed, it is a continuing source of concern that high-level appointees within the Mexican administration are periodically identified as being tainted by association with the cartels. Although the efforts to reform the security forces seems to be serious and enjoy the strong political backing of the president, we have seen before how these efforts of the executive can be undermined if stronger popular political support is not developed. There is also concern that overreliance on the Mexican military could prove counterproductive because of the corruption this may induce, as happened during the Zedillo administration (1994–2000), when a key military officer in charge of the war against drugs allowed corruption to run rampant and was ultimately convicted on drug trafficking charges

Mexico's Congress is slowly working its way through a series of security-related legislative proposals but these politicians are reluctant to grant too many powers to public authorities because they are not considered completely trustworthy. In any case, the legislative process moves at a glacial pace and making those laws effective will take even longer.

By contrast, the U.S. Congress has traditionally responded with strong conditionality and with highly prescriptive and intrusive policies. This tendency was reinforced when the Department of Homeland Security was founded in 2002 with a mandate to forestall a range of threats before they arrived within the borders of the United States. The result was to increase the pressure on the Mexican authorities to match these efforts. The Vicente Fox administration adopted a "smart borders" initiative in 2003, and signed the North American Security Partnership in 2005.

The Calderón administration has gone further, by adopting the Mérida Initiative in 2008 to fight drug trafficking. The Mérida Initiative was influenced by the U.S.-Colombian drug-trafficking initiative called Plan Colombia, but the two are not identical. Thus, whereas Plan Colombia gave prominence to crop eradication, the Mérida Initiative is more narrowly focused on internal security, law enforcement, and justice administration. Above all, no U.S. military personnel are to be officially stationed on Mexican territory, whereas they are stationed on Colombian territory. The Mexican agreement also includes U.S. commitments to addressing north-south weapons trafficking and money laundering. In addition, since Mexico's budget is more than three times that of Colombia and its GDP is almost four times as large, the U.S. share of the input is proportionally smaller and thus yields far less leverage to the Americans. Although primarily focused on Mexico, the Mérida Initiative includes the countries of Central America, whereas Plan Colombia is purely bilateral.

For such approaches to gain traction, trust and effective cooperation between the two governments must increase, and that will take time. Mexico will need more support in controlling arms trafficking (there are numerous gun shops on the American side of the border where U.S. citizens can legally purchase weapons, including AK-47s) and intelligence sharing, and to strengthen its justice system.

As we have argued here, Mexico's experience with legal and judicial institutions is deeply rooted and does not inspire much social trust. This may help to explain the divergences between U.S. and Mexican responses to the broader rule-of-law problems that affect the bilateral relationship. And the asymmetry doesn't stop there: the main market for narcotics is north of the border, but most of the violent deaths generated by this trade occur to its south.

Even so, the Obama administration has a real opportunity to improve the terms of its cooperation with Mexico to establish the rule of law, if it builds on the institutional resources that are already present while adopting a judicious and institutionally sophisticated strategy.

The new administration can borrow from the experience of other democratic communities such as the European Union, which has proactively helped to build up the rule of law in various new member states. It would be wise for the Obama administration to do likewise, rather than be forced to respond reactively to the deteriorating situation on the United States' long southwestern border.

Notes

1. Ana Laura Magaloni and Ana María Ibarra, "La configuración jurisrpudencial de los derechos fundamentales. El caso del derecho constitucional a una defensa adecuada," *Cuestiones Constitucionales*, vol. 19, 2008, pp. 107–47.

2. Marcelo Bergman and others, *Delincuencia, Marginalidad y Desempeño Institucional. Resultados de la Segunda Encuesta a Población en Reclusión* (Mexico City: Centro de Investigación y Docencia Económicas [CIDE], 2005).

3. Linn Hammergren and others, "The Juicio Ejecutivo Mercantil in the Federal District of Mexico," Document X (Washington: World Bank, 2001).

4. One such effort is the 1996 reform of the Federal Electoral Institute (Instituto Federal Electoral, IFE), but it was undermined with the 2007 election reform.

5. See also Jeffrey A. Miron, *Drug War Crimes: The Consequences of Prohibition* (New York: Farrar, Straus & Giroux, 2005).

6. According to Attorney General Eduardo Medina Mora, 15,000 heavy weapons, 2,000 grenades, 12,550 cars, 209 boats, and 315 planes were all seized in the first two years of the Calderón administration. See Pablo Ordaz, "El crimen organizado estaba tocando a las puertas del Estado," interview with Eduardo Medina Mora, *El País*, November 23, 2008 (www.elpais.com/articulo/internacional/crimen/organizado/estaba/tocando/puertas/Estado/elpepiint/20081123elpepiint_6/Tes).

PART **III**

Looking Ahead

thirteen

A Project for the Americas

Laurence Whitehead

As Abe Lowenthal states in his contribution to this volume (chapter 1), the Western Hemisphere is unlikely to be the source of the most serious and pressing challenges facing the new administration of President Barack Obama. His team will have to cope with worldwide financial disorders, not to mention security headaches in Afghanistan, Iraq, and Iran. For Washington to regain lost capital and deal effectively with the urgent global economic and security challenges it faces, the new presidential team must rectify the unfortunate legacies of the Bush administration.

Challenges and Opportunities

A core decision is whether to shift emphasis from overreliance on "hard power" in order to restore U.S. "soft power." Fiscal and monetary overstretch, together with the negative consequences of recent unilateralism, all stand in the way of renewing Washington's prestige and moral influence.

If the new administration wishes to rebuild its soft power and to upgrade its commitments to democracy and rule of law in this context, a key element could be a well-designed and carefully implemented strategy to reemphasize its adherence to multilateral approaches, to work with its democratic allies on a basis of mutual coordination, and to promote the international rule of law.

Why the Western Hemisphere?

But why highlight the Western Hemisphere, when Washington's biggest leadership challenges arise elsewhere? The short answer is that the United States benefits greatly from its location in a large region where open and competitive politics are the norm and where there are broadly liberal, constitutional, and rights-respecting institutions and practices.

The region's political and legal institutions often fail to live up to the principles on which they were founded, but the foundations are in place in the Western Hemisphere, as they are not in most other large world regions. So multilateral coordination to reinforce democracy and strengthen rule of law can make a difference, and the challenge for incoming policymakers will be to devise country- and context-specific strategies and instruments to strengthen democracy and rights.

The United States has long benefited from having a relatively "good" neighborhood, and the recent regional consensus has boosted U.S. security and prosperity further. There have always been countercurrents, but in broad geostrategic terms the Americas constitute a zone of peace and cooperation more favorable to democracy and the rule of law than any other region of the world, apart from Europe's recent history under the European Union (EU).

There are early dividends to be reaped in the Americas by the new administration if it adopts a more pluralist and inclusive political strategy than its predecessor, and this could also have a positive impact on more intractable relationships with other regions. Leaders and opinion formers in Latin America and the Caribbean welcome the Obama administration with hope and anticipation.

Countertrends visible in Venezuela and some other countries are mainly reactions to recent U.S. priorities and tactics, and are not yet deeply entrenched, so this is an opportunity to shift toward softer and more inclusive diplomacy in the Americas. The new administration can count on favorable initial conditions, good receptivity, and relatively low risk, but if it is to achieve substantive goals it should focus on specific issues and dilemmas.

Strengthened Democratic Party representation in Congress will not necessarily make it easier for the new administration to pursue its international agenda. The growing economic crisis and its repercussions are likely to stretch resources and divert energies from second-tier foreign policy concerns. But President Obama is riding a wave of international goodwill, and the U.S. executive possesses considerable scope for discretion in foreign relations.

Many democratic allies and partners in the Western Hemisphere and else-where who are well disposed toward the United States have found some of the Bush administration's international postures uncongenial and hard to defend. So President Obama starts out with an opportunity to reposition the United States, especially in the areas of democratic values and respect for the rule of law, even though his margin of maneuver will also be highly constrained, and some of the hopes projected upon him by outsiders will no doubt be disappointed.

The potential gains from even quite minor gestures and mainly stylistic changes are significant. There is a widespread admiration for the United States as an attractive model of society in Latin America and the Caribbean (a pattern heavily underwritten and reinforced by massive migratory flows), and most opinion formers are quite realistic about the constraints under which the new administration will labor.

Much goodwill can be generated if a sense that the region's concerns are being heard and differences handled sensitively replaces what Lowenthal, three decades ago, called the American "hegemonic presumption." In fairness, the Bush administration made a significant effort to mend fences in its later years, but the change at the top makes it possible to take this a step further.

Additional resources may not be the crucial factor here. In a region where the underlying structure of interests and attitudes is so comparatively favorable, better allocation of existing funds reinforced by better presentation can pay high dividends.

Constructive joint action with regional institutions and key democratic partners can leverage the impact of new initiatives, which need not require excessive amounts of scarce administrative attention or financial resources. Indeed, by working more with the grain of opinion in the region, Washington can help to head off crises that might otherwise impose far greater burdens on the administration's energies.

The hopes raised by the new administration will also generate some unrealistic demands and cause some governments to overplay their hand. There has been a loss of consensus in the region and the Obama administration could be tested in the Americas as well as elsewhere. The chapters in this volume identify many of the likely sources of difficulty.

The argument made throughout the volume and in this chapter is that the United States should avoid a simplified "us versus them" strategy when framing these issues. Attention to the separateness and specificity of the different policy issues at stake requires more discrimination than an "axis of evil" or "war on terror" perspective, and will reap better results and put to good use the new administration's potential strengths—a relatively strong capacity to engage with and respond to a multiplicity of nuanced policy challenges.

By treating the specific problems of Haitian society seriously, for example, or grasping the locally important dynamics of participatory politics in Bolivia, it is possible to tailor more effective responses to problems that, if they are responded to indiscriminately in line with a single over-schematic framework, can become intractable.

It is necessary to have unifying criteria—notably, support for democratic values and rule of law institutions—but these principles and the negotiated and peaceful resolution of disputes are widely accepted in the Western Hemisphere. What requires more effort is the practical application of these principles in awkward situations.

If economic conditions deteriorate, as seems probable, friction over secondary issues is liable to accumulate unless policymakers in the region find common ground. However, not even the most effective and open-minded of administrations in Washington can hope to embrace the viewpoints currently in contention in this large region. Some prominent figures will make unreasonable demands, and this will induce polarization rather than convergence. There are bound to be episodes of friction with conflicting demands dominating the headlines.

A calm focus on basic principles and a willingness to consider constructive proposals even when they originate from unlikely sources are necessary.

Current evidence from America's Barometer, Freedom House, and similar sources confirms that a sufficiently high degree of freedom of information and public accountability and sufficiently independent civil societies exist in the major countries of the Americas to allow public opinion to weigh in the balance.[1]

Democracy Promotion: Caribbean Contrasts

The propagation of democracy and the rule of law must be locally generated and embedded. Democracy building is often a process of affirming a particular national identity and set of communal aspirations, in opposition to external models and controls. The United States, for example, built its own democratic political culture on a rejection of European (and in particular of British monarchical) models and controls. In three Caribbean islands the new administration will inherit strong and distinctive bilateral policy commitments with a strong democracy promotion content, and it will be necessary to decide whether to continue with current policies, or make course corrections.

Cuba

The Obama administration inherits long-standing policies ostensibly directed toward promoting a democratic transition in a post-Castro Cuba, which were codified by the U.S. Congress with the 1996 Helms-Burton Law. The Bush administration tightened bilateral sanctions further and appointed a State Department "transition" coordinator. But that was before Fidel Castro's illness and the smooth transfer of power to his brother.

January 2009 marked the fiftieth anniversary of the Cuban Revolution. Most citizens in Latin America and other parts of the world, as well as increasing numbers of U.S. citizens (including Cuban American), believe that unilateral U.S. sanctions have proved counterproductive in terms of encouraging democratization in Cuba. A multilateral soft-power approach is more likely to help Cubans liberalize and eventually, no doubt, democratize. A switch in approach toward listening to the view of Washington's democratic partners (including Brazil, as well as Canada, the European Union, and Mexico) would also boost U.S. credibility in the region and beyond.

Ending the embargo and engaging with the foreign businesses that have invested in Cuba and are currently subject to U.S. sanctions would replicate the measures already adopted for China and Vietnam with positive results. Simply facilitating contacts, including family reunification visits, and business, academic, and cultural exchanges, could diminish the inflexibility of regime hard-liners, especially after the ravages of recent hurricanes and in a context of global economic insecurity.

As Pérez-Stable's chapter illustrates, Cuba presents a policy dilemma: the Cuban Communist Party still seems likely to remain in a dominant position for the indefinite future, and it is not a "reform Communist" institution that can evolve into one among various electoral contenders. But the regime enjoys a significant degree of legitimacy within the United Nations. Over the long term, this is problematic for liberal democrats throughout the Americas, since democracy promotion must be subject to the test of democratic validation.

Given that drastic regime change looks relatively unlikely and that Washington would find the consequences of a breakdown of order in Cuba hard to handle, it could be more constructive to focus increasingly on peace and security than solely on human rights and democracy.

There will also be scope for the new administration to work with allies in the hemisphere and beyond to give Havana incentives to liberalize. The Cuban regime is beginning to liberalize some forms of ownership and allowing some spaces for autonomous expression. And despite the human rights record of the regime, Cuba has a clear record of compliance with its international obligations on migration and narcotics, at least since the end of the cold war.

In short, if the goal is to reinforce moderation and dialogue and facilitate regional liberalization and convergence, Washington needs to break with the punitive ideological approach it has pursued for decades, against the advice of its democratic partners.

Cooperation with the European Union over Cuba could be fruitful. EU member states have been divided between a punitive action and "critical dialogue" with Cuba, as supported by Spain in particular, but the European Commission reached a new agreement with Havana in October 2008. A trilateral dialogue among the United States, the European Union, and Latin America on how to approach the Cuba issue could establish shared responsibility to carefully nurture liberalization and even democratization tendencies within Cuba.

Washington's condemnation of the regime lacks international resonance in part because the U.S.-run detainee camp at the Guantánamo naval base is a legal black hole of key concern to the international community. The new administration could no doubt continue to operate that facility (in defiance of Cuban and international opinion) and could continue to enforce unilateral sanctions against Havana. But the Obama administration has stated that the intention is to close the base, and thus seems to recognize that maintaining it undermines Washington's credibility as a defender of the rule of law, or as an intelligent and multilateral-minded promoter of democracy. In this spirit, elsewhere in this volume Hoffmann makes an intriguing case not just for closing the base but for returning it to Cuba.

Puerto Rico

The new administration will encounter two rival pieces of legislation under consideration by the House Insular Affairs Committee designed to settle Puerto Rico's status. And in Puerto Rico itself there are bitter divisions between rival parties concerning the ultimate shape of insular democracy; the relative weight of two rival sets of (highly politicized) judicial authorities; and the eccentric balance between rights and obligations that the U.S. Constitution imposes on this large community of citizens who are in effect second class.

The status issue in Puerto Rico is likely to force itself back into Washington's attention in 2009. In 2005 a White House interagency task force classified the current commonwealth status of the island as an interim solution.

Only full independence or full statehood count as constitutionally final-status solutions. This position was deeply resisted by the then incumbent governor of Puerto Rico, Anibal Acevedo Villa of the pro–status quo Partido Popular Democrático (PPD), who asserted that upgraded commonwealth status was a viable and potentially permanent option and a choice between the three alternatives (that is, including an enhanced version of the existing common-wealth arrangement, which the task force dismissed as merely transitional) must be made by an insular constitutional convention rather than Washing-ton. The sweeping victory of the pro-statehood Partido Nuevo Progresista (PNP) in the latest elections (coterminous with the election of Obama) means that this constitutional controversy will heat up again shortly.

Notwithstanding current and prospective federal benefit programs, the fiscal and employment prospects of the islanders are deteriorating. As free trade agreements with other Latin American nations proliferate, and as spe-cial tax incentive policies are reined back, Puerto Rico is losing its competitive edge. It remains one of the largest sites for U.S. trade and investment in the Caribbean, but for there to be good quality democratic governance Washing-ton policymakers must clarify the scope and structure of the rule of law in Puerto Rico.

For constitutional reasons, the questions of democracy and the rule of law can only be handled on a bilateral basis. Any new constitutional settlement will require the concurrence of both the Puerto Rican legislature and the U.S. Con-gress. These two entities will therefore need to agree on a process of revision and ratification that is accepted as democratic and legitimate by both sides.

If the Obama administration develops a constructive formula for consol-idating democratic progress and standardizing rights in Puerto Rico, this could reinforce its credibility and leverage in other parts of Latin America. A more legitimate, confident, and united Puerto Rico could even become a vital partner and intermediary in Western Hemispheric diplomacy instead of con-tinuing as an embarrassing sideshow, best kept out of the limelight.

Haiti

Haiti has a long history of external interventions and suspensions of its sov-ereignty. Most recently in 2004, as detailed elsewhere in this volume, Presi-dent Jean-Bertrand Aristide, who had been democratically elected, was forced from office, and an interim government invited the United Nations to send a "stabilization mission," which the Security Council charged with demobiliz-ing armed groups, restructuring and reforming the Haitian police, and fos-tering institutional development and a process of national dialogue and reconciliation. Multinational forces were deployed by the United Nations Stabilization Mission in Haiti (MINUSTAH), but five years later there is still no agreed date for the withdrawal of the UN mission, and some believe that it will take another five years to train the replacement police force.

Haiti is by far the most intractable example of cumulative policy failure in the Western Hemisphere. But it is significantly more manageable than state-building problems found in other large regions.

If Washington intends to demonstrate that it knows how to help rectify state failure elsewhere, then this is a prime site to show what it will now do better. However, as various state-building exercises have shown, one cannot implant democracy in the absence of solid state structures. So the emphasis should be on creating solid institutions, not just courts and police forces, but even the kind of educational facilities that allow Haiti's youngest citizens to develop the capabilities that their country needs.

Like other failed states, Haiti needs at the very least a generational commitment to reform, the results of which will take years to become visible. The Haitian people—the first society in modern history to bring Atlantic slavery to an end and also a significant presence both in the Caribbean and within American mainland society—have a claim on the international community that merits respect. The four hurricanes that struck Haiti in 2008 have been described by UN Secretary for Humanitarian Affairs as the country's worst disaster in the last hundred years. The Obama administration could gain widespread appreciation if it helped the UN, the World Bank, and related agencies to make real progress with these intractable legacy issues.

Strengthening the Rule of Law in the Americas

A strengthened hemisphere-wide rule-of-law system needs to rest on principles of due process and mutual recognition of diverse procedural practices. These principles are not currently uniformly observed across the region, and weaknesses in the rule of law in most jurisdictions make regionwide cooperation and joint enforcement problematic, particularly in the fraught areas of drug trafficking, international crime, terrorism, and arms trading.

There are two main reasons for this. National traditions of lawmaking and implementation are deeply rooted in the history of each republic, and these diverse origins generate divergent practices. In addition, the scope and reliability of legal processes is highly uneven both within and between these nations. Many republics' justice systems are severely deficient and require major upgrading, albeit in different ways and to different degrees.

The result of the effects of these two factors is that any regionwide convergence process is bound to be slow and difficult. But mutual support and convergence are also possible, and indeed necessary, if the rule of law is to be strengthened. The experience of EU enlargement offers some indirect encouragement concerning the potentialities and the prospective benefits.

If the Obama administration is to work on a multilateral basis and foster mutual respect and norms convergence, it must address some of the more egregious aspects of what is often seen outside the United States as verging on "legal imperialism." Various Supreme Court decisions on the treatment of foreign nationals from Latin America and on extradition issues are not new, but they became more of an impediment to joint action and international legal cooperation on criminal matters as a result of the war on terror.

The United States has repeatedly called on its allies to support its war on terror, but its judicial decisions have not always reflected a similar sensitivity about political atrocities affecting other nations in the hemisphere. One particularly sensitive case concerns Eduardo Posada Carriles (accused of a 1976 terrorist act that killed all passengers on board a Cuban civilian airplane), whose extradition to Venezuela has been blocked by U.S. legal authorities. And at the same time that U.S. courts exercise powers over foreign nationals, Washington also urges Latin American governments to sign bilateral agreements to exempt U.S. military personnel from potential International Criminal Court prosecutions.

An administration that wishes to revive U.S. soft power, and enlist the cooperation of Latin America's increasingly professional and self-confident democratic judiciaries, would be well advised to review its own record and consider which aspects of legal unilateralism and extra-territoriality might be reined in. Elsewhere in this volume, Ted Piccone and Daniel Zovatto have thoughtful suggestions to offer.

Plan Colombia

A key test of the new administration's cooperation with Latin American countries on rule of law is the way it manages Plan Colombia, launched by the Clinton administration at the end of the 1990s in the name of combating drug production in and trafficking from Colombia to the United States, which became the most prominent and costly aspect of the Bush administration's policies in Latin America.

Some hold up Plan Colombia as a shining example of a successful U.S. initiative and want it extended (to Mexico, for instance). Others stress the massive and continuing human rights violations that have taken place within the framework of Plan Colombia, and call for the United States to disengage from the program. But the Obama administration can neither repudiate what has been achieved nor extrapolate from it into the future.

Whatever the merits and failings of Plan Colombia between 1999 and 2009, President Obama must determine how to move forward as the current Uribe administration draws to a close without having curbed Colombia's leading role in drug trafficking.

The broad outlines of the Colombia debate are well known and are considered in depth elsewhere in this volume. With U.S. assistance, the Colombian government has reasserted control over large areas that had long escaped central authority. The security forces are better funded, equipped, and trained than before, their morale has risen, and they seem to enjoy strong popular support.

Although kidnapping continues at an extraordinarily high level and other indicators of criminality and terrorism remain at alarming levels, the direction of change is unmistakably favorable, and the main target of U.S.-Colombian collaboration, the Fuerzas Armadas Revolucionarias de Colombia (Revolutionary Armed Forces of Colombia), or FARC, is definitely under severe pressure. (Although on most of these indicators Mexico and even Venezuela still seem to be doing better than Colombia, comparative statistics on kidnappings, homicides, and extortion are subject to big measurement problems, and while most of the Colombian numbers are moving in a positive direction, those for Mexico and Venezuela are getting worse.)

In major urban areas, at least, the prerequisites for a functioning democracy and an effective rule-of-law regime are much more clearly in place. However, there remain very severe problems of law enforcement.

Paramilitary forces and even the armed forces are known to have committed many atrocities. It remains to be seen whether they can now be curbed. Current scandals over the high proportion of congressmen who secured elections by tying themselves to the paramilitary threaten to destabilize the country's democratic institutions.

Plan Colombia has built up and professionalized the Colombian armed forces, improving their professionalism and perhaps even their resistance to corruption. But it has also destabilized the balance of power in the northern Andes, helping to precipitate an arms race with the Venezuelans and provoking the Ecuadorian military into near confrontation with both Colombia and the United States.

The current situation in Grancolombia (Colombia, Ecuador, and Venezuela) is serious and potentially dangerous. In recent years, Washington treated the Uribe administration as democracy's best friend in the Andes and the preferred alternative to Venezuela. The new administration would do better to promote more consistent and less personalist leadership to create conditions for a more stable future for Grancolombia.

The administration could consider the establishment of an international advisory body to address regionwide issues and interactions, with broad representation and a mandate to assemble evidence and offer advice and, if requested, mediation. It could review the results of Plan Colombia, evaluate narcotics, insurgency, and terrorism issues, current security cooperation problems, legal issues such as extradition and energy security, as well as broader political issues.

To build confidence and continuity it would be best for this body to recruit a temporary secretariat representing a range of interested partners (such as the Carter Center, which already has a substantial track record here, or the Inter-American Dialogue, the Organization of American States, the Rio Group, or institutions from other countries with a similar outlook, and even the European Union). Recent mediation between Colombia and Ecuador led by the Dominican Republic indicates the scope for innovation here. The proposed advisory body would review the results of Plan Colombia and evaluate narcotics, insurgency, and terrorism issues, current security cooperation problems, and legal issues such as extradition, energy security, and broader political issues.

The Contadora Group precedent could be highly relevant to the current tensions in Grancolombia. When internal violence and interstate ideological conflict were propelling Central America toward regionwide conflict and possible external military intervention in the 1980s, a consortium of foreign ministers from Colombia, Mexico, and Venezuela, backed up by the European Union, came together in 1983 on the Panamanian island of Contadora to define principles for a settlement that would avoid war, address human rights violations, and promote de-escalation, reconciliation, pacification, and eventual democratization throughout the Isthmus.

The guiding principles for the proposed advisory body, like the Contadora Group's, would include respect for the sovereignty and territorial integrity of the three states; lawful and regionally mediated dispute resolution; agreement by all parties to use their good offices with opposition groups to facilitate peace and reconciliation in neighboring countries; reinforced legal and democratic procedures within each state to contain and channel internal differences; externally monitored programs of refugee repatriation, assistance for internally displaced communities, and reintegration of outlawed groups; and pledges of material support and assistance from the friends of Grancolombia whenever the three governments demonstrated their agreement with and wish for such help.

A Contadora-style process would allow for the formulation of principles agreeable to all three states to trigger more specific commitments. None of the contending parties would reject these principles outright, although each will doubtless interpret their application differently. So the task of the advisory body would be to work with all sides in the search for mutually acceptable assurances.

Washington might well anticipate that Venezuela will be the spoiler, but this should not be simply assumed. The chapter by Jennifer McCoy gives a balanced account of the issues here. It would be equally critical for Colombia's friends to win Uribe's participation. From the standpoint of strengthening democracy and the rule of law in these two republics, it is notable that Bogotá and Caracas have recently been competing to see which government is more negative about the work of Human Rights Watch, which has issued severe criticisms of both. In the medium term, what will matter will be the soundness and legitimacy of the underlying principles, and the consistency of regional support for them.

Opinion makers across Grancolombia need to accept that this formula would be preferable to the present direction. If Washington could demonstrate its tolerance for this type of dispute resolution approach in South America, it could set a valuable precedent for similar exercises that might be needed in more troubled contexts elsewhere.

The current polarization of views about how to defend democracy and advance the rule of law intersect with some extremely specific controversies: the role of the Manta base in Ecuador, the credibility of accusations allegedly deriving from FARC computer data captured by Colombian forces in Ecuadorian territory, and further points of contention that cannot be clarified without extensive research and conciliation.

The proposed advisory body would need to build confidence on all sides, search for common ground on a range of controversies, clarify responsibility for persisting mass refugee and internal displacement problems, and identify areas of agreement about how to cope with the often defective performance of electoral and rule-of-law institutions. All this would prepare the body for its central task: charting paths toward reconciliation and identifying a consensual framework to strengthen democracy and the rule of law in this dangerously divided subregion.

Mexico: The Paramount Relationship in Trouble

All the rule-of-law issues outlined above are relevant for Mexico as well, with the additional complications generated by the two-thousand-mile land border, economic interdependence intensified by NAFTA, and the large scale of the Mexican-born population resident in the United States

These intense and interconnected ties mean that troubles in Mexico are more likely than elsewhere to cumulate and to feed back into the United States in ways that force policy responses from Washington. Without falling into unnecessary alarmism, it must be recognized that the problems facing the Calderón administration may now be nearing a threshold of danger.

The Bush administration unsuccessfully attempted to reform immigration laws, with results that may generate more uncertainty and legal conflict. It addressed the drugs issue by launching the ongoing Merida Initiative, which could tilt either in a counterinsurgency-style direction (like Plan Colombia) or toward greater emphasis on civilian cooperation and institutional reform.

The counterinsurgency option is harder to market so close to the Rio Grande, and in a context where, in contrast to Colombia, Marxist guerrilla forces are not available as a foil for militarization. In the interim, the violence of the Mexican cartels has escalated to the level of a national emergency, and the most recent indications are that the situation could spiral out of control.

The Obama administration will face some early and critical decisions over which aspects of this relationship to prioritize and which instruments to adopt. The migration, crime, and energy security issues are all coming to a head at a time of great economic instability. The comfort blanket of NAFTA is increasingly frayed and inadequate to structure this essential bilateral relationship. One crucial dimension is to define and monitor the terms of cooperation between the justice systems of the two countries.

Some parallels between Mexico and Colombia are superficially plausible, but essentially misleading. They should be deemphasized as potentially counterproductive. A major priority for the administration should be to establish or reinforce systems of issue monitoring, information pooling, and agency coordination directed toward helping the Mexicans to help themselves.

Various Mexican agencies and political actors are making major police and judicial reform efforts with more selective and professional approaches to crime fighting and rights enforcement. As explained by Carlos Elizondo and Ana Laura Magaloni in their chapter, Mexico's rule-of-law problems have deep domestic roots, and the country's reformers will have to contend with many sensitivities and cross currents.

Similarly, although the new U.S. administration can build on the positive features of current policies on both sides of the border, it will also need to contend with the mismatch between what U.S. voters demand and what policymakers can actually deliver.

The core standpoint must be shared responsibility for cross-border problems, but this position will become harder to sustain if the apparent breakdown of public order in major centers south of the border is not convincingly reversed. Arms and illicit money flows from north to south will need to be curbed quite as forcefully as the flow of narcotics and undocumented migrants from south to north.

There may be scope for some progress at the state and municipal levels (among various twin cities such as San Diego and Tijuana, or Ciudad Juarez and El Paso) to anchor and reinforce initiatives taken at the federal level. But Washington policymakers will also need to exercise close oversight over the interrelated issues of immigration, the treatment of undocumented migrants, police and judicial cooperation, and enforcement of border controls. If the ongoing financial crisis provokes a surge in unemployment, all these low-level crises may interact and erupt into a major cross-border crisis.

The issue of energy security also has the potential to generate a further level of tension, given extreme short-term fluctuations in energy prices and indications that the volume of Mexican production may be falling well below expectations. So far, the corrective measures undertaken by the Calderón administration have been too timid, and the prospects for a stronger response are receding as a result of Mexico's electoral calendar. Clearly, this has worrying implications for North America's energy security.

The Obama administration has made reduced dependence on Middle Eastern oil one of its strategic priorities, which will have major implications for energy producers in the Western hemisphere. Any durable U.S.-Mexican response to this challenge will require mature, long-term, coordinated effort by both governments, not least because of Mexico's embedded tradition of resource nationalism.

There is no escaping the fact that public opinion in both democracies is primed to react counterproductively unless current negative trends are confronted and overcome. The Calderón administration is nearing its midterm and its political capital has eroded, so the most promising source of policy innovation could be the Obama administration.

Although the new administration's room for maneuver will obviously be highly constrained, there are a few critical areas where it could signal a fresh start and capitalize on initial goodwill at an acceptable cost. One issue of concern is the large number of deaths occurring as a result of increasingly dangerous border-crossing conditions. This is a highly emotional topic that clearly requires stronger bilateral cooperation. The U.S. Border Control should be instructed not to interfere with humanitarian rescue operations, and Mexican authorities should do more to warn their nationals of the dangers.

More generally, the Obama administration cannot afford to ignore the current fragile rule-of-law situation in Mexico, and its potentially severe implications for Mexican democracy, for U.S.-Mexico relations, and for the security and well-being of the millions of Mexican families that currently straddle the border. In particular, the counternarcotics aid program needs to be reviewed, with a change of emphasis from supplying hardware (such as helicopters) toward more collaborative and institutional support. Another crucial issue will be intelligence sharing, but this is not one where the United States can act alone, especially not in view of the long-standing and still evident reality that senior officials in the Mexican security forces have been inadequately screened. But if the new administration is to escape overdependence on the deployment of hard power, then much more coordinated strategies of rule of law support will have to be developed.

The Anglophone Caribbean

The more effectively Mexico controls the flow of narcotics across its border and into the United States, the greater the pressure on the small Anglophone islands of the Caribbean whose waters represent an alternative route for traffickers.

The problems of state failure in Haiti have not yet spread to any small neighboring islands, but their police and justice systems are already extremely overstretched. A dozen democratic members of the Organization of American States (OAS) can be found in the insular Caribbean, most of them with large diasporas in Britain, Canada, France, and the Netherlands.

For the most part these are societies with law-abiding societies and functioning institutions, but they are very small and vulnerable. The European Union is withdrawing some of the trade privileges that kept them going as exporters of tropical foodstuffs, and their economies have been destabilized by the recent very high energy prices (most of them are importers). Venezuela offers these countries some concessions in return for political partnership, but looking beyond the very short term they may be under severe pressure. The

Caribbean Community (CARICOM) provides some regional linkage, and it ought to be well placed to mobilize cooperation from Canada, and Europe.

The so-called Caribbean Commonwealth island states are easily over-looked, but if the new U.S. administration wishes to curb drug trafficking, avert illegal migration, and demonstrate that rule-of-law institutions can be nurtured through international cooperation, they deserve concentrated attention.[2] The United States should challenge the Europeans and the United Nations to work consistently to make the new international con-ventions to combat money laundering, international crime, and terrorism enforceable.

If current policies continue, the turbulence of 2008 in the worldwide eco-nomic system has the potential to create "two, three, many" Haitis (or Chávez dependents). But these are very small populations and they could be rescued effectively on quite a modest budget, provided that their many external part-ners pooled their efforts and stayed focused.

These islands have striking alternative energy advantages (solar and wind power), and microprojects supported by the Inter-American Development Bank and the aid agencies could go far toward making the Caribbean islands energy self-sufficient. In return, the United States and its allies could require strong adherence to these countries' international commitments, although this is already something most of the countries in the area accept. There already exists a regional joint reaction force, a specialized anti-kidnapping unit, and a regional intelligence center.

In April 2009, when the Summit of the Americas meets in Port of Spain, the capital of Trinidad and Tobago, the incoming U.S. administration could help strengthen these commitments, making them more substantial than the previous empty agreement with CARICOM signed by President Clinton in 1997.

Consistent and Coherent Policymaking

Most of the issues and dilemmas surveyed in this chapter require sustained monitoring and management at a relatively low level in the policymaking hierarchy. But coordination of such efforts is needed, yet inadequate coordi-nation is a long-standing key difficulty complicating Washington's successive efforts to rework inter-American relations, with various different branches of the federal government having a stake in different areas.

On matters of the highest salience (national security or fundamental val-ues) the White House can put together a policy framework and instruct key actors to follow through. Democracy promotion and the rule of law can be part of such a presidential package, along with other concerns of particular interest to President Obama. Past presidents also had their special goals—trade liberalization for Clinton and the war on terror for Bush.

In the past, Washington has tackled problems of coordination at the conceptual level through bipartisan commissions and institutions. But these are exceptional efforts, and they do not easily affect implementation. So it will be a real challenge for the Obama administration to establish the appropriate division of labor and coordination of actors to generate consistent and coherent policy on most of the issues examined here.

The task becomes more complex still in those cases where state and municipal governments have a strong interest (Florida and Miami in Cuba; Los Angeles and San Antonio in Mexico), particularly if U.S. public opinion becomes engaged as it has over border issues.

There are also highly motivated nongovernmental organizations that wish to contribute to reshaping U.S. policy, although many who wish to be consulted are single-issue advocates, incapable of proposing or conducting a consistent overall strategy. And there are substantial players with stronger ties to particular countries or issues (multinational investors, creditors, commercial partners, and specialized bureaucracies such as the Department of Homeland Security and the Drug Enforcement Administration). They must conduct their business whether or not their activities attract political attention, and although they may want more democracy and a sounder judicial system, they have to work with realities on the ground. All this must be taken into account if White House–inspired initiatives are to generate consistent and coherent results.

Various models for broader participation by multiple actors exist and are worth considering here: some essayed with the Miami Summit process, others developed by the European Union, Canada, and even some UN organizations. The new administration should review the lessons from these experiences and borrow or improve on the best of them. If the Obama administration chooses to embrace a more multilateral and consultative approach to policymaking, it will also need to coordinate with a considerable range of external democratic allies and to talk with various players in Latin America.

The existing machinery for regional cooperation is in a fairly poor state of repair. Much policymaking therefore takes place at a bilateral or subregional level. The predictable consequence is that Latin Americans tend to compete against each other for a favorable hearing in Washington. This has tended to accentuate the rivalry between, for example, Colombia and Venezuela, or

Costa Rica and Panama. A coherent and consistent multilateral strategy would be more likely to help keep all participants in balance.

There are also single-issue lobbyists and nongovernmental intermediaries at the international and domestic levels who press rival claims and aim to undercut each other. On issues such as strengthening the rule of law, it is important to develop objective criteria and reliable broad-based monitoring institutions to counteract these seesaw effects.

The Inter-American Court of Human Rights and the Inter-American Commission on Human Rights have established some valuable precedents in justice, law enforcement, and the rule of law, but they are insufficiently disseminated and followed. Most legal training remains strongly national in outlook, and there is scope for much greater emphasis on comparative and standardized approaches to the promotion of justice, and on its regional as opposed to national aspects. Some key U.S. partners, such as Canada and the European Union, could contribute a long-term and stabilizing influence here.

The Obama administration could learn from the extensive experience that has already been accumulated on the promotion of democratic governance and the rule of law. Perhaps the two most important lessons of that experience are, first, that long-term, sustained commitment is necessary, and, second, that a critical mass of investment must be reached for democracy promotion to make more than a marginal difference. This reinforces the argument for better and sustained coordination and for engaging in international cooperative efforts, to raise investment levels to the point where they make a difference.

As noted, there are various small nation-states in the Americas that provide the United States and its partners with an opportunity to make a lasting difference. If the Western Hemisphere as a whole is to become a safe haven for good-quality democratic regimes with high rule-of-law standards, then regional and international support will need to be focused on jurisdictions where the internal conditions are propitious and the outcome is finely balanced. All this can be done in concordance with public opinion and with respect for the sovereignty of small nations, provided best practices are observed and pluralist structures of external support are built up.

A Project for the Americas

With Washington's attention focused elsewhere, various highly localized problems have accumulated in the Americas. The year 2009 offers President Obama and his new administration a genuine opportunity to revive appropriate U.S. policies to promote democracy and rule of law in the Western Hemisphere. This should be easier to achieve in the Americas than in more troubled and less U.S.-friendly areas of the globe, and many in the region, in Europe, and in the United States would respond with enthusiasm.

The chances of a positive outcome will be enhanced, and the dangers of severe disappointments diminished, if the incoming administration bases its approach on a realistic and balanced diagnosis of the state of affairs in each country; clearly defines its goals and priorities; shares responsibility for this agenda with its democratic partners in the region, in the European Union, and with multilateral institutions; gains broad domestic backing for its agenda; and overcomes international skepticism, by complying with its international legal commitments and holding to the highest standards of democratic propriety at home.

The Obama administration would do well to tie all these diverse, complex issues together in a single overarching Project for the Americas, which would be about the consolidation of peaceful, law-abiding, rights-respecting, and environmentally friendly democracies with respect for local diversity and autonomy, and multilateral game rules. But such a project cannot be merely rhetorical; it must provide for substantive—even if modest and targeted—cooperation.

It would also have to be clear to U.S. citizens that although such a project would be a slow-maturing investment, it would ultimately pay the highest dividends: perhaps turning the Americas into the leading region of peace and democracy in the world, one that offers U.S. citizens and their regional counterparts the democracy and security guarantees they aspire to.

To forge this Project for the Americas, the new administration would have to back away from some recent excesses: for instance, close the Guantánamo prisoner facility and perhaps the base itself, disavow extraterritorial incursions, and reverse U.S. pressure on Latin American states to grant federal agents exemption from the ICC. It should also define an inter-American timetable to restart the stalled Miami Summit process, which should address not just trade, but also, for example, immigration and criminal justice cooperation.

Clearly, no U.S. administration can get very far without enlisting support from the new Congress. Major democratic allies, including Brazil, Canada, and perhaps Mexico, will need to sign up and establish a degree of co-ownership with the plan for the Project for the Americas. If Washington's partners are treated as subordinates, the initiative will be seen as a sham. Not only will it require the active engagement of other major and autonomous democracies, there needs to be a clear multilateral framework to structure and direct the partnership.

The OAS is the obvious multilateral forum for political dialogue and collective action, including coordinating democracy promotion in the Western Hemisphere. But the OAS would have to be overhauled to become the kind of representative and authoritative multilateral guarantor of democracy in the Western Hemisphere that it has intermittently purported to be ever since its foundation in 1948. In the 1990s it became more assertive, but proved unable to cope with the Haitian crisis of 1994 (which meant that the UN had to play the leading role), and achieved only limited success dealing with political crises in Guatemala, Peru, and Ecuador.

The Santiago Declaration and the associated 2001 Democratic Charter of the OAS were meant to mark a new era of stronger multilateralism, but these hopes have not materialized so far. There are other problems: the OAS lacks credibility as an interlocutor with Havana (Cuba's membership was suspended in 1962); it is a Washington-based entity identified with the traditional U.S. position; it has no standing on Puerto Rico, given the nonsovereign status of the island; and other large countries, including Argentina, Brazil, Colombia, Mexico, and Venezuela, have different reservations about the extent to which the OAS should become involved in their internal political affairs.

Although the OAS may be a relatively weak instrument, it has some recent achievements to its credit, and there is no plausible substitute in the region as a whole, in any event, although UNASUR, the Union of South American Nations, may be able to play a more localized role. Both worked together in October 2008 to damp down polarization in Bolivia.

Thus, 2009 might provide an unusual opportunity to reform and revitalize the OAS, since its current leadership is the most promising for a very long time.

The Inter-American Commission on Human Rights and the Inter-American Court of Human Rights, headquartered in San Jose, Costa Rica, do have very positive track records that are worth enhancing to support rule-of-law initiatives. On the broader issue of democracy, the OAS Democracy Promotion Unit (now dependent on European and Canadian support) could be strengthened, so that when a state invites the OAS to offer advice or mediate a conflict (as Bolivia and Ecuador have done recently), it is in a better position to be effective. In short, the OAS can only play a role if the parties in contention recognize its neutrality and good offices.

The Obama administration will need to concentrate on the practicalities of policymaking in a succession of exacting and urgent arenas. Good strategy will require forward planning, effective coordination within the U.S. government, and consultation with international allies.

In a number of awkward situations, Washington will do best to hold back from intrusive involvement, perhaps allowing some leadership to pass to more credible allies, perhaps tolerating pluralist experimentation, possibly even correcting U.S. conduct, in the light of external feedback.

The so-called Bolivarian Alternative proposed by Chávez, for example, is flawed in various ways, and may well implode as a result of its own deficiencies, but it would certainly not be in the interest of the Obama administration to take the lead against it. It does not merit wholesale condemnation. The project expresses some authentic popular aspirations that need to be addressed, and it is best handled as a challenge for the other democracies to do better. Playing off favorites against miscreants is a temptation to be resisted.

As a democratically elected president of part African descent, who is not identified with recent U.S. foreign and economic policy failures, and who has prioritized international cooperation to confront shared challenges (notably climate change), President Obama enters office with a strong hand to play in the Western hemisphere. Considering the damage that the Bush administration inflicted on U.S. prestige, influence, and indeed power in many parts of the world, the Obama administration will be starting from a low baseline. So it should have ample scope to make short-term gains simply by shedding unnecessary foreign policy baggage. A simple expression of willingness to meet and debate with political leaders who had been placed "beyond the pale" thus constitutes a highly significant shift in stance. The idea that critics and dissenters can sometimes be engaged in respectful dialogue will not be seen in Latin America as a sign of weakness, and need not give rise to any sacrifice of principle. Their participation can reduce misunderstanding between opposed viewpoints, and may uncover latent possibilities for convergence.

Despite the anti-U.S. reflexes that have recently been encouraged by President Chávez and some of his allies, most public opinion in Latin America and the Caribbean is at least open to the possibility that the incoming administration in Washington might prove relatively more constructive than its predecessor. A well-presented and thoughtful Project for the Americas could capitalize on that mood, and so convert short-term gains into a more durable bolstering of the Western hemisphere's democratic rule-of-law traditions.

Notes

1. For information on America's Barometer, see www.intute.ac.uk/socialsciences/cgi-bin/fullrecord.pl?handle=20071024-143522. On Freedom House, see www.freedomhouse.org.

2. The islands of the Caribbean Commonwealth are Jamaica, Trinidad and Tobago, the Windward Islands (Dominica, St. Lucia, St. Vincent and the Grenadines, and Grenada), Barbados, the Leeward Islands (Antigua and Barbuda, St. Kitts and Nevis, the British Virgin Islands, Anguilla, and Montserrat), and the so-called Northern Islands (the Bahamas, the Cayman Islands, and the Turks and Caicos Islands).

Contributors

Carlos Elizondo is professor and former director at Centro de Investigación y Docencia Económicas in Mexico.

Daniel P. Erikson is senior associate for U.S. policy and director of Caribbean programs at the Inter-American Dialogue.

Bert Hoffmann is professor at the German Institute of Global and Area Studies at the University of Hamburg.

Abraham F. Lowenthal is professor of international relations at the University of Southern California, president emeritus and senior fellow at the Pacific Council on International Policy, and a nonresident senior fellow at the Brookings Institution.

Ana Laura Magaloni is professor at Centro de Investigación y Docencia Económicas in Mexico.

Jennifer McCoy is professor of political science at Georgia Tech University and director of Latin American programs at the Carter Center.

George Gray Molina is a Young Professional Fellow at University College, University of Oxford.

Rodrigo Pardo is former foreign minister of Colombia and director of the magazine *Cambio* in Bogotá.

Marifeli Pérez-Stable is professor of sociology at Florida International University and vice president for democratic governance at the Inter-American Dialogue.

Theodore J. Piccone is deputy director of foreign policy studies and senior fellow at the Brookings Institution.

Michael Shifter is vice president for policy and director of the Andean program at the Inter-American Dialogue.

Juan Gabriel Valdés is a Chilean diplomat and political leader who recently served as special representative of the United Nations secretary general and head of the UN Stabilization Mission in Haiti (MINUSTAH).

Laurence Whitehead is an official fellow in politics at Nuffield College at the University of Oxford and editor of the Oxford University Press book series Oxford Studies in Democratisation.

Daniel Zovatto is regional director for Latin America at the International Institute for Democracy and Electoral Assistance (IDEA).

Index

Acción Democrática, 151

African Union, 57

Agriculture, Cuba, 122, 124

Alexandre, Boniface, 101

Alexis, Jacques-Edouard, 96, 101, 102–03

American Administration of Justice Program, 110–11

Amorim, Celso, 130

Amparo, 189–90, 191

Andean Trade Preference Act and Drug Enforcement Act (ATPADEA) (2002), 178

Andean Trade Preference Act (ATPA) (1991–2002), 87

Argentina, 28, 29, 91

Aristide, Jean-Bertrand, 97, 104, 116–17

Arms trafficking, 35, 116, 193, 198

ATPA (Andean Trade Preference Act) (1991–2002), 87

ATPADEA (Andean Trade Preference Act and Drug Enforcement Act) (2002), 178

Australia, 60

Bachelet, Michele, 180

Barbados, 62

Base Realignment and Closure Commission, U.S., 138–39, 140

Belgium, 127

Benedict XVI, 125

Bertone, Tarcisio Cardinal, 125

Blair, Tony, 43

Bogotá, homicide rates, 29

Bolivarian Alternative, 39, 223

Bolivarian Revolution, 147, 150

Bolivia: elections, 31, 52; International IDEA activity, 63; MCA program eligibility, 58; Pando crisis, 24, 174, 180; socioeconomic conditions, 178–79

Bolivia, democratic governance: proposed support strategies, 38, 179–80, 181; public opinion, 31; status of, 33; tradition of, 172, 195

Bolivia-U.S. relations: breakdown in, 38, 167–68, 171–76; importance of, 168–71; proposed policy focus, 15–17, 37–38, 176–82

Brazil: Cuba relations, 130; drug trade, 86, 174, 177; elections, 146; OAS leadership, 55–56; proposed policy focus, 14–15; as social democracy, 91; socioeconomic conditions, 14, 29, 30; UN Haiti mission, 97, 105

Bush, George W. (and administration): Bolivia, 38, 167; Colombia, 87–88; Cuba, 120, 127, 132, 207; democracy assistance generally, 60; Latin America generally, 5, 16, 19, 25, 53, 58; Mexico, 194, 215; public opinion of, 48; Venezuela, 52, 156

Calderón, Felipe, 35, 193, 197. *See also* Mexico *entries*
Canada, 58, 62, 97, 110–11, 126
Caracas, 153, 157
Cardoso, Fernando Henrique, 92
Carriles, Eduardo Posada, 211
Carter, Jimmy (and administration), 172
Carter Center, 56
Castro, Fidel, 48, 124
Castro, Raúl, 119–20, 121–25, 130, 141–43. *See also* Cuba
Catholic Church, 125, 126
Chávez, Hugo, 28, 37, 52, 74, 145. *See also* Venezuela
Chile: democracy programs support, 60, 62; human rights, 28, 29; Iraq War, 159; as social democracy, 9, 91, 146, 195
China, 157
Chungara, Domitila, 172
Civil liberties: Cuba, 124–25; Venezuela, 152–54. *See also* Judicial systems; Media
Civil society: Haiti, 113–14; Latin America generally, 28, 29, 39–40, 59, 60; Venezuela, 150, 159

Clinton, Bill (and administration): Cuba, 120, 126, 132; Florida vote, 128; Haiti, 97; Latin America generally, 5, 53
Cocaine prices, 77f. *See also* Drug trade
Colombia: economic assistance, 53; Free Trade Agreement, 37, 69, 81–82, 87, 89–90; homicide rates, 29; regional importance, 90–91, 94–95; Rio Group meeting, 24. *See also* Plan Colombia
Colombia, democratic governance: proposed support strategies, 15–17, 36–37, 76–82, 88–94; status of, 70–76, 84–87
Comfort, USS, 54
Commitment to the Public Security of the Americas, 44
Communities of Democracies, 57
Conservative Party, Colombia, 70
Constitutional Court of Colombia, 71, 93–94
Constitutions: Bolivia, 33, 70–71, 174–75; Colombia, 36; Cuba, 120, 137; Ecuador, 33–34, 38; Haiti, 102; Venezuela, 146–47, 148, 150, 158
Contadora Group proposal, 213–14
Copei, 151
Correa, Rafael, 38
Corruption: Colombia, 72; Haiti, 110; Latin America generally, 29, 30, 43; Mexico, 197; Venezuela, 154
Costa Rica, 31, 62
Counter-narcotics. *See* Drug trade
Crime. *See* Drug trade; Public security
Cuba: economic conditions, 122–24; Guantánamo Bay return proposal, 136–44, 208; leadership change, 119–20, 141–42; political environment, 124–25, 127; proposed policy focus, 17, 34–35, 41, 120–21; travel/remittance policy, 127–29, 132; Venezuela relationship, 130, 142, 155

Cuba, democratic governance: embargo impact, 125–26, 132, 139–40, 141, 207; proposed support strategies, 35, 129–32, 140–42, 207–8; status of, 124–25, 127
Cuban convertible (CUCs), 122–23
Cuban Democracy Act, 125
Cuban Writers and Artists Union (UNLEAC), 125
CUCs *(cuban convertible),* 122–23

Decriminalization proposal, drug, 43
Democracy, Human Rights, and Labor, Bureau of, 59, 60
Democratic Charter of the Organization of American States, 92
Democratic governance, Latin America generally: proposed support strategies, 39–45, 51, 52–63, 212–14; public opinion, 31, 33, 47–48, 93, 155; status of, 7–8, 30–34. *See also* Latin America–U.S. relations, overview; *specific countries, for example.,* Bolivia, democratic governance
Democratic Pole, Colombia, 70
Denmark, 61
Development assistance. *See* Democratic governance, Latin America generally; Economic assistance
Development Security and Peace Program (DESPAZ), 29
Díaz-Balart, Lincoln, 128
Díaz-Balart, Mario, 128
Doble moral, 124
Dominican Republic, 24, 114–15
Drug trade: Bolivia, 167, 173–74, 177–78, 181; Colombia, 34, 73, 74, 77–78, 85–87, 91–92; Haiti, 110, 116; Mexico, 35–36, 192, 193, 196–98; proposed policy changes, 12, 35–36, 43–44; as

shared challenge, 24, 28, 30; transit countries, 86, 99. *See also* Plan Colombia

Economic assistance: Colombia, 78–79, 80; Cuba, 35, 131; Haiti, 97, 108, 110–11, 113–14, 115; importance of, 18–19, 32–33, 39–41; Mexico, 35–36; military dominance, 53–54, 55*f*; proposed changes, 57–58. *See also* Socioeconomic conditions
Economic relations: Bolivia-U.S., 37–38, 178–79, 181; Brazil-Cuba, 130; Colombia-U.S., 37, 69, 81–82, 89–90; Cuba-European countries, 127; Latin America generally, 4–5, 7, 10–11, 217–18; Mexico-U.S., 185, 194, 196; Puerto Rico, 209; Venezuela, 37
Ecuador: democratic governance status, 31, 33–34, 38, 169; FARC presence, 24, 73–74, 90–91; proposed policy focus, 15–17, 38
Eder, George, 171–72
Education, 40–41, 42
Eisenhower administration, 131, 171–72
EITI (Extractive Industries Transparency Initiative), 43, 163
Ejército de Liberación Nacional (ELN), 72
Elections: Bolivia, 172, 175; Cuba, 120; El Salvador, 52; Haiti, 97, 99, 102, 104, 106–07, 110, 115–16; Latin America generally, 28, 31–32, 42, 169–70; Mexico, 184–85; Nicaragua, 52; Puerto Rico, 209; Venezuela, 28, 33, 52, 146, 148–49, 152, 157–58
Elizondo, Carlos: biographical highlights, 225; chapter by, 183–99; comments on, 215–16
ELN (Ejército de Liberación Nacional), 72
El Salvador, 31, 52, 54, 58

Embargo, Cuba, 34–35, 41, 125 –126, 127–28, 132, 141

Energy. *See* Petroleum

Erikson, Daniel P.: biographical highlights, 225; chapter by, 96–108

European Commission, 61

European Union: aid funding themes, 62*t*; Bolivia, 177, 178; Colombia relationship, 80; Cuba, 34–35, 126, 127, 143, 208; Latin America generally, 39, 43, 61, 217–18; legal norm convergence, 192; public opinion of, 48, 50*f*; regional democracy promotion, 195; Venezuela, 162

Export statistics, 4, 37, 178

Extractive Industries Transparency Initiative (EITI), 43, 163

FARC, 24, 72–74, 83–84, 90–91

Fernández, Leonel, 24

Foreign Corrupt Practices Act, 43

Fox, Vicente (and administration), 198

France, 97, 110–11

Free Trade Agreement, U.S.-Colombia, 37, 69, 81–82, 87, 89–90

Free Trade Area of the Americas (FTAA), 5

Fuerzas Armadas Revolucionarias de Colombia (FARC), 24, 72–74, 83–84, 90–91

Gangs, Haiti, 105–06, 111, 116

García, Joe, 128

Gates, Robert, 54

Gaviria, César, 92

GDP statistics, 24–25, 37, 44

Germany, 61

Goldberg, Phil, 174

Gore, Al, 128

Gousse, Bernard, 102

Guantánamo prison, 19, 41, 136–44, 208

Guatemala, 30, 31

Gutiérrez, Lucio, 32

Guyana, 54, 58

Haiti: HIV/AIDS initiative, 54; regional importance, 98–99, 112–13, 114–15; security conditions, 104–06; socioeconomic conditions, 38–39, 96, 98, 109–10, 117–18

Haiti, democratic governance: proposed support strategies, 27, 39, 106–08, 112–18, 209–10; status of, 38–39, 96–97, 98–104, 109–10, 209–10

Helms-Burton Act, 120, 125, 132, 139, 141

HIV/AIDS initiative, 54, 58

Hoffman, Bert: biographical highlights, 225; chapter by, 136–44

Homicide rates, 29, 30, 70, 153

Honduras, 31, 54, 58

HOPE II, 114, 118

Human rights: Bolivia, 179–80, 181; Colombia, 74–75, 77, 80, 88, 89–90; Cuba, 126, 129, 143; Latin America generally, 28; Venezuela, 153–54

Human Rights Council, 57

Human Rights Democracy Fund, 58–59

Hurricane damages, 96, 98, 103, 109, 122, 210

Hyper-presidentialism, 33

Ibero-American General Secretariat, 130

Iglesias, Enrique, 130

Immigration: proposed policy focus, 36, 44–45; as shared challenge, 4, 10, 13–14, 24, 216–17

Import statistics, 37, 122

India, 60

Insulza, Jose Miguel, 24

Inter-American Commission on Human Rights, 28
Inter-American Court of Human Rights, 28, 41
Inter-American Democracy Fund, 39–41
Inter-American Democratic Charter, 32, 42, 52, 55–56, 129
Inter-American Treaty of Reciprocal Assistance, 143
International Covenants, 124
International Institute for Democracy and Electoral Assistance, 61–62
Iran, 157

Japan, 60
John Paul II, 126
Judicial systems: Bolivia, 71–72; Colombia, 71, 93–94; Haiti, 109–11; Latin America generally, 30, 41; Mexico, 186–94, 215–17; Venezuela, 153–54, 163
Justice and Peace Law, Colombia, 72, 80, 84, 93–94

Karína, 73
Kennedy, John F. (and administration), 172
Kerry, John, 128

Ladies in White, 124
Lage, Carlos, 121
Lagos, Marta, 48
Latin America, overview: challenges, 27–34; international relations, 5–6; subregional problem solving, 23–24. *See also specific countries*
Latin America–U.S. relations, overview: challenges, 5–9, 24–25; importance, 4–5, 204–06; proposed policy focus, 10–20, 34–45, 217–23; status, 5–6, 25–27. *See also specific countries*

Latortue, Gérard, 97, 101–02
Lavalas Party, 102, 104, 116–17
Leader relations, proposed diplomatic strategy, 52–53
Leahy Amendment, 75, 80, 88
Liberal Party, Colombia, 70
Lowenthal, Abraham: biographical highlights, 225; chapter by, 3–21; comments on, 143, 203

Machado Ventura, José Ramón, 121
Magaloni, Ana Laura: biographical highlights, 225; chapter by, 183–99; comments on, 215–16
Martinez, Raúl, 128
Marulanda, Manuel "Tirofijo," 73, 83
MAS (Movimiento al Socialismo), 33, 151, 172, 175
McCain, John, 128, 138
McCoy, Jennifer: biographical highlights, 225; chapter by, 145–66
Media: Colombia, 74–75; Cuba, 125; Latin America generally, 33, 40, 59; Venezuela, 152–53
Mérida Initiative, 35–36, 53, 194, 198
Mexico: Bush administration, 91, 159; Cuba relations, 130; drug transit, 86; elections, 31; International IDEA membership, 62; proposed policy focus, 35–36; regional importance, 196–97
Mexico, democratic governance: institutional support strategies, 190–99; judicial system operations, 186–94, 215–17; status of, 183–85; trade liberalization effects, 188
Migration, Haitians, 97, 98. *See also* Immigration
Military forces: Colombia, 71, 75, 78–79, 88–89, 90; Mexico, 197; proposed pol-

icy focus, 44, 53–55. *See also* Paramilitary groups, Colombia
Millennium Challenge Account (MCA), 54, 58
MINUSTAH, 97, 103, 105, 111–14, 115–16, 209–10
Molina, George Gray: biographical highlights, 225; chapter by, 167–82
Moneda Declaration, 24
Morales, Evo: characterized, 170; coca policy, 173, 174; elections, 33, 172, 173, 175; potential conflicts summarized, 37–38. *See also* Bolivia *entries*
Movimiento al Socialismo (MAS), 33, 151, 172, 175
Movimiento V República (MVR), 151

NAFTA, 185, 194, 196
Narcotics. *See* Drug trade
National Endowment for Democracy (NED), 60, 131, 161
National Liberation Army (ELN), 72
National Security Council, 54–55
NED (National Endowment for Democracy), 60, 131, 161
Nicaragua, 33, 52, 54, 58, 169
Un Nuevo Tiempo, 151

OAS. *See* Organization of American States (OAS)
Obama, Barack: Colombia trade argument, 81–82, 88; Cuba policy statements, 127, 141; Florida votes, 128; Guantánamo Bay pledge, 138
Office of Transition Initiatives, Venezuela, 159
Oil. *See* Petroleum
Organization of American States (OAS): combatant reintegration processes, 79; Cuba relations, 129; electoral missions, 32, 42; Haiti visit, 117; Pando crisis, 24; proposed support strategies, 42, 55–57, 79–80, 222; public opinion of, 48, 49*f*; and Venezuela-U.S. conflicts, 159, 162
Ortega, Daniel, 48

Pando crisis, 24, 174, 180
Paraguay, 31, 54, 58, 91, 169
Paramilitary groups, Colombia: government policy, 80, 83–84, 85, 88; proposed opposition strategies, 93–94; prosecution of, 80, 85, 94; threats from, 72–74, 86
Pardo, Rodrigo: biographical highlights, 226; chapter by, 83–95
Parliamentary functions, Haiti, 103–04, 107
Partido Nuevo Progresista (PNP), 209
Partido Popular Democrático (PPD), 209
Partido Revolucionario Institucional (PRI), 184–85
Partnership proposals. *See* Latin America–U.S. relations, overview
Party of Unity, Colombia, 70
Party system. *See* Political parties
PDVSA, 37
Peace Corps, 55
Peace process, Colombia, 79
Pérez-Stable, Marifeli: biographical highlights, 226; chapter by, 119–35
Peru: democracy assistance programs, 60, 62; democratic governance status, 32; elections, 169; human rights, 28, 29; MCA program eligibility, 58; proposed policy focus, 15–17, 91
Petrobras, 130
Petroleum: Brazil-Cuba relations, 130; Latin America generally, 11–12; Venezuela, 37, 145, 154–55, 156–57

Piccone, Theodore J.: biographical highlights, 226; chapter by, 47–65
Pierre-Louis, Michèle, 96, 97, 101, 117
Plan Colombia: effectiveness, 36–37, 74,
87–88, 211–13; human rights element,
75; Mérida Initiative compared, 198;
spending statistics, 36, 53
Platt Amendment, 137
PNP (Partido Nuevo Progresista), 209
Podemas, 151
Police forces: Colombia, 71; Haiti,
105–06, 110, 111–12; Venezuela, 153
Political parties: Bolivia, 33, 70, 172,
175–76; Cuba, 119; Haiti, 102, 104,
107, 116–17; Latin America generally,
31; Mexico, 184–85; Puerto Rico,
208–9; Venezuela, 146, 147, 150–51
The Post-American World (Zakaria), 23
Poverty. *See* Socioeconomic conditions
PPD (Partido Popular Democrático), 209
Préval, René: on Aristide's return, 116;
elections, 97, 103; food request, 117;
judicial reform, 110; leadership style,
101, 103; prime minister selections,
96, 102–03
Primero Justicia, 151
PRI (Partido Revolucionario Institucional), 184–85
Project for the Americas, proposal,
220–24
PSUV (United Socialist Party of
Venezuela), 151, 157
Public opinion: Colombian president, 70;
Cuba policy components, 127–29;
democratic governance, 31, 33, 47–48,
93, 155; immigration policies, 45; of
international entities, 48–51; knowledge of Latin America, 42; tax revenue
spending, 71*f*; trade benefits, 81*f*; of
U.S., 48, 50*f*, 82*f*

Public security: Colombia, 70, 72–75,
78–79, 93–94; Haiti, 104–06, 111–12,
116; Latin America generally, 29, 36,
44; Mexico, 36, 192, 197, 215–17;
Venezuela, 153–54, 163
Puerto Rico, 208–9

Radical Change party, Colombia, 70
Radical populism, 33
Radio Caracas Television, 153
Refugees, 75–76, 97, 98
Remittance restrictions, proposed
change, 127–29, 132
Revolutionary Armed Forces of Colom-
bia (FARC), 24, 72–74, 83–84, 90–91
Rio de Janeiro, homicide rates, 30
Rio Group, 24, 35, 130
Rio Pact, 143
Roosevelt, Franklin D., 137
Rosales, Manuel, 151
Ros-Lehtinen, Ileana, 128
Rule of law, overview, 27–29, 210–11,
213–14. *See also specific topics, for
example,* Civil society; Democratic
governance, Latin America generally;
Judicial systems
Rusell, Roberto, 23
Russia, 157

Sanchez de Losada, Gonzalo, 169
Sâo Paulo, homicide rates, 29
Senegal, 60
Shannon, Thomas, 16, 117
Shifter, Michael: biographical highlights,
226; chapter by, 69–82
Silva, Luiz Inácio "Lula" da, 130, 180
Slovenia, 60
Socioeconomic conditions: Bolivia,
178–79; Brazil, 14; Colombia, 75–76;
Cuba, 121–25; Ecuador, 38; Haiti, 96,

97, 98, 109–10, 117–18; Latin America generally, 24–25, 32–33; Puerto Rico, 209; Venezuela, 37, 146, 154–56, 160–61. *See also* Economic *entries*

SOUTHCOM, 53–54

Spain, 127, 130, 208

Spheres of responsibility approach, 23

Stabilization Commission, 171–72

State Department, democracy program funding, 58

Suazo, Hernan Siles, 172

Supreme Court, Mexico, 189–90

Supreme Court, U.S., 195–96

Sweden, 61, 62

Swiss Syndrome, 117

Taddeo, Annette, 128

Taxes, Mexico, 189

Terrorism perspective, 5, 12, 19, 24, 91, 211

Trade agreements. *See* Economic relations

Travel/remittance policy proposal, 127–29, 132

Truth commissions, 29

UNASUR (Union of South American Nations), 24, 55–56, 180, 222

UN Commission on Human Rights, 126, 180

UNDEF (United Nations Democracy Fund), 60–61

UN Human Rights Council, 129

Union of South American Nations (UNASUR), 24, 55–56, 180, 222

Union workers, Colombia, 89

United Nations: Cuba, 34–35, 41, 126–27, 129; democratic governance support, 57–58; Haiti economic assistance, 115; Haiti peacekeeping mission, 97, 103, 105, 111–14, 115–16, 209–10; public opinion of, 48, 49f; Venezuela, 162

United Nations Democracy Fund (UNDEF), 60–61

United Socialist Party of Venezuela (PSUV), 151, 157

United States Agency for International Development (USAID), 58–59, 130

Uribe, Álvaro: elections, 36, 70–71; military crimes, 75; paramilitary groups, 72, 73, 85; public security policy, 70, 83, 84. *See also* Colombia *entries*

Uribe, Mario, 72

Uruguay, 31, 62, 91, 146

U.S.-Colombia Free Trade Agreement, 37, 69, 81–82, 87, 89–90

USAID (United States Agency for International Development), 58–59, 131

Valdés, Juan Gabriel: biographical highlights, 226; chapter by, 109–18

Venezuela: Bolivia relationship, 90; Bush administration, 52, 156; Cuba relationship, 130, 142, 155; democratic governance status, 31, 33, 37–38, 146–56, 157–58; drug transit, 86; elections, 28, 33; FARC presence, 73–74; market approach, 39, 223; proposed policy focus, 15–17, 37, 158–64; regional importance, 145–46, 158–59, 162; Rio Group meeting, 24; socioeconomic conditions, 146, 154–57, 160–61

Vietnam, 131

Villa, Acevedo, 209

Vulnerable groups, Colombia, 75–76

Walters, John, 85–86

War metaphor, drugs, 12, 43–44

Washington Consensus, 39

Whitehead, Laurence: biographical highlights, 226; chapter by, 203–24; comments on, 38–39

World Movement for Democracy, 60

World Summit on Sustainable Development, 43

Zakaria, Fareed, 23

Zedillo, Ernesto, 92

Zovatto, Daniel: biographical highlights, 226; chapter by, 22–46